DIGITAL
ETHNOGRAPHY

⑤SAGE | **50** YEARS

SAGE was founded in 1965 by Sara Miller McCune to support the dissemination of usable knowledge by publishing innovative and high-quality research and teaching content. Today, we publish more than 850 journals, including those of more than 300 learned societies, more than 800 new books per year, and a growing range of library products including archives, data, case studies, reports, and video. SAGE remains majority-owned by our founder, and after Sara's lifetime will become owned by a charitable trust that secures our continued independence.

Los Angeles | London | New Delhi | Singapore | Washington DC

DIGITAL ETHNOGRAPHY

Principles and Practice

Sarah Pink
Heather Horst
John Postill
Larissa Hjorth
Tania Lewis
Jo Tacchi

Los Angeles | London | New Delhi
Singapore | Washington DC

Los Angeles | London | New Delhi
Singapore | Washington DC

SAGE Publications Ltd
1 Oliver's Yard
55 City Road
London EC1Y 1SP

SAGE Publications Inc.
2455 Teller Road
Thousand Oaks, California 91320

SAGE Publications India Pvt Ltd
B 1/I 1 Mohan Cooperative Industrial Area
Mathura Road
New Delhi 110 044

SAGE Publications Asia-Pacific Pte Ltd
3 Church Street
#10-04 Samsung Hub
Singapore 049483

Editor: Jai Seaman
Production editor: Ian Antcliff
Marketing manager: Sally Ransom
Cover design: Shaun Mercier
Typeset by: C&M Digitals (P) Ltd, Chennai, India
Printed and bound in Great Britain by Ashford Colour Press Ltd

Library of Congress Control Number: 2015936011

British Library Cataloguing in Publication data

A catalogue record for this book is available from the British Library

ISBN 978-1-4739-0237-4
ISBN 978-1-4739-0238-1 (pbk)

At SAGE we take sustainability seriously. Most of our products are printed in the UK using FSC papers and boards. When we print overseas we ensure sustainable papers are used as measured by the Egmont grading system. We undertake an annual audit to monitor our sustainability.

Contents

List of Figures

Author Biographies

Sarah Pink is Professor of Design and Media Ethnography, and Director (2015–present) of the Digital Ethnography Research Centre at RMIT University, Melbourne, Australia. Her interdisciplinary work combines design, ethnography and digital media. She is Visiting Professor in Social Sciences in the School of Design and School of Civil and Building Engineering at Loughborough University, UK; Visiting Professor in Applied Social and Cultural Analysis at Halmstad University, Sweden; and Guest Professor on the Visual and Media Anthropology programme at the Free University, Berlin, Germany. Her research is funded by a range of research councils and through collaboration with industry partners. Her recent books include *Situating Everyday Life* (2012), *Advances in Visual Methodologies* (ed., 2012), *Doing Visual Ethnography* (3rd edn, 2013) and *Doing Sensory Ethnography* (2nd edn, 2015).

Heather Horst is Associate Professor and Director, Research Partnerships in the College of Design and Social Context and a Founding Director (2012–2015) of the Digital Ethnography Research Centre at RMIT University, Melbourne, Australia. She is interested in how digital media, technology and other forms of material culture mediate relationships, communication, learning, mobility and our sense of being human. Her books examining these themes include *The Cell Phone* (with D. Miller, 2006), *Living and Learning with New Media: Findings from the Digital Youth Project* (with M. Ito et al., 2009), *Hanging Out, Messing Around and Geeking Out* (with M. Ito et al., 2010) and *Digital Anthropology* (co-ed. with D. Miller, 2012). Her current research explores transformations in the telecommunications industry and the emergence of new mobile media practices such as mobile money, mobile music and locative media in the Asia-Pacific region.

John Postill is Vice-Chancellor's Senior Research Fellow at RMIT University, Melbourne, Australia, and Digital Anthropology Fellow at University College London (UCL). From 2010–11, he was Senior Research Fellow at the Internet Interdisciplinary Institute IN3,

Universitat Oberta de Catalunya (UOC, Open University of Catalonia), Barcelona, Spain. His publications include *Localizing the Internet* (2011), *Media and Nation Building* (2006), and the co-edited volume *Theorising Media and Practice* (co-ed. with B. Bräuchler, 2010). Currently, he is conducting anthropological research on new forms of digital activism and civic engagement in Indonesia, Spain and globally.

Larissa Hjorth is Professor and a Founding Director (2012–2013) of the Digital Ethnography Research Centre at the School of Media and Communication at RMIT University, Melbourne, Australia. She is an artist and digital ethnographer who studies the sociocultural dimensions of mobile media and gaming cultures in the Asia-Pacific. Her books include *Mobile Media in the Asia-Pacific* (2009), *Games & Gaming* (2011), *Online@AsiaPacific* (with M. Arnold, 2013), *Understanding Social Media* (with S. Hinton, 2013), *Gaming in Social, Locative and Mobile Media* (with I. Richardson, 2014). She has co-edited *The Routledge Companion to Mobile Media* (with G. Goggin, 2014), *Gaming Cultures and Place* (with D. Chan, 2009), *Mobile Technologies* (with G. Goggin, 2009), *Art in Asia-Pacific* (co-ed. with N. King and M. Kataoka, 2014) and *Studying Mobile Media* (with J. Burgess and I. Richardson, 2012).

Tania Lewis is an Associate Professor at the School of Media and Communication at RMIT University, Melbourne, Australia. She has published across a wide range of areas, including lifestyle media and consumption, and grassroots green movements. Her books include *Telemodernities* (co-authored with F. Martin and W. Sun, forthcoming 2016), *Green Asia* (ed., forthcoming 2016), *Lifestyle Media in Asia* (co-ed. with F. Martin, forthcoming 2016), *Smart Living* (2008), *Ethical Consumption* (co-ed. with E. Potter, 2011) and *TV Transformations* (ed., 2009).

Jo Tacchi is Professor and Director of Research and Innovation and Deputy to the President of RMIT Europe in Barcelona. She is trained as a social anthropologist and studies media, communication, development and social change, the senses and emotions, and everyday digital life. She has led a number of multi-country projects with partners such as United Nations Educational, Scientific, and Cultural Organization (UNESCO), United Nations Children's Fund (UNICEF), Intel and KPMG. She has conducted research mostly in South Asia. Her most recent book is *Evaluating Communication for Development* (with J. Lennie, 2013).

Acknowledgements

This book has been a collaborative work, and we are grateful to our co-authors for the work and ideas that they have contributed towards its making. However, the biggest thanks of all is to the people who made this book possible – that is, to the people from across the world who participated in the various different research projects that we and our co-authors discuss in this book, from Asia, Europe, the USA and Australia. Their generosity in giving their time and knowledge to the projects we discuss here is of immeasurable value. Some participants in research wish to have their real names given and others to be anonymous. Real names are used where this was agreed with the participants.

Second, we thank all the co-researchers and co-authors who have collaborated in the projects and publications discussed in this book. We have cited their published work and acknowledged their contributions where relevant in the text of this book and give details below.

We would also like to thank the School of Media and Communication and the College of Design and Social Context at RMIT University for the support of this project and the Digital Ethnography Research Centre, the intellectual space that has been core to the development of the book. Spearheaded by Jo Tacchi who was Deputy Dean of Research and Innovation in the School of Media and Communication at the time, RMIT actively began recruiting for a concentration in media and digital ethnography in 2011. This led to the founding of the Digital Ethnography Research Centre (DERC) by Larissa Hjorth and Heather Horst in December 2012; Tania Lewis, Sarah Pink and John Postill joined DERC shortly afterwards. Since this time, we have researched, written and worked together in various configurations. The motivation for this book came from our desire to think through what we as a collective might say about digital ethnography, given our different research topics, sites, and trajectories as well as different disciplinary influences. At the same time, it is also a positioning statement for DERC and an exploration of this new field.

Finally, we thank all Sage's editors who have supported and encouraged this project from the outset – in particular, Chris Rojek and Jai Seaman. During the development of our ideas for this book, we received important feedback and advice from Tom Boellstorff, Graeme Turner, Scott McQuire and Supriya Singh; their insights fundamentally shaped our approach to the book and our contribution to the field. We have also benefitted enormously from the support of Erin Taylor and Luke Gaspard who worked with us in its final stages of preparation. In particular, we are grateful for Erin's insightful comments, pointing out to us things that we could no longer see ourselves, and her encouraging presence at the end of the journey of writing, made a pivotal difference.

The research discussed in this book was funded through a variety of sources: Heather Horst's research was funded by the John D. and Catherine T. MacArthur Foundation under the 'Kids' Informal Learning with Digital Media: An Ethnographic Investigation of Innovative Knowledge Cultures' project, the Institute for Money, Technology and Financial Inclusion, Irvine, the Department for International Development (UK) and a Vice-Chancellor's Senior Research Fellowship at RMIT University. Institutional support for her research has also come from the Annenberg Center for Communication at the University of Southern California, the Institute for the Study of Social Change at University of California Berkeley, the Digital Media and Learning Research Hub at the University of California, Berkeley and the School of Media and Communication at RMIT University.

Tania Lewis's research into lifestyle television, 'The role of lifestyle television in transforming culture, citizenship and selfhood: China, Taiwan, Singapore and India', was funded by an Australian Research Council Discovery Project grant (2010–14), working with Research Associate Kiran Mullenhalli.

Sarah Pink's research into energy and digital media was part of the Low Effort Energy Demand Reduction (LEEDR) project at Loughborough University, UK. LEEDR was jointly funded by the UK Research Councils' Digital Economy and Energy programmes through the Engineering and Physical Sciences Research Council (grant number EP/I000267/1) for 2010–14, and undertaken with Kerstin Leder Mackley and Roxana Morosanu. Her research into standby mode in Australian households was undertaken with Yolande Strengers and funded by the Design Research Institute, RMIT University. Pink's 'Slow food and Cittaslow UK: changing local lives?' was funded by the Nuffield Foundation, UK (2005–07), and supported by her stay at the Internet Interdisciplinary Institute, UOC, Barcelona in 2010–11 and RMIT University in 2012–13.

Larissa Hjorth would like to acknowledge the Australian Research Council discovery (with I. Richardson) Games of Being Mobile: Mobile Gaming in Everyday Life (DP140104295), the Australian Research Council Linkage Grant (with H. Horst and S. Pink) Locating the Mobile with Intel (LP130100848) and Australian Research Council Linkage Grant Spatial Dialogues: Public Art and Climate Change (LP100200088 with Grocon and Fairfax).

John Postill's research in Malaysia was funded by the Volkswagen Foundation, at University of Bremen, Germany, and his research in Spain was funded by a Senior Research Fellowship award at the IN3 (Internet Interdisciplinary Institute, Open University of Catalonia, Barcelona).

Jo Tacchi and Tania Lewis's 'Digital Rhythms' research was funded by KPMG, with research assistants Tripta Chandola, Victor Albert and Shae Hunter. Jo's ethnographic studies in the Delhi Slum were supported through funding from the UK's Department for International Development (2003–04). Tripta's research was funded by a QUT PhD Scholarship (2006–09).

Sarah Pink and Heather Horst

ONE
Ethnography in a Digital World

CHAPTER CONTENTS

INTRODUCTION

Digital Ethnography outlines an approach to doing ethnography in a contemporary world. It invites researchers to consider how we live and research in a digital, material and sensory environment. This is not a static world or environment. Rather, it is one in which we need to know how to research in it as it develops and changes. *Digital Ethnography* also explores the consequences of the presence of digital media in shaping the techniques and processes through which we practice ethnography, and accounts for how the digital, methodological, practical and theoretical dimensions of ethnographic research are increasingly intertwined.

This book is not just for the specialist in digital media. Rather, it is a proposal for how we might do ethnography as the digital unfolds as part of the world that we co-inhabit with the people who participate in our research. Doing research with, through and in an environment partially constituted by digital media has led to the development of new and innovative methods and challenged existing conceptual and analytical categories. It has invited us not only to theorise the digital world in new ways, but also to re-think how we have understood pre-digital practices, media and environments. *Digital Ethnography* addresses this context by explaining the possibilities of digital ethnography for both researching and redefining central concepts in social and cultural research.

In doing so, *Digital Ethnography* takes us to the core issues in this debate. It asks how digital environments, methods and methodologies are redefining ethnographic practice. It takes the novel step of acknowledging the role of digital ethnography in challenging the concepts that have traditionally defined the units of analysis that ethnography has been used to study. It goes beyond simply translating traditional concepts and methods into digital research environments, by exploring the ethnographic–theoretical dialogues through which 'old' concepts are impacted by digital ethnography practice.

This book therefore addresses anyone who is interested in the implications of the digital world and an ethnographic approach for their research practice or for understanding the contemporary contexts in which we do research. It can be used at different levels and in different ways. Some readers might wish to use the concepts that we introduce as templates for developing projects or theses. Others will be able to use the book as an introduction to understanding how we live and act in a context that is, today, almost always co-constituted and entangled with digital technologies, content, presence and communication. While others will wish to engage with our broader argument and definition of the digital as situated in everyday worlds. As such it might be treated as a framing understanding through which further developments in theoretical scholarship and methodological improvisation may potentially emerge.

WHAT IS *DIGITAL* ETHNOGRAPHY?

Ethnography is a way of practicing research. Readers interested in ethnography will likely have encountered the mounting literature in this field. While sometimes proponents of different disciplines might claim to 'own' ethnography as 'their' approach, in reality such ownership only comes about contextually. That is to say, ethnography is not a very meaningful practice by itself; instead, it is only useful when engaged through a particular disciplinary or interdisciplinary paradigm and used in relation to other practices and ideas within a research process.

There are multiple definitions of ethnography with slight variations proposed by a range of different authors. In this book we are not necessarily interested in contributing to the creation of new definitions. We acknowledge that digital ethnography might be practiced and defined in different ways that relate more or less closely to the range of existing definitions. The ways in which readers will wish to define ethnography will also depend on their own critical backgrounds and interests. For example, as Pink has pointed out (2015), some definitions are more open (O'Reilly, 2005), and others are more prescriptive (Delamont, 2007). Following Karen O'Reilly, we posit that ethnography is: 'iterative–inductive research (that evolves in design through the study), drawing on a family of methods ... that acknowledges the role of theory as well as the researcher's own role and that views humans as part object/part subject' (2005: 3).

Yet, once ethnography becomes digital, parts of O'Reilly's definition become conditional on our acknowledgement of how digital media become part of an ethnography that involves 'direct and sustained contact with human agents, within the context of their daily lives (and cultures)'; what it might actually mean to be digitally engaged in the equivalent of 'watching what happens, listening to what is said, asking questions'; and where we might want to do more than 'producing a richly written account that respects the irreducibility of human experience' (all quotes are from O'Reilly, 2005: 3). Most of these ethnographic activities are to some extent transferable to a digital ethnography approach, but the conventional ethnographic practices that they stand for begin to shift. In digital ethnography, we are often in mediated contact with participants rather than in direct presence. As the following chapters suggest, we might be in conversation with people throughout their everyday lives. We might be watching what people do by digitally tracking them, or asking them to invite us into their social media practices. Listening may involve reading, or it might involve sensing and communicating in other ways. Ethnographic writing might be replaced by video, photography or blogging. Indeed, taking O'Reilly's open definition as a starting point offers us a useful way to consider what differences the digital actually makes to our practice as ethnographers, and thus to contemplate digital ethnography as it evolves. As new technologies offer new ways of engaging with emergent research environments, our actual practices as ethnographers also shift.

O'Reilly's definition is useful because it remains open to the relationship between ethnography and theory without insisting that a particular disciplinary theory needs to be used in dialogue with ethnographic materials. To engage in a particular approach to ethnography, we need to have a theory of the world that we live in. The ways in which we theorise the world as scholars, working in or across academic disciplines, impacts on our practice as individual (or team-working) ethnographers in particular ways. Methods and theory are two aspects of ethnographic research and analysis that change when carried out by different researchers. The authors of this book, for example, do not all ascribe to the same theoretical visions of the world. In fact, it would be surprising if we did, because our work is oriented towards and originates from different disciplinary approaches, ranging between social anthropology, media and communication studies and cultural studies. This means that the perspectives and the emphases that we take in doing research vary. However, there is a set of principles that underpins the approach to ethnography that we advocate and which inform the very ways in which we theorise ethnographic practice. We elaborate on these in more detail below.

DIGITAL ETHNOGRAPHY ACROSS DISCIPLINES

There are a good many prisms through which ethnography might be viewed. The literature about research practice and methods reveals two key trajectories. First, over the years, in parallel and in dialogue with changing theoretical and substantive foci in research, methodologies for researching have shifted in relation to the key debates that they generated. To be specific, in the history of ideas in the social sciences, when there has been a 'turn' in focus towards gender, the visual or the senses, for example, there has likewise been a 'turn' in the methodology literature. Where ethnographic methods are concerned, a focus on gender in ethnography also corresponded with greater reflexivity with respect to the contexts of knowledge production. There has been a parallel turn in reflexive practice, such as that in the work of Ruth Behar (1996) or Kamala Visweswaran (1994), who examine women's lives and the practice of feminist ethnography (see also Behar and Gordon, 1995; Bell et al., 1991). The increasing focus on the visual (e.g., Pink, 2001; Banks, 2001) and the senses (e.g., Classen, 1993; Classen et al., 1994; Howes, 2003; Pink, 2009; Vannini et al., 2012) at the turn of the century similarly came with new methods as well as a challenge to the dominant ways of 'knowing' and 'researching' that privilege particular senses.

The second trajectory is that these 'turns', however, do not necessarily stop once they have happened, but instead become consolidated and integrated as part of ethnographic practice. Sometimes they expand. Therefore, as readers will note in the following chapters, the ethnographic examples we outline might discuss the gendered relations of the people we have researched with as well as our own encounters as gendered researchers. We likewise discuss the different methods that reflect the practice of ethnography. Similarly, there has been a strand of ethnographic methodology literature regarding the digital. Many argue that this strand launched around 2000 with Christine Hine's *Virtual Ethnography*, although of course there were early predecessors (e.g., Baym, 1999; Correll, 1995; Gray and Driscoll, 1992; Hakken, 1999; Ito, 1997; Lindlof and Shatzer, 1998; Lyman and Wakeford, 1999). Hine's book effectively began a strand of consolidation of this theme through books and journal publications that collectively constituted a field of ethnographic inquiry. *Digital Ethnography* sits across these sets of literature. It incorporates a number of theoretical turns that have played a key role in defining ethnographic practice in the last twenty or so years. Yet, at the same time, it expands the debate about the consequences of the digital for ethnography.

Despite an interest in digital culture and practices across a range of disciplines, it is interesting to note that most of the attempts to define ethnography as 'digital' have been focused in anthropology and sociology. This is not to dismiss contributions to ethnographic practice in disciplines and fields such as Human Computer Interaction (HCI), human geography and media and cultural studies. These fields and disciplines have often engaged with 'ethnography' as part of an 'ethnographic turn' to understand media or digital practices. For example, in HCI and related fields such as Informatics, Information Studies and ubiquitous computing, ethnography has been usefully incorporated to nuance and expand the notion of the 'user' (see Dourish and Bell, 2011). Like human geography's grappling with the consequences of the 'online', 'offline' and the 'virtual', what is interesting about this particular focus on the 'digital' is what it means for the other end of the equation, be it digital anthropology or digital sociology.

Building on the formative work of Sherry Turkle (2005) and others, sociologists have broadened their focus on looking at the implications of 'the digital' through a focus on digital media or transformations that accompany 'the digital age' (Robinson and Halle, 2002; Robinson, 2007; Turkle, 2005, 2011). Many of these studies have taken up sociology's concern with structural forms and inequities to understand how inequality is extended, reproduced or complicated by digital media technologies (see Orton-Johnson and Prior, 2013). These debates are also influenced by the particular approach to ethnography undertaken in digital sociology. For instance, Bella Dicks et al.'s *Qualitative Research and Hypermedia: Ethnography for the Digital Age* (2005) introduced the use of digital media as an approach to sociology that was rooted in the multimodality paradigm. In contrast, the sociologist Dhiraj Murthy describes digital ethnography as being centred on 'data-gathering methods [that] are mediated by computer-mediated communication' (2011: 159). This, he writes, includes 'digitally mediated fieldnotes, online participant observation, blogs/wikis with contributions by respondents, and online focus groups' and can also include accounts of offline groups (ibid.: 159).

By comparison, Hine and other sociologists who have become interested in the consequences of the Internet and digital media and technology generally have been influenced by the interdisciplinary perspectives of Science and Technology Studies (STS). In her introduction to *Digital Sociology*, Deborah Lupton (2014) has recently argued that those who describe themselves as digital sociologists engage in four types of practices. These include: first, new forms of professional practice where sociologists use digital tools to network and build conversations; second, researching how people are using digital media, technologies and tools; third, using digital tools for analysis; and fourth, engaging in critical analysis of the use and consequences of digital media.

As Lupton suggests, one of the key concerns in digital sociology has been the extent to which algorithmic data has the capacity to enhance, change or replace traditional qualitative (as sociologists frame ethnography) and quantitative practice. In other words, digital sociology is framed as a debate about the discipline's focus and practice. In contrast, Marres (2013) defines the concerns of digital sociology as being not 'just about theorizing the digital society, and ... not just about applying social methods to analyse digital social life', instead stressing that: 'The relations between social life and its analysis are changing in the context of digitization, and digital sociology offers a way of engaging with this.' Marres is particularly inspired by the possibility of new, interdisciplinary 'inventive methods' such as those exemplified in the work of Celia Lury and Nina Wakeford. In fact, Marres expresses discomfiture with the disciplinary label of digital 'sociology' itself.

The growth of digital anthropology as a subfield has been well established through the works of: Horst and Miller (2012b), who, in their edited book *Digital Anthropology*, build on their earlier ethnographic research around digital technologies (Horst and Miller, 2006; Madianou and Miller, 2011; Miller, 2012; Miller and Slater, 2000); as well as the growing literature on virtual worlds (Boellstorff, 2008; Nardi, 2010); on mobile and social media use (Gershon, 2010); networked forms of community and activism (Coleman et al., 2008; Postill, 2011); and broader reflections on the digital age (Ginsburg, 2008). These and other topics are demonstrated in the book's various chapters on: digital archives (Geismar, 2012); disability (Ginsburg, 2012); politics (Postill, 2012a); location technologies (DeNicola, 2012); open source software (Karanovic, 2012); development (Tacchi, 2012); gaming (Malaby, 2012); and design (Drazin, 2012); personal communication (Broadbent, 2012); social networking (Miller, 2012); religious contexts (Barendregt, 2012); and everyday life (Horst, 2012). Horst and Miller's edited volume reveals that 'the digital' is spread across 'traditional' as well as new domains. As such, they argue that digital anthropology is now a field of study in its own right, akin to classic areas of anthropological inquiry, such as religion, legal or economic anthropology (Boellstorff, 2012). Like these more traditional areas of investigation, digital anthropology also takes up the discipline's broader concern with what makes us 'human' (Miller and Horst, 2012). This last point has been a particular focus of anthropological debate centring on technology since the emergence of 'cyberia' and 'cyberspace' studies (Escobar, 1994; Hakken, 1999; Haraway, 1991; Whitehead and Wesch, 2012).

While one must be careful not to conflate anthropology with ethnography (Ingold, 2008), most anthropologists are likely to study the digital using an ethnographic approach. For example, Gabriella Coleman's (2010) review article, entitled 'Ethnographic Approaches to Digital Media', that focuses on a broad set of practices and practitioners outside the discipline of anthropology. For anthropological ethnography, there is increasing discussion of the digital as a field in which we practice as much as we analyse. This shows that there are a range of ways in which digital anthropology itself might be interpreted, and as such we would expect digital ethnography to be equally varied when carried out by anthropologists. In effect, what we see through both the discussion of digital sociology and anthropology is that the broadening out to other disciplines is a welcome and productive catalyst for disciplinary debates. In fact, the benefits of interdisciplinary collaboration are well demonstrated in a recent co-authored book on ethnographic approaches to studying virtual worlds (Boellstorff et al., 2012). In their book, the authors – who have studied virtual worlds via ethnography from both sociological and anthropological perspectives – come into conversation to design an approach to the ethnography of virtual worlds, which counters some of what they view as the limitations of many approaches that claim ethnographic perspectives and methods.

Within this context, *Digital Ethnography: Principles and Practices* takes a specific stance in relation to the debates and discussions in the work discussed above. *Digital Ethnography* sets out a particular type of digital ethnography practice that takes as its starting point the idea that digital media and technologies are part of the everyday and more spectacular worlds that people inhabit. It follows what media scholars have called a non-media-centric (Couldry, 2012; Moores, 2012; Morley, 2009) approach to media studies by taking a non-digital-centric approach to the digital. It also acknowledges the intangible as a part of digital ethnography research, precisely because it invites us to consider the question of the 'digital intangible' and the relationship between digital, sensory, atmospheric and material elements of our worlds. In effect, we are interested in how the digital has become part of the material, sensory and social worlds we inhabit, and what the implications are for ethnographic research practice.

In this book, we suggest ways of acknowledging and accounting for the digital as part of our worlds that are both theoretical and practical and that offer coherent frameworks through which to *do* ethnography across specific sites and questions. As ethnographic researchers, we always share aspects of being in everyday worlds and making them along with the participants in our projects. Such an understanding opens up ways to conceptualise our research relationships and the basis on which we develop our collaborations as ethnographers. Just as we divide up the chapters of this book according to the idea of using concepts of experience, practice, things, relationships, social worlds, localities and events as units of analysis, so we could also very well conceptualise the ethnographic process through these very categories.

In the next section, we take a step back to explore how we might define ethnography and how this extends to a definition of digital ethnography. We argue that, in order to understand the practice of digital ethnography, we also need a theory of the digital.

PRINCIPLES FOR A DIGITAL ETHNOGRAPHY

In this section, we outline five key principles for doing digital ethnography: multiplicity, non-digital-centric-ness, openness, reflexivity and unorthodox. Most of these have been alluded to in the discussion above. Indeed, it would be difficult to write of digital ethnography at all without mentioning them. We now define them more closely and we discuss why and how they come into play specifically in the context of digital ethnography theory and practice. These principles are also demonstrated in the examples and discussions that we develop throughout this book. When relevant, we point to where instances of them appear in the following chapters. However, readers might also keep in mind that the process of identifying these principles has also been part of the process through which the writing of this book has enabled us to reflect on how, building up from our research experiences, a set of principles might be developed. While these principles are grounded in experience, they might not always be represented in all projects and in some cases offer an ideal model of digital ethnography practice that is not always realisable. Such a model is not necessarily to be aspired to, but to be bounced off, played with and adapted according to the contexts and aspirations of each new research project and process.

1. *Multiplicity*: There is more than one way to engage with the digital

Digital ethnography research is always unique to the research question and challenges to which it is responding. It is often guided by specific theoretical frameworks connected to academic disciplines, as well as by the needs and interests of different research partners, stakeholders and participants. These influences and their impact make each project and the way it is formulated evolve in particular ways. In the examples in the following chapters, we often note how the projects we discuss were funded and conceptualised because this influences the types of knowledge that is produced.

At the same time, we need to keep in mind how digital technologies and media (and the things that people can do with them) are interdependent with the infrastructures of everyday life. For example, digital media need to be powered by a reliable energy source. They need to be able to be used by the research participants whose lives and media use we are interested in studying. They also need to be functional enough for researchers to be able to use them for fieldwork. Perhaps more significantly, the infrastructures that exist to support digital media use have a clear impact on both the participants in research and the researchers. For example, during his recent fieldwork on digital media and civic participation in Indonesia, John Postill found that because there is comparatively little digital broadband and Wi-Fi access in Indonesian cities, the participants in his research tended to depend on smart-phones for Internet access. This framed both the topic he was studying and the ways in which he was able to be active as a researcher working in a digital field with a different infrastructure to that he had experienced in Barcelona where public Wi-Fi connections are easily located.

In other contexts, Wi-Fi and social media connections might be part of the research process. Indeed, in much new work on dynamic spaces there is a need to capture and archive transient processes. For example, in Heather Horst's recent collaboration with Robert Foster on the moral and cultural economy of mobile phones in the Pacific, they have started archiving the various companies' mobile advertisements through sites such as Facebook, YouTube and Vimeo. Their aim is to understand how trans-national companies develop local versions of their products and services. Without their efforts to archive, these advertisements are transient and often disappear. Moreover, when working in interdisciplinary projects and/or in distributed teams, in any context where digital data collection is part of the research process, research participants might be required to have a Wi-Fi connection to engage in Skype, Google Chat or other conference call services, which, in turn, help to create close-to-synchronous collaboration and data sharing. Variations in bandwidth speeds also shape the practices of digital ethnography.

2. *Non-digital-centric-ness*: The digital is de-centred in digital ethnography

The idea that media studies scholars might take what has been called a 'non-media-centric' approach is experiencing something of a revival in media studies and media anthro-pology (for examples, see Couldry, 2012; Moores, 2012; Pink and Leder Mackley, 2013). Such approaches de-centre media as the focus of media research in order to acknowledge the ways in which media are inseparable from the other activities, technologies, materialities and feelings through which they are used, experienced and operate. Indeed, for anthropologists – even those who call themselves media anthropologists – the idea of studying media in a way that always puts media at the centre of analysis would be problematic because it would pay too little attention to the ways in which media are part of wider sets of environments and relations. Moreover, as we often find when doing ethnographic research, by approaching research ques-tions indirectly, that is through something that is related in some fundamental way to the very thing we wish to learn about, we can often produce novel insights that tell us more about what underlies the findings of research. These kinds of insights are difficult to find through standard interview and survey methods. In the example of

Pink's research about energy demand discussed in Chapter 2, the researchers did not directly ask participants about their energy or media use, but instead studied, together with participants, the everyday routines and activities that participants engaged in that required or implicated the use of energy and digital media. The same principles can be applied to the study of digital media more generally (Horst, 2012).

In order to understand how digital media are part of people's everyday worlds, we also need to understand other aspects of their worlds and lives. In doing so, we might focus specifically on those domains of activity in which digital media are used rather than on the characteristics or use of media. As we show in Chapter 5, digital media form part of human relationships. Moreover, the qualities and affordances of mobile phones and locative applications enable new aspects of those relationships (in our examples, new forms of co-presence, or being together). Yet, even when they are conducted primarily online, relationships cannot be purely digital. We therefore need to look beyond the digital to understand how they are played out. For instance, in Horst's example in Chapter 5, transnational communication within families can only be understood in relation to the norms of kinship in Jamaica, particularly the gendered expectations of grandmothers, men and children. Jo Tacchi's study of the significance of mobile phone use among women living in Delhi slums requires a broader understanding of what mobility means for the women in her study. Similarly, in Chapter 8, we see how the concept of the event, which involves bringing together processes of different types to constitute an event, also offers us an example of how digital activities, technologies, content and uses become part of wider configurations. While our interest in this book is in the digital as part of ethnography, our approach to understanding the event through digital ethnography practices and principles means that we can understand more than just the role of digital media in people's lives. We can also demonstrate the implications of digital media through examining the entanglements of other things.

Following the same principle, then, we also argue that digital ethnography research methods should be non-digital-centric. This means that the digital ethnography project should not be prefaced with the idea of needing to use digital methods. Rather, the use of digital methods should always be developed and designed specifically in relation to the particular research questions being asked. It might be that some research about digital media use would be best undertaken when not using digital technologies as research tools, or that research that uses digital techniques and tools might be about everyday life activities or localities that are not usually contexts or sites of digital media immersion, or are sites of limited digital media immersion or availability. One example of this is Tania Lewis's discussion of the practice of 'permablitzing', wherein the primary activity involves getting out in the urban gardens of Melbourne to work. In this case, the Permablitz website is secondary to the core practice, effectively becoming a conduit for the primary practice of gardening and greening the city.

Therefore, by keeping the place of digital media in research relational to other elements and domains of the research topic, site and methods, we are able to understand the digital as *part of* something wider, rather than situating it at the centre of our work. This, we propose, inevitably enriches both the ways in which we study digital media, their uses, qualities and affordances, and the ways in which these studies create insights into the digital impacts on other strands and elements that constitute everyday environments, experiences, activities and relationships.

3. *Openness*: Digital ethnography is an open event

The concept of 'openness' has increasing currency in contemporary academic and other discourse and practice. For instance, the geographer Doreen Massey refers to what she calls 'place' as open, seeing it as a kind of 'event' where things are drawn together (2005). The term 'open' is also being used to characterise design processes as open-ended. For instance, the anthropologist Tim Ingold writes that 'designing is about imagining the future. But far from seeking finality and closure, it is an imagining that is open-ended' (2012: 29). Indeed, this processual way of characterising the kinds of things that we do as academics and researchers offers us a way to conceptualise digital ethnography research processes as open. That is, digital ethnography is not a research 'method' that is bounded. Nor is it a unit of activity or a technique with a beginning or end. Rather, it is processual.

Openness is also a fundamental concept in what is sometimes called 'digital culture', whereby open source, creative commons and other forms of digital sharing and collaboration become ways of being and relating to others in relation to digital media. Transferring this concept of openness to the digital ethnography research process helps us to understand the process of doing digital ethnography in a way that is open to other influences (like those of speculative design or arts practice) as well as to the needs of other disciplines and external stakeholders with whom ethnographers might collaborate. For example, in the work of Horst, discussed in Chapter 3, this has meant that the basic research findings were integrated into a broader and comparative project to be able to generalise to a educational context. In Pink's study discussed in Chapter 2, the research has involved collaborations with engineers and designers. Hjorth's Spatial Dialogues project discussed in Chapter 8 illustrates how ethnographic and arts practice come closer together. Finally, in Tacchi and Lewis's work with KPMG, the industry stakeholder's needs became embedded in the ethnographic project. Digital ethnography, if it is to be undertaken at these intersections between academic disciplines and external partners, becomes an open and flexible research design, which can be shaped in relation to the particular research questions which it asks as well as to the institutional contexts which it is related to and the ways in which the participants in the research engage with it.

The openness of digital ethnography therefore signifies that digital ethnography is a collaborative process. Indeed, it could be argued that all ethnography is equally collaborative in that the research encounter with others – as opposed to the distanced observational stance – is inevitably a collaborative activity: that is, we make knowledge and ways of knowing with others, and not as lone researchers. However, returning to the parallel between digital ethnography and popular representations of digital culture, which is also regarded as a collaborative and participatory context, we can see that the association of digital ethnography with collaboration invites further scrutiny. This does not mean that digital ethnography would be essentially 'more collaborative' than other renderings of ethnographic practice. Rather, it suggests that digital forms of collaboration, as integrated into digital ethnography research processes, invite different collaborative ways of co-producing knowledge with research partners and participants.

4. *Reflexivity*: Digital ethnography involves reflexive practice

In ethnographic practice, the notion of reflexivity has stemmed largely from what was called the 'writing culture debate' – a discussion and literature that emerged in the 1980s and 1990s and attended to a series of questions around the ways in which knowledge was produced through anthropological ethnography (Clifford and Marcus, 1986; James et al., 1997). The outcome of these discussions was for ethnography to become associated with the notion of a reflexive form of research practice. This was particularly the case for anthropological ethnography but has also become important to how ethnography is carried out in some fields of sociology and human geography. For the purposes of this book, to be reflexive can be defined as the ways in which we, as ethnographers, produce knowledge through our encounters with other people and things. It is an approach that goes beyond the simple idea of 'bias' and that engages with the subjectivity of the research encounter and the explicatory nature of ethnographic writing as a positive and creative route through which to produce knowledge or ways of knowing about other people, their lives, experiences and environments. Reflexive practice is also considered to be an ethical practice in that it enables researchers to acknowledge the collaborative ways in which knowledge is made in the ethnographic process.

In the context of digital ethnography, reflexivity does not necessarily take a different form to that which it would take in any other ethnographic process. However, we might think of the distinguishing feature in relation to the ways in which digital ethnographers theorise and encounter the world as a digital–material–sensory environment. Part of the ways that digital ethnographers might reflexively engage with their worlds is concerned with asking ourselves precisely those questions about how we produce knowledge. Our relationships with the digital are pivotal to the specific ways of knowing and being that we will encounter in the course of our research practice.

5. *Unorthodox*: Digital ethnography requires attention to alternative forms of communicating

Each of the chapters in this book features three examples of ethnographic writing drawn from the authors' own research at different physical and digital sites around the world. These examples are based on projects that account for the digital as part of the environment or everyday life, or as research technologies, or as both. The examples throughout the book show how taking a digital approach enables us to acknowledge and seek out ways of knowing (about) other people's worlds that might otherwise be invisible and that might be unanticipated by more formally constituted, and thus less exploratory and collaborative, research approaches. They also account for the research process as being inextricable from the ways in which ethnographic knowledge is produced, thus in some cases incorporating a degree of reflexivity into the ethnographic writing process. As instances of writing digital ethnography, these offer readers a set of examples of both what we might learn through doing digital ethnography and how and where it might be practiced.

In presenting these examples in written form, we focus on timely and, in some cases, 'rawer' forms of communication than the ways in which many digital ethnographers (the authors of this book included) tend to publish in quite conventional paper formats. Few digital ethnographies have photographs and those that have experimented with companion websites (e.g., Miller and Slater, 2000) have found little interest in these associated sites. Scholars who work with photography and video in digital ethnography and the visual as a topic of study or a mode of investigation (e.g. Ardévol 2012; Gomez Cruz, 2012) note the limitations of the ethnographic monograph. There is an emerging digital visual ethnography practice that includes using the visual as a research method and that holds enormous potential for the visual in digital dissemination (Pink, 2012). This is because digital dissemination methods go beyond the more conventional visual anthropology approach in the making of digital film and photography. In tune with this call for a visual digital ethnography, most of the examples given in this book have included one or more images that not only simply serve as illustrations but also as modes of evoking the feelings, relationships, materialities, activities and configurations of these things that formed part of the research context.

Several of the projects discussed in this book have also taken unorthodox forms of dissemination. This includes a range of websites, such as Pink's recent Energy & Digital Living website (http://energyanddigitalliving.com) that features 'raw' footage of participants doing their laundry and using energy, as well as Postill's blog (http://johnpostill.com/blog-series/), which archives conference and paper presentations as well as preliminary analyses of current events. Horst's work on the 'Digital Youth Project', which involved disseminating material through a project blog (http://digitalyouth.ischool.berkeley.edu/stories.html), an academic book, executive summary, as well as a public forum broadcast on YouTube (http://www. youtube.com/view_play_list?p=CC2EF6A461393C86), and in her work with Erin Taylor (2014) on the border of Haiti and the Dominican Republic, likewise explored various forms of presenting material such as a two-page 'cost of sending money' flyer (http://www.imtfi.uci.edu/files/docs/2010/mmm_time_and_cost_flyer_feb20111. pdf). Finally, Tacchi's work in the area of communication for development has included the dissemination of digital content created by research participants in the *Finding a Voice* project (http://findingavoice.org), and the development of the ethnographic action research training website (http://ear.findingavoice.org), which shares examples of the process of research and field notes from local community based researchers. These timely, translational and, in some ways, more transparent forms of ethnographic practices represent unorthodox forms of making and doing ethnography that leverage digital media and go beyond a 'broadcast' model of dissemination. These, in turn, highlight the potential, opportunities and challenges of digital ethnography.

These unorthodox approaches to methods dissemination enable new forms of continuity between digital ethnography fieldwork, ongoing collaborations and dialogues with research participants, and a certain bringing together of the temporalities and sites of the research, analysis and dissemination processes. They thus show how a digital ethnography approach enables us to go beyond academia, beyond disciplines and beyond the standard written production of academic scholarship.

THE FRAMEWORK FOR THIS BOOK

In this book, we examine how seven key concepts in social and cultural theory can be used for the design and analysis of ethnographic research. These concepts were selected to represent a range of different routes to approaching the social world, that is: through experiences (what people feel); practices (what people do); things (the objects that are part of our lives); relationships (our intimate social environments); social worlds (the groups and wider social configurations through which people relate to each other); localities (the actual physically shared contexts that we inhabit); and events (the coming together of diverse things in public contexts). All of these concepts have already been part of social sciences and humanities research for a long time and, in fact, they remain at the core of our business as academics. Yet, existing theoretical concepts have often been configured in ways that have responded to the specificity of the social, cultural and material forms that they have been used to understand. This means that sometimes they present limiting paradigms that do not reach the needs of contemporary researchers.

We argue that the seven concepts that we have chosen to explore in this book can all be used effectively to understand and research in digital environments, but that they need sometimes to be more finely honed for such work. We propose that the concepts can also be reshaped in response to the ways in which we encounter digital worlds ethnographically. We would also stress that the concepts which we have chosen are not the only ones that might be (re)engaged or invented to be used in dialogue with digital ethnography practice. Our main limitation has been that it would be impossible to cover everything within a single book, and so our choice has been based on an assessment of which theoretical concepts are emerging as increasingly important through recent theoretical 'turns' and debates with which our work, collectively, has been engaged. However, we would encourage readers to continue this work by exploring the use of other concepts in similar ways.

Indeed, our wider argument is that, for a number of reasons, contemporary ethnography needs to be as Hine has put it, 'adaptive' (2015: 192). The reasons for using adaptive methods vary: they can be a response to time limitations, the distributed nature of field sites, the nature of the analytical units or the (inter)disciplinary foci they take. Yet, we contend that we also need to use 'adaptive concepts' precisely because digital ethnography is not just a 'method' or part of a 'toolkit'. Rather, digital ethnography is also always engaged in building and developing theory.

STRUCTURING DIGITAL ETHNOGRAPHY: A GUIDE TO THE BOOK

Digital Ethnography is set out around a series of concepts, all of which researchers and scholars who work across a range of fields and disciplines have found to be important and useful as units or categories through which to design, analyse and represent ethnographic research: experience, practice, relationships, things, localities, social worlds and events. These concepts share the common feature of having all been developed in various more or less indirect ways in existing literatures and therefore have both biographies as concepts in the social sciences and humanities, and have more recently been engaged for the analysis of a contemporary world of which the digital is a part.

The concepts are introduced in the order that is set out above, that is, from experience in Chapter 2, through to event in Chapter 8. This is not to say that there is a linear progression through this series of concepts; however, their ordering does represent a way of thinking about them that acknowledges their differences and similarities. Experience is a difficult category of human life to research and analyse. This is because experience is ultimately unique to individuals. We cannot actually access other people's experiences in any direct way. Neither can we have the same experiences as them. Yet, we can, as we show in Chapter 2, create an analytical category around the concept of experience that can be used as a way to think about, research through, analyse and represent the findings of research. There are many types of experience that might be researched in relation to digital media: embodied, affective, hallucinatory, sensory or other forms of experience. In Chapter 2, we focus on sensory experience as an example of how such aspects of human life can be researched. In Chapter 3, however, we take a different type of analytical unit, which focuses on the concept of practices. Practices are not actual 'things' that we can directly research, but rather they are analytical constructs through which we can access and research aspects of human life and activity. The concept of a practice in Chapter 3 works rather differently to that of experiences, because it focuses on what people 'do' rather than what they feel. It would of course be possible to research feeling and doing – that is, experiences and practices – as part of the same research project. Indeed, these could be examined in combination with any of the other concepts we explore in this book. However, we tend to keep these concepts separate in our chapters to outline the ways in which specific concepts might, as a first stage, be used as part of a digital ethnography approach.

Chapter 4 turns the attention away from human activity to focus on 'things', which are made and made meaningful through human activity. Bringing together approaches to things from anthropology, cultural studies, material culture studies and STS, this chapter situates the digital, and the practice of digital ethnography, in relation to a longer term relation to the production, consumption and circulation of things. Chapter 5 looks at how personal relationships might be researched through digital ethnography and how contemporary relationships across the world are being constituted and played out through practices such as co-presence in and through digital media and technologies. Chapter 6 takes a wider view of the social by asking how we might engage with types of social worlds through digital ethnography. The concept of social worlds works slightly differently from others in the book, since unlike theories of practice, experience or materiality, there is no established body of theory on the concept of social worlds. Instead, there are a number of different theories around how social worlds are constituted, each of which advances a different vision of how social relationships, collective activities and the like are bound together. These include theories of community, network or sociality. The various concepts that are used to understand social worlds have implications for both the methods used in research and the ways that these concepts have been formulated and critiqued.

In Chapter 7, we focus on the concept of localities. This might seem an unusual concept when considering digital environments, where indeed physical localities tend to be newly connected with each other as well as connecting digital places and encounters. We explore how the concept of locality has renewed meanings and relevance when used in conjunction with a digital ethnography approach, making it a viable, if reshaped, concept. Finally, in Chapter 8, we look at the event. This is a concept that has been at the centre of discussions in media studies since the last decades of the twentieth century. The idea of the event was also used extensively at the interface between anthropology and media studies during this period, and it has remained a popular way of framing how media and activities around them fit into national and other contexts. We argue that the digital has both implications for how actual events are constituted and for the ways in which we might theorise the event in a contemporary environment where the elements that would have made up old media events have also shifted. The event, however, is also an interesting concept to end our discussion with, given that the concept of the event as bringing together diverse other things of different qualities and affordances might also help us to understand the ethnographic process. Indeed, the concept of the event could further bring together the other concepts that we have introduced in this book. To understand an event that is lived out in a digital–material–sensory environment, one might well wish to comprehend the relationships between the experiences, practices, things, relationships, social worlds and localities through which it is constituted.

THE FUTURE OF DIGITAL ETHNOGRAPHY: AFTER THE BOOK

As will become evident throughout the book, the concepts, principles and method-ologies discussed should not be viewed as a 'one-size-fits-all' approach to studying a particular concept. Indeed, in each chapter, multiple examples are provided which highlight not only the methods employed but also the motivations for designing the research methods and questions together. In many cases, new methods and approaches were developed or 'adapted' to address new questions and situations in the field. As new digital media technologies and new theoretical turns emerge there will be increasing opportunities to rethink digital ethnography. This book remains open to such advances. Our aim in the following chapters is to show how and where digital ethnography principles and practices have emerged in ways that enable researchers to use and adapt concepts to research problems or questions. Indeed, Digital Ethnography is an emergent field of theory and practice; we do not view it as a static or defined area. We invite readers not to *do* what we have done, but to *use* what we have done as examples or sources of inspiration to develop their own approaches.

Researching Experiences

CHAPTER CONTENTS

INTRODUCTION

This chapter explores how digital ethnographers might research the concept of experience. Scholars across different ethnographically oriented disciplines have interrogated the concept of experience, and it has often been claimed that experience is at the centre of ethnographic practice. Recently, work on the multidimensional aspects of the digital screen, including people's affective and haptic- (touch-) based and audiovisual experiences, has emphasised the experiential qualities of digital media. In this chapter, we bring together these different approaches to consider how we might define and activate the concept of experience, using it in two ways. First, we deploy experience as an analytical window through which to understand experiences of a world of which digital media are a part. Second, we explore how the experience of digital technologies is part of the research process, considering how experience can be mobilised as a particular way of knowing other people's worlds through a digital ethnography approach. Because research into experience is extensive and inter-disciplinary, we concentrate on sensory experience in order to show how different kinds of experience might be researched. We present three concrete examples of how digital ethnography has focused on experience. These include: the sensory experi-ence of digital media presence in homes in the UK; affective and sensory dimensions of women's uses of mobile phones in an Indian slum; and the creation of ambiance through engagements with haptic games in Australia. We conclude with a discussion of the ways in which the concept of experience can be a focus for research into sensory and affective aspects of everyday life and the implications of this approach for researching digital experience.

THE CONCEPT OF EXPERIENCE

Interest in experience as a topic of research and an analytical category crosses academic disciplines and practices. Early definitions, such as of John Dewey's understanding of experience as the flow of everyday life punctuated by 'moments of fulfilment' (2005 [1934]:16), have had an enduring influence over the development of the concept, as have phenomenological approaches to understanding the world in philosophy. Detmer has described phenomenology as the study of 'the essential structures ... of lived experience' that incorporates objects and acts of experience such as perceiving, imagining, loving and so on (2013: 23).

Indeed, Husserl's (1966) focus on consciousness, Heidegger's (1962) exploration of experience as fundamentally connected to situated ways of being in the world and Merleau-Ponty's (1996) emphasis on the body as the site of our knowledge of the world, are notable examples of how the study of experience has played a fundamental role in expanding our understanding of the human condition.

These earlier definitions of experience and subsequent discussions of them have been influential across the social sciences and humanities. For example, anthropologists have engaged with the question of experience both theoretically and ethnographically (e.g., Geertz, 1986; Throop, 2003; Turner, 1986). Debates have focused on whether experience could be understood, as Turner proposed as being between the unfiltered 'mere experience' and the after-the-event defined 'an experience' (Geertz, 1986; Turner, 1986). In response, Throop (2003) suggests that we might open up the defini-tion to multiple types of experience (see Pink, 2006). Experience as an analytical concept was also introduced into the anthropological literature by anthropologists focusing on embodiment (that is, the mind–body relationship) in the latter part of the twentieth century (e.g., Csordas, 1994). Interest in experience has more recently manifest in a growing interest amongst anthropologists in understanding, and, indeed, theorising, their own experiences as ways of producing ethnographic learning and knowing (about) others (e.g., Harris, 2007; Pink, 2015), such as through vision and other sensory modalities (Grasseni, 2007; Geurts, 2002; Howes, 2003; Pink, 2013, 2015), imagination (Crapanzano, 2004) and the emotions (Wulff, 2007). However, the interest in experience has not been confined to anthropology: cultural studies scholars have also been interested in the study of experience (e.g., Pickering, 1997); and the focus on non-representational or more-than-representational theory in human geography during the first part of the twenty-first century brought the experiential, rather than representational, dimensions of the everyday to the fore (see Lorimer, 2008; Thrift, 2007).

In contemporary literature, discussions of experience often refer to how it is embodied and lived through sensory and affective modes. In the remainder of this chapter, we focus in on sensory experience to explain how the concept is investigated through digital ethnography practice. As Michel Serres (2008) highlights, the senses permit the experience of things that are difficult or impossible to express through language, and which cannot be observed directly. One of the challenges of studying experience is that experience is often difficult to articulate, and so attempts to understand and interpret its meaning and significance rely on the ethnographer's immersion in sites of other people's experiences. It also depends on identifying concepts associated with sensory or emotional experiences that facilitate the discussion of experience with research participants and academics.

EXISTING APPROACHES TO RESEARCHING EXPERIENCE

Ethnographers who have researched sensory experience have taken two different approaches. The first approach focuses on the five senses as they are understood in Western traditions – sight, hearing, touch, smell, taste – and their interrelationships. This approach, which focuses on the senses as a cultural phenomenon, is advocated by David Howes and Constance Classen. They argue that:

> The ways we use our senses, and the ways we create and understand the sensory world, are shaped by culture. Perception is informed not only by the personal meaning a particular sensation has for us, but also by the social values it carries. (Howes and Classen, 2013, see also 1991)

Earlier ethnographies of experience also sought to uncover sensory arrangements that are different from those to which the ethnographer is accustomed. For instance,

Walter J. Ong argued that cultures can be understood in and through the organisation of the sensorium – the operationalisation of our 'sensory apparatus' – precisely because it makes culture; if one can understand the sensorium, one can understand culture (1991: 28).

The second approach, which builds on the work of the anthropologist Tim Ingold (2000), invites us to consider experience as something that might not necessarily fit into verbal categories of expression – such as those used to describe the five senses noted above, and emphasises that neuroscientists do not necessarily see sensory experience as mappable onto these five concepts as sensory channels between the body and brain (see also Ingold, 2011; Pink, 2015). Sarah Pink has built on this approach to argue that phenomenological and neurological theories of sensory perception can enhance our ethnographic studies of the senses. The ways in which the senses are understood theoretically has implications for how they are investigated in practice. Applying modern Western categories to the investigation of the senses increases the likelihood of producing findings that fit these very categories. Conversely, if one begins with the viewpoint that these categories are part of a representational layer of culture that is not intrinsic to human perception, then the possibility of discovering new categories or ways of understanding is retained.

Research that attends to the senses often takes into account the unspoken layers of sensory experience that are expressed through cultural categories. For instance, Paul Stoller's earlier work on 'sensuous scholarship' focused on experience-in-the-world (Stoller, 1997). It fused what Stoller refers to as the 'intelligible' (that is, the scholarly) and the 'sensible' (that is, the sensory) in scholarly practice in ways that are parallel to the focus on embodiment discussed above. Stoller (1989) demonstrates how sensory immersion in a culture produces profound insights and understandings. For example, this work enabled him to experience and think about the senses in ways that were different from conventional modern Western assumptions. Stoller described how after long spells of research among the Songhay people whom he worked with in Niger, he began to:

> let the sights, sounds, smells, and tastes of Niger flow into me. This fundamental rule in epistemological humility taught me that taste, smell, and hearing are often more important for the Songhay than sight, the privileged sense of the West. In Songhay one can taste kinship, smell witches, and hear the ancestors. (Stoller, 1989: 5)

Stoller brings this approach into his ethnographic writing (e.g., 1997) by moving between different ways of writing to bring scholarly discussion (i.e., the 'intelligible') together with more evocative sensory narratives (i.e., the 'sensible') in the same text.

Since the earlier approaches of Stoller and others, a focus on sensory experience and on the senses has become increasingly consolidated as a strand of social science practice and enquiry. This is demonstrated by the move towards sensory sociology in the work of Vannini et al. (2011), the visceral geography of Hayes-Conroy (2010), and the development of sensory approaches to media ethnographies (Pink, 2015) and the acknowledgment of the senses in design ethnography and anthropology (Gunn and Donovan, 2012; Pink, 2014). There has also been an increased interest in experience through a revival of the field of media phenomenology (Couldry, 2012; Markham, 2011; Moores, 2006; Pink and Leder Mackley, 2013). Sensory approaches are gaining in currency in part due to the ways in which the digital is increasingly entangled in everyday experience. This, in turn, fosters increased theoretical interest in the senses and in the everyday digital technologies, infrastructures and activities that are part of the worlds we research and live within.

THE IMPLICATIONS OF DIGITAL MEDIA AND TECHNOLOGIES FOR RESEARCHING EXPERIENCE

Digital media are increasingly interwoven in our media and communication environments and make possible the production of new or changed contexts, modes of circulation, and forms of connection. Yet, as the examples we outline below demonstrate, this is happening to different degrees, in different ways and through different technologies and platforms in different contexts. One implication of these increasing and varied entanglements with digital media is that we need to attend to the digital technologies and devices that are part of our sensory embodied experience of the environment. As the media scholar Ingrid Richardson points out, 'in an environment of multiplying handsets and frequently upgraded portable game consoles it is salient to examine the perceptual specificity of our interactions with and experiences of such devices' (Richardson, 2011: 421). At the same time, the emergence of new digital platforms has made lived experience possible in new ways. Research into these new modes of lived experience include: studies of immersion in virtual worlds (Boellstorff, 2008; Boellstorff et al., 2012; Taylor, 2002); gaming (Hjorth, 2011; Hjorth and Chan, 2009; Nardi, 2010; Pearce et al., 2011; Taylor, 2009; Thornham and Weissmann, 2013); and the experience of moving across online and offline worlds (Hjorth and Pink, 2014; Horst, 2009; Taylor, 2009). These new platforms have become sites for ethnographic fieldwork. Indeed, experiences of the types of immersion of being with ethnographic participants – beyond interviews and elicitation methods that has been called 'being in fieldwork' (Marcus, 2008) – have now been discussed in relation to digital contexts (Marcus, 2012: xiv; Horst, 2015), as have ways of engaging with other people and their experiences in relation to the availability of digital media technologies (Burrell, 2015; Kraemer, 2015).

There are a growing number of ethnographic studies that have attended to embodied and sensory experience of new devices, media and content. For example, work on haptic technologies (Paterson, 2007, 2009; Pink et al., 2010) sound, noise and silence (Bijsterveld, 2008; Born, 2013; Bull, 2000, 2008; Helmreich, 2007) and the visual, such as through camera phone studies (Hjorth, 2007; Ito and Okabe, 2005; Okabe and Ito, 2006; Pink and Hjorth, 2012), has demonstrated the importance of both attending to both other peoples' and ethnographers' own embodied and sensory experiences of and engagements with new media. Work in disability studies and related fields has drawn attention to the particular capabilities of digital media to enhance, augment and/or replace prior capabilities (Ellis and Kent, 2011; Ginsburg, 2007; Goggin and Newell, 2003), such as Miller's (2011) discussion of a housebound man in Trinidad living in Facebook, or Ginsburg's (2012) reflections on disability activists' use of YouTube and other social media. Boellstorff (2008) observes that:

> Second Life's reliance on textual chat instead of voice during the period of [his] field-work, the limited capacity for avatar facial expression, and a general tolerance for delayed or unexpected responses (for instance, because persons were often afk [away from the keyboard]) made it possible for many residents with autism to be competent social actors to a significantly greater degree than in the actual world. (ibid.: 147)

Such examples highlight the central role of media platforms in shaping the sensory experience of the world in and through digital media.

RESEARCHING EXPERIENCE THROUGH DIGITAL ETHNOGRAPHY

Ethnography is well placed to describe in detail the implications of the digital for experience and the ways in which experience shapes the digital. In this next section, we focus on three examples of research into experience. The first describes a study of digital media and energy use in UK households, which shows how invisible sensory and affective experiences can be made visible through focusing on routines and activities of everyday life. The second describes part of a long-term ethnography in a slum cluster in India, focusing on women and mobile phones to make visible their experience of underlying and oppressive gendered structures. The third example explores the ways in which gaming and play have now constituted the background of everyday life for many Australians. Each approaches everyday experience ethnographically, in and/or through digital technologies.

Short-term ethnographies of the sensory and affective experience of in the home

Media are used in the home in a range of different ways. Conventionally, media studies scholars have studied both media content and its audiences in terms of communication. However, digital media technologies and content also play other roles as part of the environment of home. They are present as part of the tangible and (to some) intangible sensory and affective structures and textures of home. Interviews, observations and diary methods have conventionally been used by scholars in audience studies and communication studies to research what people actively do with media, for instance, when watching TV or listening to music or radio (e.g., Keightley and Pickering, 2012; Markham and Couldry, 2007; Silverstone and Hirsch, 1992). Yet, such methods do not tend to reveal other 'invisible' or normally unspoken elements of the experience of media in the home. These may not involve participants directly communicating through media technologies or engaging with media content. Indeed, when seeking to research invisible sensory and affective experience – such as feelings of wellbeing or being at ease – researchers do not necessarily know exactly what they are expecting to find. Therefore, researchers often approach unseen elements of the experience by investigating how they are manifested in those routines and activities of everyday life that can be seen and discussed. In this section, we explain how this technique might be used through the example of researching 'media presence' developed in Sarah Pink and Kerstin Leder Mackley's work (2012) on digital media and energy use in UK homes. This work is also represented online in the 'Energy & Digital Living' website at: www.energyanddigitalliving.com and Figures 2.1, 2.2 and 2.3 below show how the ethnography discussed here is presented there.

Because their ethnographic research formed part of a project that aimed to develop digital design interventions to help people to save energy, Pink and Leder Mackley were concerned with how people used digital media and energy as part of their everyday life routines in their homes. Their research design was rooted in phenomenological anthropology to examine everyday life routines from two perspectives: first, through a focus on the experience of the home environment, by asking how their participants created the sensory aesthetic of their homes; and, second, by investigating in more detail participants' experiences of practical activity at mundane moments in their days. Pink and Leder Mackley accessed the mundane experiences and activities in which their participants used media and energy, but that they would not normally have any motive or reason to show or discuss with others (see Pink and Leder Mackley, 2012). Various different concepts might be used to structure research into everyday life experiences in the home. Here, in contrast to Tacchi and Lewis's approach to the 'Digital Rhythms' project presented in Chapter 3, where uses of digital media in the home were conceptualised as 'practices', the concept of practices did not map onto the ways in which the Low Effort Energy Demand Reduction (LEEDR) researchers needed to understand the flow of everyday life. Sociological approaches to energy demand in the home also tend to use practices as a core analytical unit. However, an ethnographic approach can yield different insights, and, here, the ethnographic materials were analysed in order to build alternative analytical approaches to everyday human activity and experience in the home. This involved using the concepts of movement, flow and presence to understand the experience of home. Three digital video methods were used in this research: the video tour, re-enactment and following participants as they undertook normal everyday activities (Pink and Leder Mackley, 2012, 2014).

Video tours involve a participant showing a researcher around their home (Pink, 2004, 2013). This method has been developed by Pink in a range of projects researching homes over the past 15 years. It is an adaptive method that can also be shaped to researching digital media in everyday life. Between 2010 and 2014, this project researched media and energy use through focusing the tour on the question of how the participant made their home 'feel right' with a view to understand how they used digital media and energy for the purposes of creating a sensory and affective experiential environment of home. This method encourages participants to show the researcher their home and share the 'feelings' of its textures, air flows, temperatures, sounds and smells. Sometimes, during tours, participants also introduce experiences to share with researchers by inviting them to smell or hear elements of the home that might not be initially obvious, or by inviting them to empathetically imagine what the experience of using media is like.

For example, Pink and Leder Mackley describe how one participant explained to them his family's affective and embodied experiences and activities relating to having media devices switched off. Alan, their participant, emphasised the importance of being sure that media was switched off in order for his home to feel right, they outline how:

> One of the first things Alan showed us when we arrived was how he had set up the TV in the living room so that it and all the related equipment could be switched off using a single switch. He pointed out that this would be done every night [by one of his family members] before he got home, using a wooden stick that reaches to the switch, which is behind the TV. (Pink and Leder Mackley, 2013: 679)

The family's experiential and affective experience of media being switched off was described verbally by Alan when he told them how, 'for his adult daughter who lives at home: "because it's electricity … she's got a little thing on her mind, where it's got to be off, otherwise you don't feel at ease"' (ibid.). As they toured relevant areas of the home, the participant's story of switching off at night continued to point out the different technologies that were involved in making the home feel right (or not). Alan used verbal descriptions and visual/material cues in this narrative, and, showing his embodied experience,

Alan also told us how in his son's room the TV used to be left on standby because he couldn't quite reach the plug, until Alan inserted an extension lead so all the media devices could be turned off at the plug socket via the now accessible adaptor. He emphasized this again when we toured the son's room, going down to the floor under the desk where cables for the TV, Wii, Xbox and laptop are kept to show us the plugs, describing and actually performing for us how [this was done]. (ibid.)

By video recording this, the researchers were able to review their experience as well as Alan's performance to undertake their analysis. Using video in this way enables researchers to reimagine how it felt to be in a participant's home as well as to imagine the participant's own experience (Pink and Leder Mackley, 2012).

Figure 2.1   The Energy & Digital Living website and its video clips

Note: The website hosts shows a series of digital video clips from the LEEDR project which readers are invited to view in relation to the discussion here.

During digital video tours, participants often initiate enactments of activities such as Alan's. A second method, the video re-enactment, invites participants to engage in a more detailed demonstration of everyday activities (Pink and Leder Mackley, 2014). In the project discussed here this included bedtime and morning routines, which were selected because they involve uses of media and energy (including switching on and off). One of the key elements of experience conveyed to the ethnographers through these re-enactments concerned how media were used to create a particular sensory and affective environment at bedtime. While media ethnographers undertaking observation studies would not usually accompany participants up to the moment that they go to bed, and even participant diary-writing might happen before the moment of going to sleep, here, participants can re-enact what they do right up to the moment of going to sleep. The ethnographers were able to learn how participants used media as part of the process of going to sleep, as once they arrived in their bedrooms they described how they used the noise and presence of the television or other media sound, left on a timer or to otherwise switch itself off while they went to sleep. For example:

> when Kerstin visited to discuss the video tour she was surprised to hear that a programme that tends to be on at bedtime is about police chases. Asked whether this did not unsettle them when trying to get to sleep, Laura and Paul explained that it is more about the noise of 'something being there' in the background than about engaging with the content. (Pink and Leder Mackley, 2013: 685)

Taking an ethnographic approach in this project, which involved finding out the unexpected ways that people use media, therefore brought to the fore the ways in which the conventional study of media as content and communication misses situations in which content and communication do not necessarily matter or take priority (Pink and Leder Mackley, 2013). In this case, the use of media to create a sensory and affective experiential atmosphere also provided insights into how people use energy in standby mode (ibid).

Figure 2.2 Pink and Leder Mackley's work is discussed on the Energy & Digital Living website

Note: Here, in contrast to the Web capture shown in Figure 2.1, where viewers directly access the video clips through the archive, written text is used to discuss the findings, interwoven with video.

Long-term ethnography with women and mobile phones in a Delhi slum cluster

This example focuses on work by Jo Tacchi and Tripta Chandola (2015) that begins with an ethnographic study of the changing communicative ecologies of poor communities in two research sites in India. It was part of a larger four-country research project exploring emerging media and communication technologies in India, Jamaica, Ghana and South Africa (Miller, et al., 2005). Tacchi and Chandola used a range of methods, beginning with a communicative ecology study (Slater, 2013; Tacchi et al., 2007) that consisted of interviews in homes, on the street, in Internet cafes, public phone venues, and shops that sold a range of media and communication devices and services (including mobile phones, MP3 CDs, radios and videos). Interviews focused on how communication happened and why. Tacchi and Chandola also conducted short surveys through an 'exit poll' at public phone services in the slum cluster which were widely used at the time. They also engaged with organisations working in the slum cluster. During this initial study, which lasted 18 months, women and their experiences of phones emerged as interesting partly because of the way in which they made visible underlying gendered structures. Mobile phone use was not prevalent in this site at the time, unlike in the other research sites, especially Jamaica and Ghana (see Horst and Miller, 2006; Slater, 2013), but fixed line phones were an important part of the communications landscape. This research laid the foundation for Tacchi and Chandola's ongoing ethnography in this site, continuing to the present, and including the experience of smartphones and other digital technologies. They have been able to observe how while some things change, especially in relation to the technologies available, others remain the same, particularly underlying structures of power.

In 2004, Tacchi and Chandola met Savita and her family, which included her husband, four sons and a runaway boy of 13 who lived with them and helped them in their tea shop and catering business. Rajbeer was Savita's husband and initially the main point of contact. He answered Tacchi and Chandola's questions, even when directed at Savita. Rajbeer had suffered a serious accident some years before and was unable to work outside the home. Plans were underway for the two oldest sons to marry two sisters. Just two months prior to the wedding, Rajbeer died. Savita's position in the family was dramatically transformed as she became head of the household. While Rajbeer was alive the researchers sensed a warm, loving and supportive relationship with his parents who lived nearby. However, soon after his death, when discussions about rescheduling the double wedding were underway, Savita took a stand not to postpone it, contrary to the wishes of her in-laws. This was her first act of defiance and open acknowledgement of an acrimonious relationship with her in-laws. Savita's mobility – spatial, social and economic – was strictly contained in her role as a wife and daughter-in-law. But once she was head of the family, the possibilities for mobility increased. She now controlled the businesses, made household decisions and arranged the weddings. Her access to the phone also significantly changed.

Before Rajbeer's death, Savita did not answer the phone or have a 'direct' conversation on it. Even if the caller inquired after her, her husband or sons would relay the conversation back and forth. Rajbeer made it clear that he objected to the increasing freedoms or mobilities available to women, including the emerging use of mobile phones. In contrast, his eldest son was one of the few local men at that time who owned a mobile, which Rajbeer saw as important for his work and career. The control of telephones lay firmly with men. This shifted markedly after Rajbeer's death. Savita began using the phone to conduct her business and social relationships, especially since, as a widow, she was required to be in extended mourning for at least a year. And yet, once her two daughters-in-law joined the household after marriage, Savita strictly controlled their movements, and their use of phones, just as hers had been controlled before Rajbeer's death. It was now her responsibility to uphold the family's morality and virtue, demonstrated through a range of constraints and restrictions.

The first 18 months of study in this site was followed by a sensory ethnography of sounds in the slum by Chandola (2012a–b) extending the ethnographic engagement. The environment was so sensorially rich (sounds, smells, sights, textures and tastes), that a sensory approach seemed essential to understanding experience. It helped provide understanding of the social and political relationships between the slum-dwellers and the city (Chandola, 2010), and gendered and violent aspects of life, including those exposed through exploring instances of public and political 'noise' such as women's wailing (Chandola, 2014). More recently, Chandola and Tacchi began focusing on smartphones (Tacchi, 2014; Tacchi and Chandola, 2015). This work includes interviews and participant observation, but also sound recordings, close observation of mobile handset use, contact lists, discussions around phone messaging (most prominently SMS and WhatsApp), explorations of social media use, and research conversations through mobiles, social media and messaging services. Through this work, gendered, social, cultural and moral landscapes were seen to determine and constrain experiences and use of phones. At the same time, phones were seen to help women to resist or defy such constraints. Ethnographic research focusing on phones helps to make both oppression and resistance visible through exploring experience.

Tacchi and Chandola used this work to illustrate the experience of underlying structures and the need to understand digital communication devices, in this case smart-phones, in relation to these experiences (Tacchi, forthcoming; Tacchi and Chandola, forthcoming) and within complex lives. They drew on the lives of two young women in particular, Rani and Monica. During 2012, Rani lived with her aging widowed mother, younger brother and her daughter aged 9. She also had two younger sisters, whose marriages she had arranged and paid for. Her father was a drug addict and her husband was abusive. She left him a year after they were married, returning home at age 18. Rani's mother worked at the time as a domestic help in a nearby middle-class household. Rani tried working as a maid, too, but found it intolerable and humiliating. The ill treatment and lack of respect and control that she experienced as a maid contrasts with the line of work that she took up, which was sex work. As a sex worker she experienced far more control, and earned a great deal more and enjoyed a rarely available economic, social and spatial mobility, and yet it is also highly precarious work. While she earned enough money to improve the condition of her family, she also feared the implications for them if it were to become known that she did this kind of work.

Figure 2.3   Woman talking on her smartphone

Source: Photograph copyright of Tripta Chandola.

Rani carried two mobiles, and had three mobile connections. Only one connection was in her name, and she never used it when dealing with her clients. Her work was organised and managed through the mobile phone. Even though she was illiterate, she sent and received several text messages a day. Her social communications (rather than work arrangements and client relationships, which were strictly sepa-rated) contained a lot of forwarded messages, such as poetry and words of affection. Her brother or one of her educated neighbours, such as Monica, read these to Rani.

Monica's mother ran a general store, which, as the only store catering to a few hun-dred households, did thriving business. She was revered and respected as *badi khaala* (elder aunt), and also owned four *jhuggis jhuggis* (slum dwellings constructed with mate-rials other than concrete) and an apartment in a lower-middle class area. She kept a careful watch on her daughter, who graduated from high school and went on to study a course in fashion merchandising. After her studies, Monica found a job in an export house on the outskirts of Delhi. However, after only five months, Monica resigned her job because of her mother's constant surveillance: she would call her on her mobile sev-eral times a day, and if she didn't answer, she would call the office phone. Her mother considers this her duty, commenting that: 'young girls need to be protected. There are so many distractions, and we cannot allow her to go astray.' Monica found her mother's oversight extremely difficult and said that her smartphone connection with the outside world stopped her from 'going mad'. Constantly online through her phone, she used a range of social media sites, including Facebook, Orkut, Twitter and Skype. She had mild flirtations on Facebook and had over 400 friends, many of them unknown to her offline. She observed, 'of course, Amma does not know what I am up to on the phone. She thinks I am texting, and gets annoyed at times but that is it. She does not know Internet, or Facebook.' Monica knew that her mother would prohibit the use of the phone if she knew what she did, but for her it was a way of managing or circumventing the severe restrictions placed on her in what she considered to be a harmless way.

Structures of power, gendered oppression and violence cannot be excluded from consideration in an ethnographic study of mobile phone use. They are important components of the context of phone use. Structures of power constrain mobile phone access and use for some people, while mobile phones also provide some of these same people with opportunities to subvert or circumvent them. Through exploring Rani and Monica's use of mobile phones ethnographically, it is impossible to ignore the broader and complex conditions of their lives. Only through engagement with these broader contexts and experiences of everyday life can we fully appreciate and under-stand mobile phone use by women such as Rani and Monica. At the same time, this use helps to make the broader context and its implications visible.

Ethnographic moments of ambient play in Australian households

This example draws on ethnographic work conducted in 2014 on Australian mobile gaming practices by Larissa Hjorth and Ingrid Richardson. Mobile games are part of an assemblage of interrelated media practices, including camera phone image sharing, and contribute to what Hjorth and Richardson have defined as 'ambient play' (2014: 74). Mobile games have grown to encompass a variety of sensory modalities such as haptic (touch), locative media and sound. Through their multisensoriality, the various genres of mobile gaming afford new forms of ambience and play.

The concept of ambience is often used to describe sound and music but has also been used in computing and science. As a noun, it specifically refers to a style of music with electronic textures and no consistent beat that is used to create a mood or feeling. More generally, the term describes the diffuse atmosphere of a place. In short, ambience is about the *texture* of *context*, *emotion* and *affect*. It is thus a sensory/affective category that goes beyond the five-sense sensorium, bringing together different sensory and affective categories into the same 'feeling'. There are many features of gameplay that are ambient, most explicitly the soundtracks that play a pivotal role in developing mood, genre and emotional clues for the player. Without their soundscapes, many games would fail.

And yet, like ambience, sound is relatively overlooked in games studies despite its pivotal role in the generation of the embodied experiences of players. However, what constitutes ambience within the context of mobile games – especially as they travel across different modes of physical and online presence (see Chapter 5), engagement, distraction and online and offline spaces, while potentially being on the move – means that we need to develop a more robust understanding of ambience. Often sound and aural ambience are augmented by the haptic elements of the game experience. Here, we need to understand ambience not just as an aural experience but also as an integral part of a game's texture, affect and embodiment. Co-presence – that is, ways of being together with others – is often an important part of the ambient texture. Making forms of intimacy through particular communication technologies when playing across physical and/or psychological distances has become a key feature of what makes online games so compelling (Milne, 2010: 165).

One of the challenges of doing ethnography in this context involves developing techniques to capture different forms of ambient play as it moves in and out of distraction, in and out of the online, and off and on the screen. That is, how can we learn about people's experience as their gaming practice moves from the background to the foreground and vice versa? In order to research ambient play, Hjorth and Richardson used a mixture of methods in the first phase of this project, including scenarios of use, diaries, video interviews and day-in-the-life videos (where the participant wears a GoPro video camera for a day) as part of first-person digital ethnography, participant observation and screen capture software. In many cases, the families recruited had a diversity of play and non-play practices. Hjorth and Richardson sought to contextualise games as part of the messiness of everyday life as an ambient play assemblage. Their fieldwork was conducted in Adelaide during March–September 2014 with twelve families, including single mothers, families without children, families from high and low socioeconomies, interracial couples and same sex couples. Within this diverse cohort, they found people who did and did not game in and around mobile and non-mobile devices. Some couples played together online and offline; with other couples, one member didn't play and the other did; some siblings played together, other siblings played with their parents; and in some families, pets also played.

A more detailed examination of some of these families gives an idea of how digital games, screens and the ambience associated with them formed part of the sensory and affective environments of these families. For example, Jane was a single mother for whom it was important that there was a balance of offline family activities for her three young boys. Her eight-year-old twins played games like *Minecraft* together for social bonding while watched by their fascinated five-year-old brother. The boys played mobile games across iPods and iPad platforms at home and at school, and their iPads played a key role in every class. All students had day planners on their iPads so that teachers and parents could see where they were at all times. In another family, for games teacher Tom and his school teacher wife Wendy, online multiplayer games like *World of Warcraft* (*WoW*) were pivotal in their everyday lives and formed part of the ways in which they experienced their evening routines. At night after work, Tom and Wendy played together for hours on *WoW*. Then, to prepare for sleep, they would graduate to playing mobile games in bed. However, in contrast Margaret, who was an editor, and her husband Brian did not use digital media together in this way. While Margaret loved reading (both on the Kindle and hardcopy), Brian played games. Digital media formed part of the sensory and affective experiential environment of the home in both cases, but in different ways. Although they had no children, their home was frequently visited by their neighbour's children. They watched or played games with Brian who, due to his gaming experience, was viewed as a sage by the neighbourhood children. In another family, with two young girls (eight and ten years old), the girls saw games as essential to contemporary socialisation and an important part of social play between school friends. They also taught their mother 'cool' games. For the girls, even Photo Booth was a game because it was 'playful'.

However, the ways that digital gaming, its ambience and particularly its touch screens was implicated in, and mediated, the embodied and affective relationships between family members also went beyond only human relationships. One family, consisting of a mother, father, ten-year-old girl and two cats, is particularly interesting. The cats were active members of this family, including when it came to games. The mother, Amanda, spoke just as lovingly about the two cats as she did when she spoke about her husband and daughter. The house also contained multiple games devices, three iPhones (father, mother and daughter), an iPad, two computers and a PlayStation. While iPhones tended to stay close at hand for their individual users, the iPad was viewed as the shared family device, residing on the sofa by the TV. The iPad had hundreds of games for the various players: husband, wife, daughter and cats (Figure 2.4).

Amanda's idea of having games for the cats had come from her observations while her daughter was playing on the iPad and her cats tried to join in. At first it was a great family joke. Initially surprised by her two cats' interest, she then searched online for cat games and came across a whole genre of cat play.

Figure 2.4 The family's understanding of the iPad as a family device included the cats as users of it

Amanda's search for cat iPad games questions the iPad's multisensorial capabilities, especially in terms of the haptic. While cats playing with a digital screen have its history in TV, it is the haptic participatory dimensions of the iPad that make for more playful and ambient possibilities. Friskies® offers a series of cat-specific games such as *CatFishing2*, *Happy Wings*, *Jitter Bug*, *Call.A.Cat* and *You vs. Cat*. The cat fishing-game obviously draws on the cat's interest in fish as if it were a screen-based fish bowl. From there, games have developed to include multiplaying between humans and cats (*You vs. Cat*), thus creating possibilities for thinking about how touch-screen technologies for games can be used to mediate and/or generate the sense of sensory embodied interactions between humans and animals. Moreover, as part of the Let's Play phenomenon whereby players film themselves and upload the videos for other players to watch, filming cats playing iPad games has become a key subgenre. This invites us to consider how the audiovisuality of this subgenre forms part of the ways in which digital media evoke human–animal–digital relationships and how empathetic experiential viewing positions might be generated (Figure 2.5).

Figure 2.5 The haptic screen is not only for the human species, as the participants in Hjorth and Richardson's research found

Source: Photograph copyright of Larissa Hjorth

Amanda and her family's mobile gaming demonstrates how games cannot be constitutive of human relations only, but also create platforms through which interspecies relationships can be experienced. The haptic dimension of iPads provide new opportunities for understanding mobile gaming as ambient play in everyday life. Central to the logic of mobile games has been their degrees of ambient play: that is, the way in which they enable a reflection of inner subjectivities, resonate within and around the everyday, and generate multiple forms of engagement, distraction and reflection. As we have seen, ambient play might be associated with haptic and auditory experience as much as with the visual. Mobile games amplify a particular form of embodied and ambient play which, as demonstrated, might be experienced not only by humans but also by animals, thus suggesting that it is not simply the representational qualities of the media that are important but rather the embodied and experiential elements that cannot necessarily be expressed in words, and, indeed, could not be for animals.

Seeing play as such – 'as part of a background to life' (Hjorth and Richardson, 2014: 73) – suggests that we need to rethink our definitions of play and game engagement, especially when dealing with convergent and mobile media devices that provide multiple, and often parallel, modes of engagement and distraction. Through the rubric of ambient play as the embodied, sensory and affective texture of mobile gaming, we have sought to think through a notion of the ambient as no longer an aural soundtrack but as an embodied part of haptic screen cultures embedded in their surroundings. In this example, we explored the notion of ambient play as integral to the messy logic of mobile games as they move across physical, geographic, electronic, technological and emotional spaces and across human and animal species. As we have suggested, as mobile game genres and gameplay techniques and textures grow, we need to account for more complex modes of embodiment as it traverses engagement and distraction, online and offline, here and there in new ways.

REFLECTING ON EXPERIENCE IN DIGITAL ETHNOGRAPHY

An ethnographic approach highlights how the Internet, social media, digital worlds, platforms, devices and content more broadly are experienced, and, indeed, are engaged in ways that generate new experiential configurations. Sites for such research, or units of analysis through which we might study the way that digital media form part of experiential worlds, might include practices, material culture, relationships, things, localities, social worlds or events. We remain conscious of this as we develop our discussion of each of these sites or contexts in the following chapters. Not all digital ethnography projects put the sensory, embodied or affective realms of experience at their core, yet human experience is part and parcel of everything that humans do, including ethnographers. We argue that accounting for experience is part of being a digital ethnographer. Indeed, it would benefit any form of ethnographic practice.

The three examples outlined above illustrate a range of ways of using ethnography to research experience. They also represent different approaches to sensory and digital ethnography. In the first example, Pink and Leder Mackley develop an approach to exploring digital media as a part of the tangible and intangible sensory and affective structures and textures of home. They are focusing on the normally unspoken aspects and experiences of media in the home – what they call 'media presence' – which demands an open approach, given that we cannot know in advance what we might find. Video tours and video re-enactments allowed Pink and Leder Mackley to follow the lead of the research participants and begin to understand, and to some extent share, routine and sensory experiences. Their use of the method of the 'intensive encounter' defined what their experience of fieldwork meant for this study (Pink and Morgan, 2013). This approach helped them to consider media beyond what conventional studies might uncover in relation to media as communication and content. By focusing on the experiential rather than material, they found that what matters at certain times was the use of media to create sensory and affective environments not necessarily directly related to the particulars of the content or the technology itself.

The first example also shows how researchers might develop a focus on the sensory experience of home. However, it does not predetermine experience as needed to refer to specific sensory categories of visual, olfactory, tactile, gustatory or aural experience. Instead, it appreciates experience as being more mixed up in the processes of human perception. Pink and Leder Mackley were interested in understanding what their participants' experiences of media in their homes felt like to participants themselves, therefore they left it open for them to find ways of narrating their experiences through recounting events and showing and performing with the material and sensory environment of home.

The second example, of Tacchi and Chandola's work, discusses a multi-year ethnography that started with a focus on communicative ecologies and then developed into a sensory ethnography. Both these approaches elicited insights into the gendered experience of everyday life in a slum cluster. It demonstrates that a focus on women and mobile phones needs to take broader and embedded structures and relationships into account, because it is in relation to these that the mobile phone is made meaningful (Tacchi et al., 2012). The ethnographic study shows how, in the context discussed, such structures were preserved through the uses and restrictions around mobile phones, and how they were circumvented. The ethnographic study of women and mobiles made those structures visible through engagement with everyday experiences and discussions around what these meant to research participants. It also opens up new channels for research itself, via these technologies and the social media that they connect to. In this example, 'being in fieldwork' (Marcus, 2008) extended to phone calls, messages and online chats when away from the physical site of the slum. This broadening of context allows access to new forms of sensory and affective expression, dialogue and experience. The researchers did not use specific sensory categories to develop the notion of experience, but instead focused on using the example of mobile phones to show what women's lives felt like in an Indian slum, through an emphasis on the affective and relational circumstances through which their lives are shaped and change.

In the third example, we saw how Hjorth and Richardson contextualised mobile games as an ambient part of the domestic sphere that involves both human and non-human actors. Ambience here is a multisensory form of experience, not reducible to sound, and in which touch is important. Understanding mobile games as part of the messy space of the digital within everyday households permits the exploration of various generational and cultural notions of the family and how mobile screens move in and out of the embodied experience of the digital. Through the rubric of ambient play as the intrinsic and affective texture of mobile gaming, the researchers sought to explore the idea of an embodied haptic screen culture that is embedded within participants' surroundings. In the case of the interspecies human–cat family we discussed above, the haptic element of the screen experience is pivotal to the uptake of iPad cat games, both in terms of how it is perceived by the human family members and how the cats engage with the screen.

SUMMING UP

There are a variety of approaches to researching experience, but central to all of them is the goal of describing and understanding experience as a critical component of addressing or answering research problems and questions about what it is like for other people to 'be' in the world, and how we know and learn about this beyond words. The ethnographers' embodiment is always at the core of this process, although to different degrees. For instance, researchers may seek to experience the same environments and activities as others as a route through which to empathetically connect with their sensory, embodied and affective experiences, or use their own experiences in seeking to comprehend what it might be like to feel those of others. The next task of the ethnographer of experience, whether or not she or he is concerned with digital media, is to communicate these experiences, or the ways of knowing and being associated with them, to wider audiences of academics (see Leder Mackley and Pink, 2013), stakeholders in research (see Sunderland and Denny, 2009) or wider publics (Pink and Abram, 2015). This is not a simple task, particularly given that such ethnographic research has tended to focus precisely on the unspoken or unsaid elements of everyday life. However, as the examples presented above have shown, it is indeed possible to write experience ethnographically, in addition to accounting for it through audiovisual and Web-based digital dissemination projects as outlined in Chapter 1 of this book.

THREE

Researching Practices

CHAPTER CONTENTS

INTRODUCTION

This chapter focuses on the concept of practices. It examines how a digital ethnography approach may engage this concept to research everyday habits and routines as they are played out in everyday environments, of which digital media are part. First, we discuss the development of the concept, reviewing how practices have been conceptualised in different disciplines. Then we consider how the notion of practices might be fruitfully put to use, both to understand what people do with and in relation to digital media in everyday life and as part of a research design that accounts for the digital. We discus three examples of how practices have been researched by digital ethnographers:

everyday practices that involve digital media in the home; the participatory practices of fan cultures; and everyday forms of environmentalism using digital media. We conclude by exploring the relationship between the ethnographic study of practices and its implications for understanding the tacit and mundane.

INTRODUCING THE CONCEPT OF PRACTICES

The study of practices emerged through an interest in how human actions and habits are shaped and maintained over time and the ways in which these impact in the world. Scholars interested in practices have been concerned with understanding the relationship between human actions and the rules, structures and processes that underpin what people say and do. There have been a range of theoretical approaches associated with a practice paradigm. These can generally be divided into two generations of practice theory scholarship (Postill, 2010). The first generation includes the early work of social theorists such as Pierre Bourdieu (1977) and Michel de Certeau (1984). The second generation includes the work of social practice theorists such as Theodore Schatzki (e.g., 2001) and Andreas Reckwitz (2002), which were taken up by sociologists such as Alan Warde (2011) and media scholars such as Nick Couldry (2004) in their studies of everyday life. These different renderings of practice theory are not all directly in agreement with each other, and in some cases they have been opposed (Pink, 2012; Postill, 2010). However, as Warde suggests, practice theories generally tend to stress 'routine over actions, flow and sequence over discrete acts, dispositions over decisions, and practical consciousness over deliberation' (2014: 9). In addition, they emphasise 'doing over thinking, the material over the symbolic, and embodied practical competence over expressive virtuosity' (2014: 8).

Building on the seminal work of Bourdieu, and on the work of social practice theorists such as Theodore Schatzki, sociologists have found theories of practice particularly useful for understanding consumption, and particularly as an approach that contests 'the perceived inadequacies of individualistic models'. (Warde, 2014: 284). Cultural studies scholars have been interested in the seeds of resistance that might be found in popular media culture and related practices, particularly the forms of meaning-making and symbolic resistance (through media and pop culture) mobilised by the working classes, feminism and 'subaltern' groups (de Certeau, 1984; Hebdige, 1979; McRobbie, 1991; Williams, 1974). Attuned to the differences between what people say and do, social and cultural anthropologists have also had a long-term interest in the concept of practice, or practices, as a way to understand the activities through which life is lived (Ortner, 1984). Thus, across sociology, cultural studies and anthropology as well as in philosophy and science and technology studies, the ways in which a concept of practice has been defined and used have been differently inflected (see, for example, Couldry, 2010; de Certeau, 1984; Reckwitz, 2002; Schatzki, 2001).

More recently, an approach referred to often as 'social practice theory' has emerged and has come to influence media studies (Bräuchler and Postill, 2010; Couldry, 2003). The practice turn, as it has been referred to, emerged from a growing interest across the humanities and social sciences in how the world is shaped through everyday actions and practices (Reckwitz, 2002; Schatzki, 2001). Building on the work of Giddens (1984), Bourdieu (1977) and others, Schatzki stresses the importance of performance to the instantiation of particular practices. Following Schatzki's approach, researchers have studied activities ranging from consumer practices such as eating, shopping, play and leisure. Of particular relevance for digital ethnography theory and practice is that science and technology studies scholars argue that our everyday practices are also shaped by *non-human actors*, such as technologies and material objects. This has implications for understanding human relationships and engagement with media and communications technologies, including mobile phones and television (Bijker et al., 1987; Latour, 1992; MacKenzie and Wajcman, 1999). It therefore also invites us to consider how our relationships with the technologies we use in our research practice are implicated in the ways we perform and generate knowledge as researchers.

EXISTING APPROACHES TO RESEARCHING PRACTICES

The above review of how the concept of practices has travelled through academic disciplines brings us to a central concern of this chapter: how does the notion of practices impact digital media research? Media studies has tended to organise its understanding of media according to three categories: media production and institutions; media genres, content or texts; and the uses of media in the world. Media researchers have paid particular attention to the political economy of media (institutions), conducting textual or content analysis and/or researching audiences, a subfield also known as 'reception studies' (Couldry, 2003).

As Hesmondhalgh notes (2010), there has been a long tradition of research on media production and media institutions. A classic study is Todd Gitlin's ethnographic study of primetime network TV, *Inside Prime Time* (1983). Historically, much media research has been carried out by disciplines outside of media studies (such as business and organisational studies). The emergence of a defined scholarly field of media industries or media production has been relatively recent (Hesmondhalgh, 2010). By and large, researchers in media studies, media anthropology and cultural studies have examined media practices primarily in terms of media *use* and how media audiences have engaged with, and made sense of, media in their everyday lives. Much of this work has focused on television and a preoccupation with domestic audiences, and it has been concerned with practices of meaning making, including how audiences might 'read' media content as symbolic 'texts' to be deciphered and decoded. Anthropologists were among the earliest scholars to examine how people view television and other media due to their collaborative involvement in indigenous media projects (e.g., Deger, 2005; Ginsburg, 2002). In some of these projects, media was *part of* a study rather than the topic of study.

In recognition of various challenges to conventional media studies approaches, Couldry has called for a media research paradigm that 'sees media not as text or production economy, but first and foremost as practice' (2010: 35). Couldry suggests that divisions between media production and political economy, media studies of genre and audience studies are arbitrary, bearing little relation to how media functions in the world. He argues that media environments are complex, and neat divisions between media production and consumption are increasingly problematic. Couldry (2012) moreover proposes a 'non-media-centric' approach to media studies – an approach inspired by the work of David Morley (e.g., 2009) and shared by media scholar Shaun Moores (2012). Morley argued that a non-media-centric approach is needed 'to better understand the ways in which media processes and everyday life are interwoven with each other' (2007: 200). Focusing specifically on media can detract attention from the contexts in which media practices take place. Couldry contends that in order to move towards a non-media-centric media studies, scholars can draw from the lessons of practice theory, particularly its more sociologically oriented strain. If practice theory sees the social order as being produced and enacted through everyday practices, rather than existing prior to them, our starting point for analysis should not be media texts, media institutions or audiences. Rather, it should be with 'media-oriented practice in all its looseness and openness' (Couldry, 2010: 39). The focus, therefore, shifts to what people are doing with media in different situations and contexts.

WHAT ARE THE IMPLICATIONS OF THE 'DIGITAL' FOR THE CONCEPT OF PRACTICES?

The increased use of new and digital media in everyday life has driven a renewed interest in the concept of practices as well as a broadening of what practices might mean in the context of digital media use (Bräuchler and Postill, 2010). Focus has shifted from *meaning making* and *audiences* to a broader notion of *an ensemble of practices*, or *fields* of practices as conceptualised by social practice theory. The image of a couch-bound audience who consume media texts that are made by distant producers in a media centre has become increasingly anachronistic in a digital media world (Hepp and Couldry, 2010) (see Chapter 8). The media which we engage with today are not primarily pre-made. Rather, media technologies have become highly *personalised* experiences that are embedded in our *daily lives, routines and interpersonal relationships* (see Chapter 4). As many scholars argue, new media technologies such as mobile phones have become so ubiquitous in many parts of the world that they have become a taken-for-granted and relatively invisible part of our daily lives (Burrell, 2012; Goggin, 2011; Hjorth, 2009; Horst, 2012; Ling, 2012). At the same time, through the spread of interactive technologies such as social media and mobile phone applications, we have increasingly become active producers and shapers of media content (Bruns, 2006; Lange, 2014; Lange and Ito, 2010).

These crucial shifts in the way we engage with media in our daily lives compel a transformation in our understandings and approaches to contemporary media practices. Social practice theory offers us a useful way of responding to these transformations by addressing 'how media are embedded in the interlocking fabric of social and cultural life' (Couldry, 2006: 47). Yet, practice theory does not offer a methodological toolkit for investigating practices. In the remainder of this chapter, we examine how digital media practices that are habitual and unconscious (reflected in the fact that people routinely underestimate their use of social media, mobile phones and so on) and tied to people's everyday routines (Horst, 2010; Pink, 2013) have been researched ethnographically. As we show, a digital ethnography approach, precisely because ethnographic methods enable us to focus on *doing* – the central interest of practice theory – offers methods through which to investigate practices as they unfold, both as they are performed and as they are reported or demonstrated. This might include researching people's participation in communities and interpersonal relations (Facebook, Weibo) and the co-creation of media content. It might also involve considering how a focus on practices can enable us to account for how technologies and material infrastructures become players in social relations (Horst, 2013; Miller and Horst, 2012). A focus on (media) practices over time also provides a way to understand processes of social change (Lewis, 2015; Postill, 2012b).

RESEARCHING PRACTICES THROUGH DIGITAL ETHNOGRAPHY

In this section, we discuss three examples of ethnographic studies that provide insights into what a non-media-centric, practice-oriented approach to media might look like. These examples illustrate ways that a concept of practice can help researchers understand the use of digital media and technologies in everyday life. The first example, a study of the use of digital media in everyday life routines and what the researchers who undertook the study call 'rhythms' in Australia, highlights how digital media has become part of the mundane, routine dimensions of households. The second and third examples explore engagements in two different 'communities' in the USA and Australia that span a variety of spaces, including households, neighbourhoods and websites. These three examples focus on the routines and complexities of everyday practices, and represent a range of new practices and research methods.

Researching the digital rhythms of the home

Our first example of researching practices is an Australia-based project that was designed in collaboration with a corporate partner. The global auditing company KPMG was interested in the implications of digital media for their client base. They wanted to understand how consumers engage with the digital realm in the context of a rapidly shifting digital environment, and felt that a conventional survey-based approach was not sufficient. While quantitative data can describe and predict patterns of use across large groups of people, they tend to overlook key qualitative dimensions of customer values and behaviour. These include how customers make choices, and how customers feel about and engage with products, interfaces and devices in the context of the messy realities of everyday life. One key limitation of user surveys is that they take a static snapshot of people's *perceptions* of digital use at a particular point in time and in a space abstracted from the contexts in which usage takes place. In contrast, ethnography generates embedded descriptions and understandings of how people use digital technologies and content in the contexts of everyday places, practices, relationships and routine. The researchers in this particular study coined the notion of 'digital rhythms' to conceptualise these practices. Digital ethnography draws attention to the mundane and 'hidden' dimensions of how and why digital media and content matter (Horst et al., 2012; Pink and Leder Mackley, 2012, 2013).

The research was driven by a set of thematic areas of interest or broad frames. In particular, the project was designed with questions in mind around the role digital media may or may not play in how households manage, negotiate and experience key areas of their lives such as health, travel and transport, energy consumption, work, shopping, leisure, finance and relationships. However, the key research 'questions' that the Digital Ethnography Research Centre (DERC) developed for this project were open-ended and broadly defined. The researchers who undertook the project – Jo Tacchi, Tania Lewis, Victor Albert and Tripta Chandola – were therefore able to remain flexible and incorporate unexpected or unanticipated findings regarding how digital media transform the lives of ordinary people.

The researchers employed a range of ethnographic methods, informed by digital and visual ethnography to develop a study. The methods were designed to get below the surface of everyday life and explore what people actually do and feel *in situ*. The researchers used immersive techniques to learn about people's everyday lives and digital rhythms through repeated visits to households over a four-month data collection period. The pilot project encompassed twelve households across two states in Australia with some of the households located in remote and rural sites. Participants included families with children (from toddlers to teenagers), elderly and professional couples, a single-person household and a shared student house (Figure 3.1).

Figure 3.1   Digital media in everyday life

Source: Photograph copyright of Jo Tacchi and Tripta Chandola.

Key methods included video recordings and re-enactments of pivotal moments of digital media use, day-in-the-life studies and exploring the production and circulation of content. The researchers collected data over a series of three visits to each household (in some cases, they condensed the data collection into two visits). The first visit was designed to explore households as contexts or communicative ecologies for the consumption and circulation of digital technologies and content. The video tour method introduced in Chapter 2 has been used extensively for investigating everyday life in the home (since Pink, 2004, 2013) digital technologies in the home (Pink and Leder Mackley, 2012). In this study, householders were asked to take the researcher who visited them on a tour (often videoed) of their home environment, as they sought to develop a picture of how different digital media technologies, platforms and content combine in different ways in each household. Through audio- and video-recorded interviews in homes, they explored participants' own digital media biographies, capturing the language they used when speaking about digital media, their values, their emotions and their expectations of the affordances offered by the digital realm now and in the future (Figure 3.2).

Figure 3.2   Ubiquitous digital media

Source: Photograph copyright of Jo Tacchi and Tripta Chandola.

The second visit focused on developing the concepts of 'digital practices' and 'rhythms', exploring how digital media and content are embedded in but also shape everyday routines and habits as well as feelings, expectations and experiences of time and speed. Within the energy and digital media study discussed in Chapter 2, Pink and Leder Mackley (2014) developed the method of the video re-enactment in order to research getting up in the morning and bedtime routines. In the Digital Rhythms project, the researchers invited householders to re-enact getting up in the morning, which they defined as a daily practice which might involve waking to the sound of their mobile phone alarm, checking their email in bed and then opening a weather app to work out what to wear that day. Observing digital practices also highlighted the role of technology in shaping and mediating relationships: while much of participants' use of digital media and technology was personalised and privatised, digital practices were shaped by social relationships.

The final visit focused on the consumption, production and circulation of content, from online news articles and TV programmes to accessing online health advice or health-related apps, to uploading photos and videos and playing digital games. Here, rather than viewing content as somehow separate from everyday practices or as a static 'thing', the researchers built on concepts of communicative ecologies, digital practices and rhythms to explore the ways in which content and daily practices were co-articulated.

The Digital Rhythms study used an ethnographic approach to provide KPMG with a different perspective and new insights into how consumers are responding to a rapidly shaping digital world. Through engaging with, observing and videoing householders over a period of time, the digital ethnographic approach captures the flows and rhythms of day-to-day digital use and enables researchers to uncover practices that are routine and out of the ordinary. In contrast to surveys and quantitative studies, digital ethnography captures the unspoken meanings and emotional or affective dimensions of engaging with digital technologies. Spending time with householders also involves recognising their embedded knowledges. These correspond more broadly with what anthropologists refer to as 'local knowledge' or 'indigenous knowledge' (e.g., Sillitoe, 2007), in earlier research in the home this has involved a focus on the forms of everyday 'expertise' associated with, for instance, 'housewifely knowledge' and its appropriation (Pink, 2004: 93), or what in cultural studies has been termed 'ordinary expertise' (Lewis, 2008) around digital use. Much of this 'knowledge' can be habitual and unconscious. During this project, research relationships developed with participants over time, leading the participants to reflect on earlier research conversations and consider their activities around the digital in different ways. The researchers found that it was common for people, when first asked, to underestimate considerably the amount of time spent on, and the amount of attention paid to, digital devices and activities. However, on reflection and through discussion, they often recognised higher and more regular usage than they had initially estimated.

For instance, during Tacchi and Chandola's first visit to the home of Nancy and Paul, a low-income couple living with their two young children in rural New South Wales, the couple initially portrayed themselves as low-level users and as digitally unsophisticated (they described their young daughter as the main technology user). However, on their second visit, Paul talked about how he had realised after his initial conversation with Tacchi and Chandola how much time he and Nancy actually spent on their smartphones, often scrolling through Facebook or playing games while relaxing in the evening in front of the TV and once their children had gone to bed. Towards the end of their final interview, they recalled that they had used the Internet to book a family holiday, taking three weeks to research carefully their travel (train and flights) and accommodation. It emerged that Nancy had made videos of two horses that she wanted to sell, posted them online and sold the horses. They had also sold their car through a Facebook page. For many households, such activities are now so much a part of routine and mundane everyday lives, that they are often unremarkable and embedded into the flow of the day. In Nancy and Paul's case, their recognition of their own extensive digital practices only came up in the last hour of this final visit, following their participating in six hours of research activities and discussion. Such findings reflect a key advantage of practice-led ethnography: it can help both researchers and participants become reflexively aware of hidden habitual and embodied digital practices and meanings.

Approaching Fan Fiction Practices through Ethnography

The second example focuses on the concept of *genres of participation* as a practice-based approach to studying digital media engagement. Developed by Ito et al. (2010), *genres of participation* describes differing levels of investments in new media activities in a way that integrates understandings of technical, social and cultural patterns. It represents an alternative to taxonomies of media engagement that are generally structured by type of media platform, frequency of media use or structural categories such as gender, age or socioeconomic status (e.g., 'the gamer', 'the digital native'). Rather than focusing on age, educational status, race and ethnicity as the structural determinants of practice, genres of participation enables a more holistic approach to practice that emphasises the ways in which such sociocultural categories are part and parcel of media engagement. Participation takes shape as an overall constellation of characteristics, which are constantly under negotiation and in flux as people experiment with new modes of communication and culture.

The example and the dominant genres of participation – hanging out, messing around and geeking out – emerged out of a broader ethnographic project on youth, families and informal learning carried out during the Digital Youth Project (Ito et al., 2009, 2010). The study – which involved 800 youths in the USA who participated in the 22 case studies and included over 5000 hours of online observation – examined how young people were using new media for communication, friendship, play and self-expression within and across contexts, including institutions (schools and after-school programmes), online sites, interest groups, homes and neighbourhoods. This specific example draws on Horst's study of digital media use in 25 families living in Silicon Valley, California, carried out between 2005 and 2008 (Horst, 2009, 2015). This example discusses the practices of one of the youths in Horst's study, a 16-year-old active fan fiction writer who used the pseudonym 'Fangrrl' (for this study).

A range of scholars have looked at the dynamics of fan-based subcultures and their engagement with media texts; especially within media and cultural studies Henry Jenkins's now classic study of fan cultures (1992) chronicled how fans effectively engaged with, subverted or 'poached' meta and mass produced texts by becoming creators and producers of alternative cultural forms. Subsequent work has revealed how once 'alternative' fan practices have become increasingly mainstream with the merger or convergence of 'traditional' and digital media forms (Jenkins, 2006a). Fans now not only consume professionally produced media, but they also produce their own media products, continuing to disrupt the culturally dominant distinctions between the practices of production and consumption. In some cases, writers of canon texts embrace fan fiction, as in the case of the *Twilight* series writer Stephanie Meyer.

Through an initial background questionnaire and interview, Horst learned that, at the age of 16, Fangrrl had become an award-winning fan fiction writer, with followers throughout the world and a presence on a number of fan fiction community sites. Fangrrl began her fan fiction career at the age of 13, when she started reading the *Harry Potter* book series. She then heard about a website, fanfiction.net, where amateur writers create stories using characters from the *Harry Potter* series. After a year or so of avidly reading and, eventually, drafting a few of her own stories, Fangrrl began to concentrate on writing fan fiction for the *Buffy the Vampire Slayer* television series that aired between 1997 and 2003. It has a steady following thanks to television re-runs and the ability to watch new series through DVD rentals through services such as Netflix. Fangrrl typically wrote a story or two each month during the schoolyear and wrote at least one story a week during the summer. Like other fanfic writers, Fangrrl's

Figure 3.3a Watching Fan Fiction, Diary Study 2006

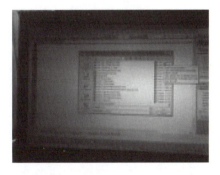

Figure 3.3b Writing Fan Fiction, Diary Study 2006

Figure 3.3c Reading Fan Fiction, Diary Study 2006

Figure 3.3d Sharing Fan Fiction, Diary Study 2006

Source: Photograph credit to Fangrrl as part of Horst's Families in Silicon Valley study.

stories are often focused on romantic and homoerotic stories described as 'slash'. Fangrrl's stories and their various 'couplings' and storylines (particularly those focused around the character of Angel), grapple with the 'power' of youth culture and the reconfiguration of masculinity and challenges of misogyny dominant in the broader culture. Although personally significant for Fangrrl and her own identity formation, the content of her writings were not atypical for fan fiction writers (Figure 3.3).

The diary study provided Horst with insights into the effort that goes into amateur cultural activities like fan fiction (Jenkins, 2006b; Lange and Ito, 2010) by bringing to light the different activities that Fangrrl engaged in to support her fan fiction practice and its significance in the context of the rest of her life. The diary study enabled Fangrrl to document the different ways in which she took on an active role in the fan fiction community, and enabled her to discuss her transition from 'messing around' (or exploring different aspects of the fan fiction sites) to 'geeking out', a genre of participation that reflects deep commitment and engagement in a particular site, community or practice and often involves feedback, commenting and other forms of interactions in networked spaces (Horst et al., 2010). For example, Fangrrl used her photo diary to document her practice of providing feedback on other fan fiction writers' stories. She wrote comments in a Microsoft Word document and later copied and pasted into the comments section on fan fiction websites and authors whom she followed. As Fangrrl described her own participation:

I'm good at commenting on other people's [stories]. [I] just do a lot of comments, but it bothers me when I, like, have lot of hits but no comments. So I try to comment if I can ... Often I'll kinda check various long, ongoing ones to see if they've updated, and if they have, I'll try to write a quick comment.

Like many involved in fandom, Fangrrl also started to take on a more active role in other aspects of production, such as creating the art for her stories. As she described it:

I will sometimes, instead of doing homework, fool around with Photoshop and the digital pictures ... Before, we had [a digital camera], it was a lot harder to, you know, use pictures. I had to like lift stuff off the Internet like a picture of Angelina Jolie ... I mean now it's a lot more fun because I can actually, like you know decide what images I want and then make them ... But, like, I would also do the Buffy stuff, or whenever I take pictures that are screen captures I edit them or mix two together or something and kinda make a picture for the title page of the story or something I've written.

In addition to being a reader and commentator, part of honing her craft (and maintaining her credibility in the fan fiction community) involved routinely watching *Buffy the Vampire Slayer* with her sister Maggie. On the weekend on which she completed the diary study, the sisters spent time 'hanging out' and watched a total of ten hours of the show on DVD together. Notably, all of the online activities took place using a dial-up modem at home or, when given permission, at the library at school during lunch (Horst, 2010; Horst et al., 2010).

An ethnographic approach to researching digital media practices enabled Horst to flexibly develop methods that could explore in greater depth and detail the practices that young people were reporting in their interviews. These are practices that participant observation in more traditional contexts could have accounted for but were not possible in the context of a study of youth living in Silicon Valley, California, particularly given the fact that most of these activities took place in the private space of the home, one where sociality and visits from non-family members are increasingly structured around formal dinners and play dates. Within the context of the broader Digital Youth Project, the development of the diary study by Horst and her colleagues allowed researchers working with youth in the context of homes, families and neighbourhoods to understand the intricacies of young people's everyday use of digital media when 'being there' is restricted by social norms, human ethics guidelines, and the different spaces, places and times in which youth engage with media.

Capturing and cultivating green urban and suburban practices

From productive gardening and urban farms to suburban food coups, grassroots green practices are emerging around the world as householders and communities become increasingly concerned with the ethical implications of how we live. While some of these practices are fairly public and visible, much of what constitutes green activism and citizen engagement today is hidden from public view. In this example, our focus is on a research project that has used digital ethnography to document sustainable practices and to make them visible to a broader audience. The focus here then is not on people's media practices per se (although, as we will see, digital media use is often integral to organising and facilitating people's sustainability practices), but rather on lifestyle practices more broadly.

Tania Lewis and her colleagues used qualitative and ethnographic methods to study a range of household and community based practices in suburban Melbourne oriented towards sustainable living. These included household hard waste reuse and recycling, direct-to-farm food cooperatives, urban craft and carpentry, and productive suburban gardening (Lewis et al., 2014; Lewis, forthcoming). They were interested in developing methods to document everyday green practices that are largely invisible to the public eye, such as practices occurring in back gardens, homes, curbsides and other ordinary spaces. Additionally, they were interested in methods of researching practices that are centred on action and transformation. The researchers also wanted to explore the ethics and politics of participating in and making visible privatised green lifestyle practices (Figure 3.4).

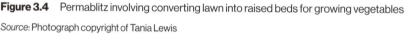

Figure 3.4 Permablitz involving converting lawn into raised beds for growing vegetables

Source: Photograph copyright of Tania Lewis

One example of suburban sustainability practices involves the transformation of ordinary backyards and gardens into productive sites via 'green' garden makeovers.

Melbourne Permablitz is a network of people who volunteer to transform suburban gardens into productive food systems that are designed according to the principles of permaculture. The idea of permaculture was developed in the mid-1970s by Australians Bill Mollison and David Holmgren as an alternative to industrialised forms of agriculture (Holmgren, 2002; Mollison, 1988; Mollison and Holmgren, 1978). Conceived of as an ethical and holistic design system for sustainable living, land use and land repair, '[p]ermaculture has come to mean a design system, for taking pattern and relationships observed in natural ecosystems into novel productive systems for meeting human needs' and has been embraced by individuals, groups and communities worldwide (www.permablitz.net/resources/our-principles). In an excerpt from her fieldwork, Lewis describes what it is to attend a permablitz event:

> I arrived somewhat late in the morning to the Sunday 'blitz', driving up through a part of northern Melbourne I hadn't visited before. Armed with a video-camera, shovel, hat and sunscreen I followed a lanky stranger down the side drive of an ordinary suburban brick house to find a good sized group of people already at work weeding, hacking away at plants and thoughtfully inspecting the various spaces and 'projects' underway in the to my (inner urban) eyes rather huge quarter acre block.

Cut to the end of the day and I and others, no longer strangers, are taking photos of (and in my case videoing) the transformation that has taken place during the day:

An old chicken coup has been repaired and extended, once desolate patches of dying off lawn turned into wooden-framed raised garden beds, overgrown spaces cleared and turned into potentially productive land ready for planting ... In one day with the aid of planning and the labour and skills of many bodies, a large neglected suburban backyard is on its way to turning into an integrated permaculture garden complete with chickens.

The Permablitz movement's 'home' is a website (www.permablitz.net), with permablitzes themselves usually taking place in people's backyards around suburban Melbourne with participants, most of whom are strangers, often travelling long distances across town to volunteer their time. The Permablitz network undertakes a number of activities, including holding Guild Sessions around various sites in Melbourne to share knowledge and skills, and to link people across the network. However, the network's main activities are organising and holding one-day garden makeovers in private gardens of all shapes and sizes across Melbourne. Lewis attended and participated in a number of blitzes at a range of suburban sites across Melbourne over the course of one year, talking to volunteers, home owners and blitz organisers (blitzes are extensively planned and led by volunteers who usually have permaculture training), taking field notes and also taking photos and videos of blitz activities and the dramatic transformational process undertaken at backyard sites.

As her field note suggests, a central aspect of Lewis's research on sustainability practices has been to actively participate in them and acquire new skills. Lewis's concern with making change visible and actively contributing to it (such as the transformation of a domestic garden into a sustainable food space) can be viewed as 'action research'. Her positioning as a co-participant focuses on gaining knowledge about the culture of suburban green practices through what the field of cultural studies has called 'intense immersion' (Sands, 1999; Sparkes, 2009).

The embodied nature of participant research on green gardening also involves engaging with and communicating somatic sensory practices and the visceral nature of the everyday (Hayes-Conroy and Martin, 2010) in what Panhofer and Payne have referred to as 'non-languaged ways' with respect to dance (Panhofer and Payne, 2011). How do researchers capture the feel of learning to work with the grain of the wood as one builds a chicken coup or cuts branches from a tree? How does one engage with the shifting sense of habitus, of explicit and tacit bodily knowledge that accompanies the retraining and repositioning of the body within the space of ordinary everyday practices? And how might the research process itself speak to a recognition of the ways in which human practices are articulated through non-human actors and objects, such as chickens, soil, gardening tools, and other environmental and material elements (Strengers and Maller, 2012)?

Lewis's research on sensory and non-human practices of transformation combined interviews, fieldwork, video, photography, and elements of participatory and experiential ethnography to shed light on the multifaceted nature of green practices. Combining mobile technologies such as video cameras and mobile phones with ethnographic research on the sensory and haptic dimensions of everyday practices enables a complex engagement with the sights, sounds, taste, smell, feel, rhythms and temporalities of a range of actors, spaces and practices (Pink, 2015). For Lewis, the use of mobile visual technologies in combination with the moving, labouring body of the researcher extended empirical research, which often privileges the beliefs and actions of humans, beyond that of purely visible markers of social change towards what P. Ticineto Clough (2009) terms 'infra-empiricism'. This approach is consistent with the practice and ethos of permaculture, which views productive sustainable gardening as an ongoing process embedded in complex environmental-technical systems and practices of which human activity is just one part. The very act of videoing strangers building a chicken house in a suburban backyard, or photographing a piece of previously disused land that has been converted into a productive garden, involves intervening in and transforming everyday practices into moments and sites of 'activism'. Activism is thereby tied to an array of visible and invisible forms of agency.

The use of video and photographic images by research participants themselves also points to the role of everyday green 'activists' as producers and curators of content in a digital media context. Visual practices are central to the Permablitz network, whose website features a continually updated array of photos and videos of previous garden makeovers which act to document and archive practices ('eating the suburbs, one backyard at a time' is the website's tagline), to construct a sense of 'community' and to entice and recruit new members to the group. Such practices on the part of both participants and participant-researchers point to the increasing difficulty of distinguishing between scholarly researchers and communities of everyday experts. It also highlights a shared concern with legitimating and foregrounding invisible forms of activism through visual modes of documentation.

REFLECTING ON PRACTICE AS A CATEGORY FOR DIGITAL ETHNOGRAPHY RESEARCH

The three examples in this chapter describe different approaches to the study of digital media technologies. All three examples acknowledge and analyse the diverse ways in which people are engaging with digital media, and the consequences of these engagements for our conceptual understanding of digital media practice. For example, the research design of the Digital Rhythms project accounts for the broader spaces or ecologies in which digital media are situated, the routines and rhythms of digital media as well as the kinds of engagements with different content across the twelve households in the study. Comparing a range of practices, or genres of participation, the fan fiction study practices moves from the domestic into the fan fiction community who are linked together by common interests. As research in media and cultural studies continues to highlight, fans are active meaning makers in the construction of media who often reframe or 'poach' media texts (Jenkins, 1992). The final example of permablitzing looks at the ways in which the community website involves practices of engaging and monitoring community via a website and through the sociality created through the practice of gardening in urban Melbourne.

The three examples highlight how digital ethnography might be engaged in conjunction with theories of practice in order to understand processes of change, instances of human action, and embodied ways of knowing across a range of different national, cultural and public or domestic contexts. A research design that focuses on practices offers us an analytical unit that creates a ready entry point for studying what people *do* and how these *doings* might be constitutive of wider social configurations, contexts and processes. Their focus is on the practice rather than the individual and group as a prism through which to understand the world. However, while analytically we can conceptualise a practice as a unit, as the studies we have discussed above show, in fact such practices are not 'naturally' bounded. For instance, in the example of the Digital Rhythms project we saw that Internet use was actually inseparable from horse-selling or other practices that made the use of the Internet part of everyday life. In the example of Horst's research with a young fanfic writer, we see not only the ways in which her interest changed over time, but also how her interest in a form of popular culture enabled Fangrrl to move into writing and other creative outlets and, in turn, how these practices became part of her relationship with her sister and other relationships. In the example of Lewis's research, we saw how the practices of photography and Web maintenance were interdependent with the practices of permaculture. As these examples show, researching digital media practices often actually means researching the relationship between digital media and other things and processes, and considering how the practices through which these are played out become blurred.

This is not to say that media studies' insights into institutions, texts and audiences should be disregarded, but rather that they highlight how practice-inflected ethnographies of media are particularly useful for capturing the complex intersections between media, culture, the social and the material. They bring to the foreground media practices that are often habitual and invisible and therefore difficult to access using more conventional interview and survey-based research, as we saw in the example of the Digital Rhythms project. There are, of course, questions that need to be asked about the limitations of the concept of practices and its application as a method alongside ethnography. As Couldry (2010) suggests, a key question in moving to a practice approach, for instance, is how we might think about orderings or hierarchies of practice and questions of power. Do some practices, for instance, 'public' spectacles and rituals, carry a particular kind of social weight or power, anchoring, grounding or shifting more everyday processes and practices? What is the ongoing representational role of media and how is it played out? Such questions then suggest a research area that is comparatively new and emergent; a field that we would argue needs to grow and develop through the research process itself.

SUMMING UP

This chapter's focus on practice theory in digital ethnography can be used to understand the everyday ways that people are engaging with digital media and technology. Although the global spread is uneven, for many people now mobile phones, laptops or tablets have become integral to daily life and to their interpersonal and broader social relationships. The ubiquity of digital media in everyday life makes it at once obvious and easy to find, but at the same time it is difficult to separate out the ways that people use digital media from the wider rhythms and routines of everyday living and embodied senses of self. Contemporary societies might be characterised as inhabited by people continually checking email, using GPS technology to navigate a city or locate a 'lost' friend, chatting to distant friends in the car or downloading a TV show to watch after work. In this context, digital media permeate everyday life in ways that have both continuities and differences with how old media technologies like locationally fixed TVs and mobile pens, paper and letters. As we have sought to demonstrate, a digital ethnography approach to practices enables an understanding of where digital media and technology are embedded in the routines and habits of our everyday lives, and recognises the processes through which digital media technologies are both central to our existence but increasingly taken for granted and invisible.

Researching Things

CHAPTER CONTENTS

INTRODUCTION

This chapter examines how ethnographers have approached the study of media and media technologies as things. We begin by discussing the how anthropologists, media and cultural studies scholars study things that are produced, distributed, circulated, consumed or discarded, and what the study of media and technologies as things enables us to understand about media and technologies as well as social processes and relationships. While in many cases the existing literature references people's relationships to objects, in this chapter we will use the term 'things' to avoid confusion or conflation with a separate category of analysis, that of 'media objects'. We argue that while the past twenty years of research has been dominated by a concern with the multiple meanings of consumption, the heart of contemporary ethnographic research has returned to a focus upon the conditions and processes of production, such as the less visible aspects of digital media infrastructures and engagement with design practitioners who take consumer desires and aspirations into account in their wish to design usable platforms, software, spaces and objects. We illustrate these new directions through three examples: a study of radio and sound in domestic settings; a project on energy and the portability and materiality of domestic technologies; and a study of migrants and the use of mobile technologies across national borders. Throughout the chapter, we use the phrase 'media technologies' to draw attention to the multivalent nature and function of things despite the convergence of their capabilities and uses.

WHAT IS THE CONCEPT OF THINGS AND WHERE DOES IT COME FROM?

Attention to media technologies as 'things', or forms of material culture, has a long history in the social sciences and humanities. Early on, Karl Marx's attention to labour and production processes hinged on a model of technological determinism, wherein the meaning of a particular thing or artefact was predetermined by the production process (Tucker, 1978). Subsequent work by Frankfurt School scholars looked more specifically at the role of culture industries in the production of mass culture and the ways in which aesthetic forms in art, music and other forms of mass-produced culture were resulting in false consciousness conducive to capitalism (Adorno, 2002; Benjamin, 2008[1936]). A later focus on 'things' then developed in, and was shaped by, academic disciplines and interdisciplinary fields as they came increasingly to account for the material and its implications, including in media and cultural studies, anthropology, museum studies and material culture studies.

A significant transformation in approaches to understanding 'things' and material culture occurred with the development of British cultural studies in the 1960s and the broader attention in the social sciences and humanities to the intersection between capitalism, imperialism and colonialism (Ortner, 1984; Williams, 1974). Retaining the concern with power and domination that characterised cultural studies scholarship at the time, scholars started to focus upon understanding the practices of the non-elites and the meanings that people ascribed to media, material and consumer culture, with increasing attention to how class, race, gender and other forms of identity were co-constituted (Centre for Contemporary Cultural Studies, 1982; Hall, 1973, 1980; Willis, 1977). These included attention to the production of youth subcultures and ethnic and racial identity through music, fashion and other forms of consumption (Gilroy, 1987, 1993 Hebdige, 1979, 1987).

Framing the social or cultural as the locus of agency, they suggested that it was society rather than production processes that gave 'things' meaning, and that 'things' could be seen as artefacts that reflected relations of power, domination and inequality in society. A key example of the cultural studies approach to media technologies was outlined in Paul du Gay, Stuart Hall, Linda Janes, Hugh Mackay and Keith Negus (1997), *Doing Cultural Studies: The Story of the Sony Walkman*. In the groundbreaking study, the authors introduced the concept of 'circuits of culture' as a framework that enabled cultural studies scholars to identify and explore the moments – production, consumption, representation, identity and regulation – wherein culture defines and shapes the meaning of media technologies.

Alongside cultural studies, the field of material culture studies also experienced a renaissance of sorts in the 1980s, moving away from the focus upon museums, collecting and archaeology characteristic of its early origins in anthropology to contemporary forms of material culture and mass consumption (Miller, 1988). Rather than viewing 'things' as reflections or products of society, material culture studies scholars argued that objects and things, the materials used to construct them and the properties of these materials are central to understanding culture and social relations: humans play as much of a role in the creation of objects as objects create the conditions of human life. With the recognition of the mutually constitutive role of people and things, the focus then becomes a question of how a particular object or thing comes to have value. Arjun Appadurai's (ed.) (1986) *The Social Life of Things: Commodities in Cultural Perspective* is widely recognised as setting the stage for a new conversation in the social sciences not only about 'things', but also how we think about 'things'. In his introduction, Appadurai made the case that just like persons, objects and commodities have lives which are implicated in different regimes of value which result in different meanings 'as they move through different hands, contexts and uses' (Appadurai, 1986: 34). In particular, Kopytoff's (1986) contribution to the edited volume introduced a new framework and methodology – cultural biography – as an approach to understanding these changing meanings and regimes of value. In Kopytoff's words:

> In doing the biography of a thing one would ask questions similar to those one asks about people ... Where does the thing come from and who made it? What has been its career so far, and what do people consider to be an ideal career for such things? What are the recognized 'ages' or periods in the thing's 'life', and what are the cultural markers for them? How does the thing's use change with its age, and what happens to it when it reaches the end of its usefulness? (1986: 66–7)

In effect, Kopytoff approached 'things' as always in a processing of becoming – of 'things in motion' rather than a set state of being, with identification as a 'commodity' (commoditisation) to be sold, exchanged or branded as being only one possible stage in the lifecycle of a thing. Subsequent studies have explored how these processes may be changing for particular kinds of regimes of value such as art markets (e.g., Myers, 2001; Geismar, 2013) and the global flows of people, ideas, money, technology and media (Appadurai, 1996; Marcus and Myers, 1995).

HOW HAS THE CONCEPT OF THINGS BEEN DEVELOPED IN EXISTING RESEARCH (WITH MEDIA)?

One of the seminal contributions to debates about the relationship with media technologies as things was the domestication approach, consolidated in the edited volume *Consuming Technologies: Media and Information in Domestic Spaces* (Silverstone and Hirsch, 1992). The volume introduced a productive conversation between cultural and media studies' concerns with text and narrative, social anthropology's focus on social relationships and material culture studies' attention to the relationship with things in context, prompting a spate of interdisciplinary conversations around consumption studies. As Silverstone and Hirsch (1994: 20) describe, contemporary media technologies 'must be viewed as essentially material objects, capable of great symbolic significance, investment, and meaning', while domestic technologies are 'embedded in the structures and dynamics of contemporary consumer culture'. A particularly important concept within the domestication approach is 'double articulation', which acknowledges that media technologies are objects that link the private sphere with the public sphere and, in turn, facilitate the negotiation of meaning both within and through their use in domestic settings (Silverstone et al., 1992). They further argue that:

> objects and meanings, in their objectification and incorporation within the spaces and practices of domestic life, define a particular semantic universe for the household in relation to that offered in the public world of commodities and ephemeral and instrumental relationships. (Ibid.: 18–19)

This has implications for the processes through which new media technologies are incorporated into everyday life.

Through appropriation, or the process by which people assign meaning to things, people, places and activities, media technologies are incorporated and redefined in different terms, in accordance with the household's own values and interests. The meanings and significance of all media depends upon the varied ways that individuals, households and other entities use and engage with media technologies. Silverstone and Hirsch outlined four phases to describe the concept of domestication: appropriation, objectification, incorporation and conversion. Appropriation is when a technology leaves the world of a 'commodity' and can be taken by an individual or a household and owned. It includes the whole process of consumption as well as the moment at which an object crosses the threshold between the formal and the moral economy (Miller, 1988). Objectification is expressed in usage but also, following Bourdieu (1984), the dispositions of objects in the spatial environment of the home. All media technologies have the potential to be appropriated into an aesthetic environment. Incorporation focuses on ways in which objects, especially technologies, are used. Technologies are functional. They may be bought with particular features in mind, but may also serve other cultural purposes in appropriation. Indeed, they often become functional in ways that are somewhat removed from the intentions of designers or marketers. Conversion is the process through which, in practice, the relationship between the household and the outside world becomes articulated. Technologies that are present in the household help to define and claim the household and its members in the 'wider society'. This is often related to the ways in which technologies are 'evaluated' within the moral economy of the household and the values of the wider society. As Silverstone and Hirsch and Morley (1992: 20) suggest, media technologies must be viewed as capable of great symbolic significance, investment and meaning that become 'embedded in the structures and dynamics of contemporary consumer culture' (see also, Postill, 2011).

Like many early studies of information and communication technologies (ICTs) in everyday life, Elaine Lally (2002) used domestication theory to examine the introduction of the home computer and the processes underpinning the appropriation and ownership of computers and other related assemblages in the home. She draws attention to the ways in which these objects play a role in the constitution or project of the self, a core characteristic of personhood in many Western contexts. Lally argues that computers and other objects become extensions of the self through acts such as personalization, self-transformation and 'material projection(s) of an imagined possible self' (ibid.: 214). Lally critiques domestication theory's distinction or dichotomy between the self and the environment, instead revealing how computers and other related objects become de-alienated in everyday life, noting that their role in the transformations of the self represent 'essentially a process by which the ontological security of parts of the self which might previously have been in question stabilize and we come to feel at home through the accumulation of experience and knowledge in inhabiting them' (ibid.: 216), what Horst and Miller (2012a) describe as normativity. The changing media ecologies also challenge some of the assumptions about the nature of the 'things' being domesticated. For example, research on specific stages and processes, such as forms of personalisation and customisation using mobile phones (Hjorth, 2009; Ito et al., 2005) and the distributed nature of households (Horst, 2010), raise questions about the micro-processes of domestication and the equation of the (single) household producing the primary normative order, especially outside of Western contexts (Lim, 2005). The short life-cycle of different media objects and broader policies of planned obsolescence by companies such as Apple lead to questions about the pace and processes of the cycle of domestication (Horst and Hjorth, 2013). Moreover, contemporary work on the portability of devices such as the mobile phone, tablets, laptops as well as profile pages, avatars, apps and other platforms, also challenge domestication theory's focus on the household, especially the living (lounge) room, as the primary location for negotiating relationships, morals and values around media technologies.

WHAT ARE THE IMPLICATIONS OF THE DIGITAL FOR THINGS?

Theories of the processes of appropriation, domestication, double-articulation and the differing values and materialisation of things were developed through ethnographic approaches to analogue media. More recently, a growing corpus of ethnographic research has developed with the focus upon understanding the diversity of uses and appropriations of digital media in everyday life in different cultural contexts, often focused on specific technologies. For example, Daniel Miller and Don Slater's (2000) *The Internet: An Ethnographic Approach*, was a seminal study that highlighted local meaning and interpretations of what they termed the 'Trinidadian Internet'. Subsequent ethnographic research has explored the emergence and use of digital media technologies, such as mobile phones (Hjorth, 2009; Horst and Miller, 2006; Ito et al., 2005; Wallis, 2013), video recorders (Buckingham et al., 2011; Pertierra, 2009), the webcam (Miller and Sinanan, 2014), video games (Taylor, 2006; Witkowski, 2012), virtual worlds (Boellstorff, 2008; Nardi, 2010), social network sites (boyd, 2008; Miller, 2011) and different engagements with particular communities, networks and relationships with the Internet (Coleman, 2012; Hjorth and Arnold, 2013; Kendall, 2002; Latour, 2005; Postill, 2011). Through these engagements, scholars have critiqued, modified and developed new theories to understand digital media as objects and structures, and the relationships between the objects and their use.

The combination of more extensive ethnographic analyses, the increase in access to a number of different digital media technologies, and the ways in which people integrate them into their everyday routines and practices (see Chapter 3), has troubled the virtues of studying *individual* platforms or technologies such as the mobile phone. Concepts such as mobile media and social media signal the convergence of mobile phones as well as the capabilities or affordances of particular devices via applications (apps), software and open platforms (boyd, 2014; Goggin and Hjorth, 2014; Jenkins, 2006a). Analytical frameworks such as media ecologies (Horst et al., 2010), communicative ecologies (Hearn and Marcus, 2009; Lennie and Tacchi, 2013; Slater, 2014) and polymedia (Madianou and Miller, 2012) also highlight a renewed attention to context and practice. For example, research on new forms of creative production such as video (Lange, 2014), networked gaming, photography and other forms of expression, are increasingly analysed in relation to genres of participation (Ito et al., 2010), scenarios of use (Hjorth and Arnold 2013) as well as ecologies and repertoires (Baptiste et al., 2010; Kendall et al., 2012; Maurer, 2012). More specifically, digital media technologies have become spaces that we move in, through and between. From Boellstorff's (2008) work on Second Life and analyses of youth friendship (boyd, 2014; Ito et al., 2010) to Nardi's (2010) work on clans and avatars in *World of Warcraft* and Miller's (2011, 2012) analysis of social network sites like Facebook, contemporary research continues to highlight the everyday integration of digital media technologies in everyday life as objects, places and spaces that we use not only to communicate through but also to dwell. Avatars, profile pages and the landing pages and virtual homes we customise become ways through which we discover who we are, what it means to be connected to and in relationships with others and the consequences of the digital form for our understanding of the body and other forms of materiality (Boellstorff et al., 2012; Ginsburg, 2012; Horst, 2009; Humphrey, 2009; Miller and Sinanan, 2014).

RESEARCHING THINGS THROUGH DIGITAL ETHNOGRAPHY

In order to understand the implications of researching media technologies as things that are produced, consumed and circulated, and what this perspective might mean in the context of conducting a digital ethnography, this section turns to three examples of digital media technologies in domestic spaces as well as in the digital objects that accompany many of us in our everyday life. Each example demonstrates how the researcher(s) designed their ethnographic research on the understanding of people's relationships with different digital media technologies, as well as the key literatures that help to define the relationship to 'things' across each project.

Researching radio and textured soundscapes in domestic spaces through ethnographic immersion

The things that make up the material culture of domestic spaces have different temporalities and forms. For example, generally enduring objects such as furniture and technologies have different properties to generally less enduring things such as food, clothing, cut flowers, drapes and ornaments. There are a range of media and technology objects in domestic spaces, and their content can be considered as part of the constantly shifting environment as they flow through it, contributing to its particular character at different times of the day – maybe the TV set showing a soap opera in the early evening, the radio station distracting us from mundane domestic chores on the weekend, the mobile phone alarm waking us up, and perhaps alerting us to the weather, the state of our email inbox this morning or our Facebook notifications. An interest in the ways in which less tangible and time based media content contribute to domestic environments led Jo Tacchi to undertake an ethnographic study of sound-scapes and how we might think about radio sound as part of the material culture of the home in the UK. It explored how, in the mid-1990s, radio sound contributed to textured domestic environments or soundscapes (Tacchi, 2001; Waterman, 1990).

Over a decade later, Tacchi undertook further work in order to understand if some of the same practices and meanings associated with radio sound persisted in now *digital* domestic environments. There are therefore two components of this example that are relevant to this chapter: first, how to think about and research sound as material culture, given its less 'fixed' quality compared to the object delivering the sound. Second, how to think about and research the meanings and experiences of the object and the content of 'radio' as they shift over time and space. Digital and Internet technologies have trans-formed radio. Podcasts, MP3s, streaming audio and digital radio receivers have replaced many radio sets (Tacchi, 2012), and we live in digitally enabled private spheres with multiple channels for the reception and circulation of audio visual media content. The ethnographic study of the role of radio in domestic spaces sought to understand some-thing of the *quality* of radio sound, which today might be referred to as its *affordances* or its constraining and enabling material possibilities. Why did people often talk about radio as a friend, a companion? What was it that made radio the ideal accompaniment to domestic chores? How did soundscapes help to create domestic affective rhythms (Tacchi 2009). How did radio work, and in what roles, as an intimate, invisible medium? Tacchi's research with women and families in Bristol, a city in the south-west of the UK, revealed that domestic soundscapes engendered and embodied senses of being in the world.

From the perspective of material culture studies the soundscapes themselves can be seen to have no intrinsic value or meaning; these are established and re-established continually in each domestic arena, through each individual instance of use, and it is these meanings that ethnography attempts to 'get at'. Miller (1988: 3) suggests that 'the very physicality of the object which makes it appear so immediate, sensual and assimi-lable belies its actual nature' as 'one of the most resistant forms of cultural expression in terms of our attempts to comprehend it'. Thinking of radio sound as textured allows the possibility of considering how it operates, and how people operate within it. This thought process allowed Tacchi, as an ethnographer, to momentarily 'fix' something that is dynamic and flowing. Yet, this is true also of objects and artefacts more generally. As discussed above, their meanings are not static, as one might assume from their concrete physicality. Radio sound is not tangible in the same way as other domestic furniture, yet to think about radio sound as material culture is not to artificially make it something it is not. Rather, the ethnographic research suggested that radio sound contributes to the creation and maintenance of domestic environments.

The ethnographic principles guiding the research approach included the need for immersion or long-term engagement, and for understanding the ways in which research participants consumed mediated sound and created domestic soundscapes in meaningful ways in terms of their everyday lives. This meant attempting to understand the categories those participants themselves understood and made meaning through, rather than imposing pre-conceived categories – such as the active audience – upon the site of study. Participant observation, in-depth interviews, techniques such as media diaries and creating visual diagrams of sounds in domestic spaces (sound mapping), helped Tacchi to think about, with and through sound over time, helping her to understand contemporary domestic lives. Following a circuit of culture approach, Tacchi's ethnography incorporated the production of radio; how radio companies and stations research and understand audiences; and how they relate to and conceive of (and package) listeners. Over a period of 18 months, Tacchi attended events and meetings where listeners and producers came together in the UK – listener groups for two commercial radio stations, voice of the listener and viewer events related to the BBC – and interviewed radio managers and producers from both commercial and BBC radio, and people within these organisations who undertake or use research on audiences.

Participant observation was a challenge because radio-listening was often a solitary activity that was not conducive to participant observation in the traditional sense. Yet, it was not enough to visit people in their homes and interview them; Tacchi wanted to get to know them in their social settings as well as to talk to them in their homes. She was particularly interested in issues of sociability, and the way in which mediated sound connected participants to both innermost states of being and a more public sense of their place in the world. Mediated sounds come from outside the home, and she wanted to get to know some of the participants in social environments. Therefore, Tacchi joined a single parent group in Bristol as a participant, and met with several informants in this public setting on a regular basis as well as visiting them in their homes for interviews. This gave her access to social networks, and allowed her to get to know research participants in a deeper way. For those who were not members of this group, Tacchi spent time in their homes, often drinking many cups of tea (never refusing), interviewing couples both jointly and individually (requiring more than one visit), and following up introductions to friends or relatives that participants offered (extending the research participants through social relationships, and in the process learning something about those relationships). Perhaps the most obvious technique that Tacchi used for thinking of sound as material culture was sound mapping. This involved walking through domestic spaces, drawing a diagram of that space and discussing and noting the key sounds that participants talked about – both sounds that are produced through media in the home and external sound. In effect, this helped to 'fix' the flow of sound in the discussions that Tacchi had with her research participants, and open up another way of talking about what is generally not discussed.

An ethnographic approach led Tacchi to understand radio sound and domestic soundscapes as important to the establishment and maintenance of affective equilibrium (or emotional balance). It helped her to understand how time and space are implicated, so that contemporary efforts to maintain emotional balance involve memories and imaginations of the future (for example, memories of a father shaving in the morning while listening to the radio, ideas about romantic attachments imagined for the future), as well as intimate and public relationships and mediations (for example, requesting a song dedicated to someone far away or feeling comforted to know that there are other listeners to a late-night call-in show), that relate to spaces and places external to the home. In addition to finding that radio sound has particular characteristics or affordances that make it suitable for the affective management of the everyday, Tacchi's ethnographic work showed that radio sound was appealing partly because it allowed for moments of 'social silence' (Tacchi, 1998), that is to say, blocking out aspects of sociality and the social world through radio listening. More recent interviews suggest that contemporary mediated audio is appealing in much the same ways, which Tacchi later explored through the concept of 'stillness' (Tacchi, 2012). She argued that while what constitutes 'the radio' has changed, radio-like media and mediated audio continue to permeate domestic spaces and perform a similar role to radio in the mid-1990s, and that by thinking of sound as a constituent component of the material culture of domestic spaces, we can access the ways in which contextualised and particular meaning is created and recreated.

The ethnographic research also called attention to the changing definitions of 'radio' itself (Tacchi, 2000). While a research participant in the late 2000s felt that people now listen less to the 'radio' because they had a lot more choice with the Internet, providing place-based, genre-based or customised audio on demand, and talks nostalgically of the radio of his childhood, he nevertheless listened to podcasts and other streaming audio via the Internet – he just did not think of it as 'radio'. In the mid- to late 1990s, Tacchi's research participants also told her nostalgic stories about the recently passed golden age of radio, and the soundscapes of *their* childhood (Tacchi, 2003). For both sets of participants, almost 20 years apart, remembering the radio meant remembering their childhoods, their youth and their parents. While the technologies of radio transmission have undergone some dramatic changes, and we have largely moved from analogue to digital, the uses and roles of mediated audio in domestic spaces remain strikingly consistent. Contemporary mediated audio, including analogue and digital radio, streaming MP3s and podcasts, continues to display some of the same affordances that radio sound brought to domestic life 20 years ago, even while the social perception of what counts as 'radio' has shifted. Ethnography helped demonstrate that what is understood as 'radio' has varied across time and location, and how its affordances and constraints have shifted and yet in some ways remained consistent.

Using digital video re-enactments to understand how people live with technologies

In the context of research about digital media and energy consumption in England, Sarah Pink and her colleagues (Pink and Leder Mackley, 2013; Pink et al., 2013) focused on how digital media are used to make the home and how media move around the home with people as part of their everyday life routines. For example, media can be thought of as travelling with people at home in two ways: the technologies they take with them as they move around their homes; and the technologies that stay fixed in one location for long periods of time but are used as people move through rooms. As discussed in Chapter 2, Pink and Leder Mackley used two key methods to research how people used digital media in their homes: the video tour, in which they went from room to room exploring with participants how they use digital media to create the sensory aesthetic of each room (Pink and Leder Mackley, 2012); and the re-enactment, whereby participants were video-recorded re-enacting and showing how they performed their everyday routines (ibid., 2014) (Figure 4.1). In this section, we explore a particular element of everyday routines that are oriented towards digital media use, and show how they might be researched effectively through video re-enactments.

As part of this research, Pink and her colleagues were interested in learning about how people used digital media at key transitional moments in their days. One of the everyday activities they focused on with the 20 households who participated in their research was what became referred to as the 'morning routine'. During their research in participants' homes, Sarah Pink, Kirsten Leder Mackley and Roxana Morosanu asked members of each household to show them what they did from the moment they woke up in the morning on an ordinary working day, to the moment they left home to go to work. To explore these activities with participants they used the re-enactment method, which Pink has developed across a series of research projects and is discussed in detail elsewhere (Pink and Leder Mackley, 2014). The method draws on techniques and ideas from both art therapy and neuroanthropology, to create a way of focusing on tacit, embodied and unspoken sensory memories, and making these explicit by using the actual performance of a habitual activity, which is recorded with a digital video camera, as a research probe. When performing these activities, their participants were able both to describe verbally and to show the researchers through their performances how they went about everyday tasks that they never usually spoke about or shared with others, and that they would, indeed, not normally need to talk about. As these routines unfolded through the re-enactments, the participants began to show the researchers how and where digital media were used as they went about their mornings, weaving their ways through rooms and amongst other family members while preparing for work and school, making breakfast and ensuring that younger children were entertained.

Figure 4.1a–b Using digital video re-enactments: A participant's measure of detergent and her preferred machine setting

Note: During their video tours of UK family homes, Pink and her colleagues explored the material culture that participated in making up the environment of home, using the camera to invite participants to 'show' their homes, and the digital technologies that were part of them. These images were first published in Pink and Leder Mackley, 2014, figure 3.

Source: Photographs © LEEDR, Loughborough University.

The participants' morning routines varied according to the composition and age of their households, however as they were all family households with children there were common themes. Pink and Leder Mackley (2013) describe an example of how families move between rooms and digital media in the morning, showing how media technologies, as part of the materiality of the home, become things that are activated in some way through human movement. They are as such things that, along with configurations of other things and processes, form part of the materiality of the rooms of the morning time home. In the home of Laura and Paul, a couple with three children, Pink and Leder Mackley describe how:

> the morning starts with the children invading the still darkened master bedroom. As Laura explains, the TV goes on first thing: 'They come into ours in the morning, and they're up really early, so we put the telly on for 10 minutes, so everyone can wake up properly – ... cos they're up at six.' Then Laura takes the children via the bathroom downstairs into the living room where, avoiding the harshness of the ceiling light, she turns on the wall lights and switches on the TV, using lighting and media to create a particular feel to the room. She moves around the downstairs part of the house, interweaving a set of tasks ... Although the children are more directly engaged with the TV, it is also part of her environment. While Laura goes upstairs to make everyone's beds, open the bedroom windows and get dressed, the children typically move between TV and playroom, and the oldest makes his way upstairs to play with the Xbox. (Pink and Leder Mackley, 2013: 686)

All the families who participated in Pink's project engaged with media in different ways, but the routine of going from room to room, watching a different television in each room as the morning progressed, was a common element across different households. The same routines of moving through the house between media also resonated in the Standby project that Pink and Yolande Strengers undertook in Melbourne, Australia, in 2014. Laura and Paul's household represents an example where media technologies tended to stay in relatively fixed places, and thus generated a particular way in which the home could be said to be mediated in the morning. In other households, morning uses tended to involve participants moving from room to room and taking the technologies with them. For instance, iPhones are charged next to the bed, used as alarm clocks and then woken up with and taken down stairs for breakfast. In this sense, we find that mobile media technologies often *accompany* us as we go about our everyday lives. This can enable forms of co-presence and new types of intimacy, as discussed in Chapter 5. However, in this chapter, our interest is in focusing on the object–nature of technologies, and the affordances that they may have, beyond being simply communication or entertainment media.

Understanding digital media technologies as 'things' – that is, as material objects – and tracing their movement with people, therefore means that we can begin to see how digital technologies are entangled in the everyday activities of home. When people carry technologies with them, they are also carrying with them their potentials, qualities and affordances. Likewise, when people move between technologies as they traverse their homes, they are moving between these affordances, and the experiences and meanings associated with them. The implication of this is that we need to subsequently rethink the ways in which everyday actions are undertaken *in relation to media*. If we see digital technologies as things that accompany people, then we can think of mundane human activities differently. This approach invites us to take activities, like making the breakfast, and reconsider it as a mediated activity, that is incomplete without the material and sensory affordances of the television or iPhone.

Understanding transnational movement through objects of mobility

The mobile phone has become a seminal object for maintaining social networks and relationships, facilitating the flow of goods, people, and money, and managing households and money across national borders (Hjorth, 2009; Horst and Miller, 2006; Ling and Horst, 2011; Wallis, 2013). Between 2010 and 2012, Heather Horst and Erin Taylor carried out research that explored mobility on the border of Haiti and the Dominican Republic in the towns of Anse-à-Pitres and Pedernales. Throughout this project, they examined the materiality of the border in terms of the objects that people carry or use, how these individual objects relate to other objects in a set, and the repertoires of practices and meanings that emerged from their collective use in economic and social arbitrage across the border. Situated within a broader study of life in the region (Horst and Taylor, 2014; Taylor and Horst, 2014), their aim was to understand the mundane ways in which people strategised mobility in light of the different currencies, citizenship status, languages, telecommunications infrastructures, economic opportunities and power relations that distinctly shape the ways in which mobility and movement are possible (Figure 4.2).

To gain a deeper understanding of mobility on the border and the significance of the mobile phone as an 'object of mobility' (Horst and Taylor, 2014), Horst, Taylor and their research team – including Hermes Baez, Yoselyn Espinal and Felix Quiroz Rodriguez – conducted interviews with 40 individuals living in the border region. They also carried out a survey with 200 respondents, primarily with people who worked in and around the market that spans the border. With a subset of 12 individuals, they drew on work in design and anthropology to develop a portable kit study focused on the items that border residents carry with them as they live, work and socialise in and around the border region (Ito et al., 2009). Given the potentially sensitive nature of the portable kits, the potential disclosure of individual legal status and time, Horst and Taylor recruited participants for the portable kit study primarily from their initial interview and survey pool, inviting participants whom they believed would be amenable

Figure 4.2 Image of the Haiti–Dominican Republic border

Source: Photograph by Hermes Baez, 2010.

to the intimacy of opening up their wallets, purses and backpacks. At the beginning of the interview, a member of the research team requested that participants take the objects that they carry with them on a 'normal' day out of their bags, pockets and wallets, and display them on a flat surface. After an initial discussion of the items, they worked with each participant to distinguish between the items that they carried with them on an everyday basis and those that they carried less frequently. They then asked participants to sort the objects in terms of their importance, from the most to the least important.

The highly politicised context of the border between Haiti and the Dominican Republic (Taylor, 2013) and the differing infrastructures meant that having 'papers' (or forms of identification), a mobile phone that would work at the destination and enough money to facilitate this movement, took on a heightened significance. Participants discussed the challenges of keeping their phone charged and maintaining funds on two phones in the event of an emergency. They also noted that using the phone also involved coordination and planning as border residents were restricted from crossing the border after 6 p.m. Because the regulation of movement in the border region depended on the practical and symbolic properties of multiple objects, the team also extended their study to pockets, shoes, hats, jewellery, clothing, bibles, hand cloths and, in one case, a motorbike. Participants in the study noted that they carried their most valued objects, viewing home as a less stable or secure location for the things that they felt were important.

Throughout the twelve portable kit studies, the mobile phone was always in the top five objects that Haitian migrants in the region carried with them on a daily basis. At the time, the mobile telecommunications company Digicel had launched their service in the Haitian town of Anse-à-Pitres. Prior to this moment, Haitians only had access to Dominican mobile service providers, Claro and Orange, which provided service in Pedernales. While most people living in Pedernales owned a Claro or Orange phone (people identified by their telecommunications carrier's name) to coordinate their lives and stay in touch with work, friends and relatives living in the Dominican Republic, it was not uncommon for Haitians to own two mobiles in order to communicate at national call tariffs with relatives, trading partners and services in both countries. For example, Bronte, a married mother of two in her early thirties, identified the five most important items in her portable kit, which was a small black wallet (see Figure 4.3): her Dominican identity card (cédula); her social security card; her handkerchief; her mobile phones (Claro/Digicel); and her house keys. She explained that her identity card was the most important of these objects of mobility, because with it she acquired her social security card and her phones. Bronte routinely carried a Digicel (Haitian) phone and a Claro phone, both of which she bought in 2011 to speak to people on both sides of the border, as her family are spread between Pedernales, Santo Domingo (capital of the Dominican Republic) and Port-au-Prince (capital of Haiti). She primarily talked with her mother, who lived in a town 40 km away; her father and sister in Pedernales; and, on occasion, a friend in Santo Domingo. She also shared her Haitian mobile phone with her husband Emmanuel when his credit was running low or he needed to cross the border. While calls could theoretically be made from either side of the border, in this particular region the services were often limited to up to 1 km across the border on each side, depending on the provider and the type of phone. Through strategically employing two entirely different national telecommunications systems in tandem, Haitian migrants like Bronte use mobile phones to maintain networks across national contexts and circumvent many of the border's restrictions on mobility.

Understanding the mobile phone as a 'thing' or object of mobility (Horst and Taylor, 2014) that can accompany mobile persons highlights the multiple ways in which mobile phones come to have meaning and value. In this example, the mobile phone is a repository for family members, employers, spouses and friends. It is a conduit for communication where relationships can be intensified and enlivened through conversations and calls. In many ways, it is a domestic place, the place(s) where family, in the Haitian sense of *lakou* or a cluster of homes that includes extended families who share resources, parenting, care and religious practices which emerged in rural Haiti during

Figure 4.3 Bronte's portable kit

Source: Photograph by Heather Horst, 2012.

plantation slavery (Edmond, et al. 2007) comes together. In this context the mobile phone becomes seminal to keeping the family together given the distance that separates members of Haitian families who migrate. It is an object that is both a thing that represents and reifies differences between two national contexts as well as an object that can transgress the boundaries between the two countries. It is also a thing that sits alongside a range of other objects – money, keys, identity cards and wallets – required for everyday movement for migrants. Importantly, the mobile phone's significance in this set of objects of mobility remains relational rather than fixed, part of a repertoire of practices that are contingent on the contexts in which a person or a thing circulates.

REFLECTING ON THINGS AS A CATEGORY FOR DIGITAL ETHNOGRAPHY RESEARCH

The three examples in this chapter describe different approaches to the study of digital media technologies as things. Collectively, they build upon the work of media and cultural studies scholars in their emphasis on understanding the meaning of media technologies in particular cultural contexts. They also extend the work in social anthropology, material culture studies and media studies on domestication and the social life of things through their focus upon routines, different states and affordances of things and the relationships between people and things in motion.

Yet, the examples also illustrate new avenues of exploration, especially around the ways in which we understand the 'domestic' context and the salience of concepts such as 'domestication' for capturing the material properties of things. Pink and colleagues emphasised the ways in which people develop relationships with media technologies as part of their everyday routines – getting ready for work and school, coming home at the end of the day and getting ready for bed. Rather than the stable and enduring environment facilitated in classic studies of domestication, these practices are enacted daily and become part of the daily work of living with a range of different digital media technologies. Horst and Taylor's study of portable kits on the border of Haiti and the Dominican Republic also attends to the media technologies (especially the mobile phone) carried with them as they go about their daily lives, but situates the mobile phone within the range of objects of mobility such as ID cards, wallets, keys and money that are equally (if not more) important to Haitian migrants as they navigate significant physical, material and structural differences. While in many ways Tacchi's study of radio and the textures of home could be viewed as a classic example of the domestication approach, her focus is less on the 'hard materiality' of media technologies and turns instead to the immaterial properties of sound that permeate the space of the homes. This, in turn, spurs a consideration of the ways in which media are variously used to secure affective equilibrium and senses of being connected to a world outside the home. In all three cases, the ways in which people relate to and engage with digital media technologies is revealed to be in motion, mutable and even transient.

A second important implication emerges through the attention to the role of media in facilitating and creating sociality. In the discussion of Bronte, the Haitian migrant who owns two mobile phones with different national carriers, we see how the mobile phone becomes an inscription of her family living throughout Haiti and the Dominican Republic, a symbol and conduit for bringing her family of kin and fictive kin together. Keeping the two phones charged and with credit enables Bronte to keep these relationships alive despite significant distance and legal barriers. In the discussion of domestic soundscapes, voices of radio speakers and callers become familiar companions over the course of the day. This becomes particularly poignant for single parents who find themselves alone, once their busy parental duties have ended for the day. Emotional management of the sense of loneliness involves a sociality with the material properties of sound and voice and the ways in which media itself also changes character over time (analogue to digital, radio to streaming audio). Pink and colleagues draw attention to the range of people in the family who are often simultaneously involved in socialising the various digital media technologies in the home. This is an elaborate dance of people moving throughout the rooms of the home filled with digital media technologies like gaming platforms and televisions and objects such as mobile phones and tablets moving through the house with people. Digital media technologies and people become socialised together.

The three examples in this chapter also reveal how we might conceptualise digital ethnography as a research approach and framework. In particular, the examples in this chapter highlight some of the limitations of participant observation, as practiced in anthropology and cognate disciplines. For example, Tacchi notes that in her study of radio and domestic soundscapes, it was often not possible to sit around in people's homes waiting for people to engage with sound; this was particularly antithetical to those who saw sound as an important companion in their home. Tacchi adapted to this situation by developing relationships across a range of contexts and also developed techniques such as sound mapping to find different ways to talk about soundscapes and their meanings with participants. The time that Tacchi took to develop these relationships reflects the challenges of conducting research in middle- and working-class homes in England (e.g., Miller, 2001). Pink and her team were interested in domestic energy consumption in a project designed to inform their collaborators about everyday energy use. However, using energy as a practiced category could not be understood without following the action. Pink's team used re-enactments to understand how and why the narratives of, or lines made by 'things' as they move around the home and other domestic settings. This became a way to make visible what people do, without necessarily being 'there' on a daily basis. Similarly, Horst and Taylor's study of Haitian migrants' portable kits on the border of Haiti and the Dominican Republic acknowledged the limitations of crossing the border with research participants, which could have caused undue alarm or attention to participants making them vulnerable to increasing surveillance by state agents on the border. They also recognised the limitations of use of particular items in people's portable kits; while they were carried, not all things in people's purses, wallets and backpacks were used or viewed as being as significant as others. Without the process of encouraging participants to display the parts of their kits that they first described as 'not very interesting' or 'not what you want to know about' and, in turn, organising the things they carry, participants were able to make explicit practices and rituals that they viewed as mundane. Together, these examples illustrate the diversity of ways in which tacit relationships with digital media technologies can be examined ethnographically.

SUMMING UP

In this chapter, we outlined the history and development of the concept of researching (digital) media technologies as things that have social lives, circulate in our culture and are embedded in processes of change over time. We argued that in a digital context the notion of the digital media technologies as things provides an important vantage point for ethnographic research and analysis. We highlighted how things have material properties that correspond with and move beyond their physical presence in everyday life. This requires a rethinking of the ways in which devices and environments are intertwined through everyday practices in particular places or contexts, the ways in which environments are designed by a range of stakeholders, and the salience of 'things' in our everyday lives.

Exploring the different ways in which we now research things also reveals a shift in academic debates and directions. In particular, while the past 20 years of research has been dominated by a concern with understanding the multiple meanings and processes of consumption, the heart of contemporary ethnographic research has in many ways returned to the processes of production and design that have effectively been mystified through the global networks of production, distribution and consumption as well as the 'immaterial' nature of digital media technologies. This also means an engagement with designers and others who work in industry who are interested in understanding consumer desires and aspirations to design usable platforms, software, programs and objects. For Horst, this has also meant a more focused engagement with the mobile telecommunications companies that market and brand technologies, their negotiations with regulators as well as the less visible aspects of digital media technologies such as mobile signals (Horst, 2013). The new affordances of digital media technologies – their temporality, interactivity, replicability, persistence (or storage), searchability, mobility and scalability (Baym, 2010) – have spurred ethnographers on to experiment with alternative frameworks such as infrastructure (Bell and Dourish, 2012; Star, 1999), Actor Network Theory (ANT), design and other approaches to understand our relationship with digital media technologies as 'things'. As this chapter demonstrates, the strength of a digital ethnography approach revolves around its adaptable set of frameworks to understand our dynamic digital worlds.

FIVE

Researching Relationships

CHAPTER CONTENTS

INTRODUCTION

This chapter explores how digital ethnography can be used to research contemporary relationships. First, we outline how relationships have been conceptualised and studied in the social sciences and the role of media and communication in the formation of relationships. Next, we discuss how ethnographers might approach human social relationships when they are digitally mediated. We then focus on one concept that has come to predominate recent discussions of digital social relationships: co-presence. By exploring the changing practices of co-presence in a digital era, we bring to the fore the specificity of how everyday human relationships are shaped, in part, by the qualities and affordances of digital media technologies. Through three ethnographic examples, we consider how digital ethnography methods can be mobilised for researching co-presence through a range of ethnographic techniques including re-enactments, examining mobile phone contact lists, scenarios of use, individual and group interviews and participant observation. Whereas in Chapter 6 we will discuss the structural elements of relationships and the creation of social worlds, in this chapter we focus on the role of media and communication for the development, maintenance, expression and negotiations of relationships. This will include a focus on particular forms of intimacy, including relationships with significant others such as boyfriends, girlfriends, spouses and other partners as well as family members.

WHAT ARE RELATIONSHIPS AND HOW DO THEY DEVELOP?

Understanding the ways in which relationships are formed, maintained and structured has been a fundamental concern for scholars across the social sciences and humanities. Early work in anthropology explored different social structures around the world, with a particular focus on understanding the languages, rules or grammars of these social (and cultural) systems. These interests resulted in studies of: family, kinship and descent (Dumont, 1980 [1957]; Leach, 1951; Parsons, 1953; Pitt-Rivers, 1958; Radcliffe-Brown, 1940); different forms of political governance (Fortes, 1953); religious practices (Malinowski, 1925; Tylor, 1958); race and ethnicity (Barth 1969); and processes such as gifting, reciprocity and other forms of exchange (Mauss, 1990 [1950]; Malinowski, 2002 [1925]. In sociology, scholars focused on the processes through which society is held together. Many sociologists have studied families, often viewed as the fundamental unit of society, such as landmark works such as Michael Young and Paul Wilmott's study of *Family and Kinship in East London* (1957), and Jan and Ray Pahl's *Managers and their Wives* (1972). More recently, sociologists such as Ray Pahl and Liz Spencer have focused on friendship, arguing that these relationships form a kind of 'social glue' (Pahl, 2000; Spencer and Pahl, 2006).

One particularly influential set of theories that aimed at understanding the ways in which society is built and stays together is 'symbolic interactionism'. This approach develops a specific focus on human interaction and has been important not only for anthropologists and sociologists but also for social psychology and communication. Founded by Charles Cooley and George Herbert Mead in the early twentieth century, symbolic interactionists argued that our world is socially constructed and does not exist outside of actions and social interactions (Cooley, 1922; Mead, 1934/1962).

Relationships between the self and others, and the internal dialogue within the self, are constituted in and through these social interactions between different kinds of objects (Cooley, 1922). As Mead (1934/1962) described the process, 'The individual experiences himself as (an object), not directly, but only indirectly from the particular standpoints of other members of the same social group' (1934: 138–40). Sociologist Erving Goffman's (1959) classic text *The Presentation of Self in Everyday Life* introduced the concept of 'social dramaturgy' which called attention to the ways in which social context shapes the roles and performances that we take on in our everyday lives. Specifically, Goffman explored how individuals experiment with and perform different roles and identities using language, actions and gestures, drawing attention to the 'front' and 'back' stages through which we operate. This includes how a person prepares for an interaction with others through clothing and other props, how they present themselves on the 'front' stage where other people (an audience) can see the performance, how the audience responds to the performance, and how the person reconfigures their front and back stage performances in response to the audience.

These early studies of social life also revealed the importance of language, symbols and communication in our interactions. Malinowski argued that 'ties of union are created by a mere exchange of words', further suggesting that 'the communion of words is the first to establish links of fellowship' (2013 [1926/1999]: 303). This includes the formation of speech communities and the importance of cultural competence in communication (Duranti, 1994; Gumperz, 1971), and especially code-switching within particular groups and contexts (e.g., Bauman and Sherzer, 1975; Hymes, 1964). Other studies have explored the different mechanisms through which connections are forged. In addition to non-verbal communication, scholars identified practices such as phatic communication, that is, staying in touch without content or information being disseminated (Malinowski, 1923). This includes engaging in 'small talk', such as asking how the weather is, a wave to say 'hello' while passing by, or asking an acquaintance 'What's up?'. In these exchanges, the act of communication is more important than the content of the conversation (see also Horst and Miller, 2005; Horst and Miller, 2006). Yet other studies have focused on the social function of practices such as joking, ritualised banter and gossip in creating social cohesion within particular groups (Gluckman, 1963; Radcliffe-Brown, 1940). Through this work, we see the ways in which relationships are formed through interactions with things and objects (including people). These interactions form the basis for creating meaning and, in turn, people learn to make sense of, manage and transform these meanings over time through interpretation (Blumer, 1962). In effect, interaction and people's interpretations of these interactions come to represent the primary unit through which meaning is made, shaping the ways that people develop relationships with others and constitute their social worlds (see Chapter 6).

BRINGING TOGETHER THE STUDY OF
RELATIONSHIPS AND MEDIA

Many of the early studies of relationship formation and development focused upon small communities who lived in close physical proximity to one another. Indeed, Goffman noted that proximity is important in creating what he termed the 'full conditions of copresence' where 'persons must sense that they are close enough to be perceived in whatever they are doing, including their experiencing of others, and close enough to be perceived in this sensing of being perceived' (Goffman, 1963: 17). Yet, even in close-knit societies where most communication takes place in person, forms of mediation are always present. For example, messages are conveyed through third-party objects or people, such as notes, sound signals or word of mouth. They are also mediated through language, facial expressions, gestures and a range of other communication norms and practices. The invention and dissemination of the printing press and other technological improvements did not invent mediation; they simply expanded its geographical reach.

Indeed, recent studies of the role of media – even the most mundane and pre-digital forms such as letters and postcards – further challenge the importance of proximity and co-location for the development of personal relationships (Hjorth, 2005b; Milne, 2010). These studies point out that co-presence does not depend on people meeting face to face, rather, it can be created through media. As Hjorth asserts, 'The postcard was marked by the politics of co-presence – shifts in public and private spheres, fusions of work and "leisure" (symbolized by the flâneur), being *here* and yet *there*, being *present* whilst simultaneously *absent*' (2005a: n.p.). Laura Ahearn (2001) has explored the ways in which love letters, and the increase in literacy associated with their emergence, helped to facilitate a shift from arranged marriage to elopements and love marriages in Nepal. These letters often became the main way through which these intimate relationships developed in a cultural context where face-to-face interactions between men and women were closely managed. Claude Fischer's (2002) social history of the landline in the USA also emphasises the importance of the landline for women and others seeking to engage with others beyond the neighbourhood and domestic spheres.

Studies of migration and transnationalism have been particularly important for challenging assumptions about '[T]he degree to which geographically dispersed agents experience a sense of physical and/or psychological proximity through the use of particular communication technologies' (Milne, 2010: 165). Panagakos and Horst (2006) argue that migrants are often at the forefront of creative practices and communication technology adoption given the desire to stay connected, communicate and create co-presence. For example, Karen Richman's (2005) work with Haitian migrants outlines the ways in which cassette tapes of religious ceremonies and rituals that travelled from Haiti into different communities in Florida often incorporated personal messages within the ceremonies, such as songs questioning why remittances had not been sent or longing for a visit. Similarly, Madianou and Miller (2011) chronicle the practice of circulating letters and cassette tapes among Filipino migrant women and their children, drawing attention to the differential appropriation of particular media in relation to particular relationships, the qualities of the particular media selected and the kinds of materialities and temporalities created through the process of mediation. In a project that used digital video making as part of its research method and for its dissemination, Rebecca Savage (2011) recounts the maintenance of relationships among Mexican parents who migrated to the USA and children who remained in their hometown in Mexico. Family members sent videos of first communions and house-building between Mexico and the USA (see: www.docwest.co.uk/projects/rebecca-savage/). Such examples highlight both the importance of media for creating opportunities for co-presence and the importance of remediation, or the process by which new forms of media rework and configure our relationship to older media use and practice, in shaping contemporary patterns of communication (Bolter and Grusin, 2000).

HOW DOES DIGITAL MEDIA CHANGE THE FORMATION AND QUALITIES OF RELATIONSHIPS?

There have been two primary approaches to understanding the influence of digital media technologies on the creation, maintenance and quality of personal relationships. The first approach focuses on the *management of communication and connection* through different platforms. Today, there is a broad range of digital media technologies that can be employed for different communication ends. Nancy Baym's book *Personal Communication in the Digital Age* (2010) describes the ways in which digital media has created new forms and patterns of personal connection. Among other characteristics of these new connections, she highlights how people use digital media to manage relationships, particularly by navigating communication through synchronous and asynchronous features (boyd, 2008, 2014; Broadbent, 2012). Baym further emphasises that digitally mediated communication should not be viewed as an impoverished or second-order to face-to-face communication. Rather, 'mediated communication is not a space, it is an additional tool people use to connect, one which can only be understood as deeply embedded in and influenced by the daily realities of embodied life' (Baym, 2010: 152). The tools of digital communication comes with its own set of cues, signals and ways of expressing emotion that must be understood within the contexts of their use, people's desires and the affordances of media.

Madianou and Miller's concept of polymedia suggests that cost and access are no longer the primary determinants of media choice. Rather, Madianou and Miller argue that:

the primary concern shifts from the constraints imposed by each individual medium to an emphasis upon the social, emotional and moral consequences of choosing between those different media. As the choice of medium acquires communicative intent, navigating the environment of polymedia becomes inextricably linked to the ways in which interpersonal relationships are experienced and managed. (2011: 170)

Wilding's (2006) work on the ways in which transnational families caring for older family members decide to communicate through email highlights the social and emotional relationship between relationships and platforms. In Wilding's case, children opt for email because the content of the communication is more important than the sense of connection or co-presence. Similarly, Gershon's (2010) analysis of the relationship between media ideologies and practices among college students highlights the importance of identifying the appropriate medium or channel for disconnecting, or breaking up, with someone in a changing media ecology.

The second approach highlights the importance of digital media for the *creation of co-presence*. Fields such as mobile communication and Internet studies acknowledge the significance of multiple forms of presence, or ways of being together. Kenneth Gergen (2002) considers how the mobile phone transformed the relationship between those who are physically co-located and the 'absent presence', referring to relationships we hold with partners, children and family who are not physically present in one space. Christian Licoppe (2004) explores how mobile phones permit interactions to continue across space and time, as relationships are reinforced and maintained through a series of interactions via calls and SMS messages. As he describes:

maintaining this connected presence, ratified by the inter-locutor, allows for a lesser formality of mediated interaction: it becomes less necessary to reassert the formal and institutional aspects of the frame of interaction at each call if one is feeling connected to the other person through a continuous flow of small communicative acts. As regards interpersonal relations, the question is also how the redistribution of the modes of interaction changes the nature of relations, if at all. (Ibid.: 154)

Subsequent work has explored the role of photographs and MMS as ways to maintain forms of visual intimate co-presence (Goggin and Hjorth, 2009; Ito and Okabe, 2005). The concept of co-presence therefore stands for a range of ways of being together that do not necessarily involve being in the same physical–material locality, including during ethnographic research (Beaulieu, 2010).

The maintenance of co-presence increasingly occurs across media platforms such as SMS and MMS to apps such as Facebook, Twitter and Instagram. As Giovanni

Mantovani and Giuseppe Riva (1998) note, early debates in Internet studies failed to acknowledge that presence is always mediated and that it is culturally constructed. And yet, equally significant is recognising that 'the ability of the subject to elide or ignore this mediation is crucial to the presence effect' (Milne, 2010: 165). It is in this way that presence can be been understood as a psychological state whereby some form of technology, such as the use of multiple screens, has shaped subjective experience and perception (Aguado and Martinez, 2014). For example, Mizuko Ito and Daisuke Okabe (2005) highlight the importance of 'ambient virtual co-presence', which they describe as 'a way of maintaining ongoing background awareness of others, and of keeping multiple channels of communication open' (ibid.: 264). An example of this kind of backgrounding is evident in Miller and Sinanan's (2014) study of webcam, which outlines the ways in which some transnational families keep their webcam switched on while they carry out mundane activities such as cooking.

Yet, not all forms of co-presence dispersed across apps, platforms, spaces and modes facilitate a sense of connection and intimacy. Wallis's (2013) work among female migrants in China details the use of mobile phones for surveillance and monitoring by employers who often exploit the migrant's precarious positions. In a different context, Melissa Gregg (2011) highlights how, for workers in creative industries, the presence of smartphones, laptops and other digital media technologies contributes to the conflation of home and work – what she terms the 'presence bleed' – in post-industrial capitalism. She draws attention to the ways in which these practices both reflect and create the increasing significance of work in the lives of flexible workers. In essence, such conceptualisations of co-presence that take mediated relationships into account challenge assumptions about the role of digital media in facilitating connection and break down binaries such as here and there, virtual and actual, online and offline, absent and present.

RESEARCHING RELATIONSHIPS THROUGH DIGITAL ETHNOGRAPHY

In the next section, we examine three different ways in which the co-presence and intimacy can be studied through digital ethnography. As we show, digital ethnography offers us new ways to understand both changing communication practices in relationships (Turkle, 2001) and the amplification of existing rituals and intimacies (Pertierra, 2006). The first example examines how the customisation or personalisation of the inside and outside of mobile phones can map relationships onto, and through, hardware and software. The second example explores how mobile phone use reveals gendered relationships among transnational families spread between Jamaica and the UK. The final example demonstrates how transnational Chinese families use online gaming sites like *Happy Farm* as spaces for dwelling and connection. In all of these examples, we attend to small-scale and personal relationships, highlighting the ways in which digital media integrate with existing practices and extend others.

Understanding personalisation and intimacy through scenarios of use

Ito, Okabe and Misa Matsuda (2005) argued a decade ago that the mobile phone is one of the most 'personal', 'portable' and 'pedestrian' objects in our digital media ecology. People develop relationships with their mobile phones as much as they use their mobile phones to enhance relationships with other people and, given the personal nature of the mobile, they are often one of the most intimate forms of everyday digital media (Fortunati, 2002). However, while mobile phone use generates forms of intimacy, it does not follow that these intimacies are always experienced privately. Rather, mobile phones include features that make it possible to render intimacies *public*. They are part of a broader socio-technical trend in which the sites for the practice of intimacies extend to a wider audience through use of various media. As Lauren Berlant argues, intimacy had taken on new geographies and forms of 'publicness' (1998: 281). In fact, such intimacies extend beyond personal relationships to include macro structures like institutions and cultures. Michael Herzfeld, for example, suggests that cultural intimacy can be understood as 'the recognition of those aspects of a cultural identity that are considered a source of external embarrassment but that nevertheless provide insiders with their assurance of common sociality' (1997: 3).

Media, such as television, newspapers and radio, expand the possibilities of creating such cultural intimacy because they facilitate communication between different layers of society. Extending these observations beyond the 'culture' of nation-states, Eva Illouz (2007) associates such forms of closeness with specific political and economic configurations, suggesting that capitalism fosters an intensely emotional culture that blurs workplace, family, and relationships rather than creates boundaries between public and private and emotions and rationality. In a related approach, Lynn Jamieson (1998) extended earlier work by Giddens (1992) to detail how intimacy is gendered as well as culturally and socioeconomically informed. These studies are part of an 'intimate turn' that has impacted upon various facets of cultural practice and politics as integral to social life (Ahmed, 2004). For Ahmed, emotions are 'the flesh of time' (ibid.: 10) that get attributed to objects, media, contexts and people in ways that are 'sticky'. Ahmed defines 'sticky' as situations and interpretations that are full of affect.

Over the past few decades, researchers have increasingly sought to understand how digital media are implicated in the constitution of intimacy. For example, literature around mobile media has highlighted that it magnifies the importance of place (Ito, 2002). Amparo Lasén (2004) argues that mobile media devices operate as repositories for the emotional and intimate and highlights that emotion has always involved motion – and thus can be understood as 'mobile'. As Jane Vincent and Leopoldina Fortunati (2009) work shows this connection between movement and emotion also indicates why mobile phones have been so successful in being repositories and vehicles for intimacy. Emotions are always mobile even when they are seemingly immobilised in moments of crisis as was the case with the 11 March 2011 Japanese earthquake, tsunami and Fukushima disaster known as 3/11. During 3/11, people hung onto their mobile phones as though they were repositories containing their intimate friends and family. This occurred despite the fact that the technology failed and they couldn't make actual contact (Hjorth and Kim, 2011).

Researching the mobile phone can provide insight into how the phone both *literally* and *symbolically* creates the affective qualities of intimacy in different contexts. Larissa Hjorth's work (2009) on the gendered dimensions of mobile media in the Asia-Pacific region has focused on the different ways that personalisation reflects sociocultural notions of intimacy. This involved studying how participants' symbolic, material, expressive and communicative media practices played out through use of mobile media hardware and software. Hjorth conducted interviews with participants over a period of seven years in order to understand these practices across a broad period of time. Along with standard interview techniques, Hjorth used the 'scenarios of use' method – a deep interviewing technique, developed with Michael Arnold – that involves reviewing a participant's typical day from the moment they wake up until the moment they go to sleep. Participants are asked to share information about when they use media and why, with interviewers asking further questions about the detail of the everyday and mundane. Interviews often last for two to three hours. Scenarios of use and re-enactments assist discussion of some of the tacit and familiar practices that can be overlooked in ordinary interviews. Alongside the scenarios of use method, participants were also asked to collate a diary over a month, including visual images such as screen shots, so that the researcher could gain a sense of some of the key phone applications that participants were using, as well as how and why they used them.

Figure 5.1 shows a Japanese mobile phone (*keitai*) littered with the Japanese cute (*kawaii*) icon Hello Kitty. Hjorth suggests that by examining these material transformations of hardware, we can learn about how mobile media reinforce existing practices of intimacy and locality. The phone's owner has deployed Hello Kitties to symbolically and literally connect herself and her phone to a sense of place and the social relationships that are part of this. When asked to describe her motivations for each of the Hello Kitties, the owner narrated a series of experiences in different places in Japan with her friends and family. Each Hello Kitty represented a different location (i.e., Yokohama Hello Kitty) and a memorable experience with a loved one. The phone was a repository and part of a memorialisation process for the owner, with her special moments always there and on show. Here, we must recognise that the cute (*kawaii*) has multiple and contested readings (Allison, 2003; Hjorth, 2003, 2005a, 2008; Kinsella, 1995; McVeigh, 2000). In Japan, where premature adulthood is the norm, the *kawaii* represents a place for subversion and play against Japanese tradition, especially around gender. This form of material personalisation of mobile media means the user can easily locate and recognise her phone. However, the collection of these *kawaii* also generates a sense of co-presence and of situatedness, a sense of being in place. For the female owner of this mobile phone, each Hello Kitty represents an experience with someone, a moment in the user's life story. Like a charm bracelet, the user collects mementos of special moments so that they may always be there. This creates a form of lingering co-presence, as each charm becomes a kind of memory object and a way of experiencing and materially manifesting the digital co-presence via the phone of friends. Moreover, while mobile media are often associated with the notion of a sense of place in relation to their locative capacity, this example shows a different cartography in which the relationship between co-presence and place take on new dynamic dimensions. This Hello Kitty phone shows how material culture can create a sense of place as it collects together objects that stand for people's own stories.

Figure 5.1 The mobile located: Hello Kitty entangles the mobile relationship

Source: Photograph by Larissa Hjorth.

In the example illustrated by Figure 5.2, we can see another way in which the mobile phone becomes a site for, and of, emplacing intimate co-presence. Mobile media personifies the user's relationships as a repository for intimacy while channelling particular norms and nuances. Some studies have found that anxieties around losing one's mobile phone are at least partially generated by the owner's fear of losing a part of themselves along with the hardware. In locations like South Korea, it is not uncommon for a female partner to colonise her boyfriend's phone, tagging it with 'feminine' customisation both inside and outside the phone (see Figure 5.2). Here, the mobile phone becomes a symbol of rituals and symbols such as the engagement ring. As an object that is always close and visible, with users often putting it on the table, these highly feminised (Brunner, 2002) examples clearly signposted to others that the boy was engaged. In one scenario (Figure 5.2), a girlfriend had put a picture of her eye as a screen saver on her boyfriend's phone. It might be interpreted as the all-watching, omnipresent eye. For the boyfriend, the phone with his girlfriend's eye is the ultimate personalisation. He sees the phone as an extension of his relationship with her and the screen saver constantly reminds him not only to think about her but also to call her perpetually.

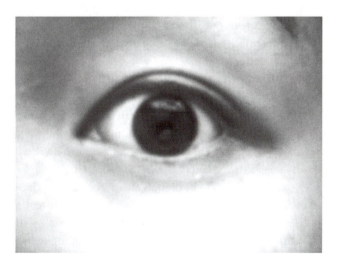

Figure 5.2   Girlfriend always present: The screen saver eye

Source: Photograph by Larissa Hjorth.

In this section, we explored the various ways in which the mobile phone enables older rituals of intimacy that are culturally specific while, at the same time, providing new ways in which to understand the negotiation of co-presence by geographically dispersed users. Through two examples we can see how contemporary intimacy is enacted across material and immaterial digital and mobile media. Studying the mobile phone provides a lens through which we can gain new insights about sociocultural understandings about what it means to be co-present and intimate (Bell, 2005). As we will explore in the next examples, mobile phones are also interwoven into how transnational familial relationships are traversed and maintained. This requires us to rethink how we define geography, not only in terms of co-presence and affect, but also in terms of gender.

Researching communication and care in transnational families

As feminist scholars have argued for some time, gender fundamentally structures communication, movement, migration and the dynamics of power that emerge across transnational spaces (Mahler and Pessar, 2001; Pessar and Mahler, 2003). The extensive literature on gender and family in the Caribbean such as Edith Clarke's *My Mother who Fathered Me* (1999 [1957]) and work on the matrifocal family (Smith, 1996), for example, highlight how mothers and grandmothers play one of the most central roles in the family and household unit. Indeed, mothers and grandmothers have always played a central role in childcare, often facilitating their children's ability to take advantage of educational and occupational opportunities on a temporary or permanent basis, reinforcing the key role of mothers and grandmothers in the family. Plaza (2000) suggests that this central female figure of the household is also prevalent among Caribbean migrant communities and notes the emergence of 'transnational grannies' who travel between the USA, Canada, the UK and the Caribbean to visit relatives and look after their siblings, children and grandchildren, bearing food, gifts and other household items associated with Jamaican culture.

This example integrates Horst's work with return and transnational migrants (Horst, 2006a, 2006b, 2007, 2011) and her study of mobile communication with Daniel Miller in rural and urban Jamaica (Horst and Miller, 2005, 2006). One of the key techniques used in the latter study was an analysis of individuals' contact lists through a discussion of all the names and numbers saved in their phone (Horst and Miller, 2005). Participants documented each contact's name and relationship to them, the last time they spoke with that person, what they talked about and how frequently they sent or received calls and messages from them. This contact list study also involved going through the entire phone, such as looking through pictures saved, screen savers, music, ringtones and other forms of customisation. Combined with the broader ethnographic research that Horst carried out between 1999 and 2002 and again in 2004, 2007 and 2009, the contact list study enabled Horst to understand the structure of relationships and networks activated through mobile phones. It also generated insights into some of the broader social implications of these structures, particularly gender relations in families, for understanding the meaning of the mobile phone in people's everyday lives (Figure 5.3).

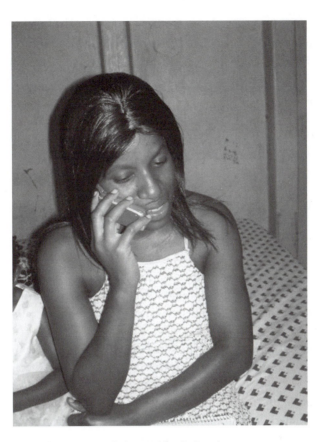

Figure 5.3   The mobile phone as an intimate object in Jamaica

Source: Photograph by Heather Horst.

One example of the way in which mobile phones enter into relationships between grandparents, children and grandchildren is during a family crisis. On a visit to Jamaica in 2007, Mrs D., one of the returning residents in Horst's study of returnees in Mandeville, Jamaica, received some very distressing news. Her son and his wife who were living in England took her teenage grandson to a doctor for tests, and a few days later they learned that he had acquired a serious form of cancer. Mrs D. learned that her grandson would spend his holidays in London undergoing chemotherapy. As a nurse and a grandmother separated from her children and grandchildren, her first instinct was to begin to book a flight from Jamaica to London. However, there were other matters to consider. Her husband had a medical condition and could not take the nine-hour-long flight from Jamaica to London, and flying to London without him would mean that she would be trading one worry for another.

In the end, Mrs D. stayed in Jamaica, relying on her eldest daughter in London to take on the family's maternal caregiver role and to keep Mrs D. abreast of the latest news about her grandson's health and her son's emotional state. This meant that calls needed to be made at least a few times per week, which was costly for the couple living off a fixed income (UK pension). Aware of the new mobile communication ecology in Jamaica, Mrs D. began weighing her options as to the most reliable and cost-effective phone plan and decided on a $JA1000 pre-paid phone card for 1000 international minutes. In contrast to letters and previous forms of communication, Mrs D. felt that one of the best features of the mobile phone is the ability to hear sounds, background noises and changes in tone, aural dimensions of mobile communication that gave her an ambient sense of presence, despite the distance. It also happened to be significantly cheaper than placing international calls on her landline. Although for many returned migrant grandmothers, migration or return to Jamaica to retire incited feelings of loss and ambivalence (Horst, 2011), developing proficiency in navigating the price structure of mobile phone plans and cards in the name of transnational communication, care and grandmothering became a way to counteract the distance and ambivalence felt about their return and role in the family.

Gendered geographies of power also influenced how many young men in Jamaica use the mobile phones to maintain transnational relationships with family members and friends living outside of Jamaica. 'Indian', a 20-year-old man who sold hard candy and nuts on the roadside in rural Jamaica, viewed the mobile phone as a way to maintain connection with his 'links' (connections) outside of Jamaica. Stressing the difficulties of life as a young man in Jamaica, where unemployment hovered around 13 per cent, Indian was particularly attuned to the inequity between the opportunities available in Jamaica and abroad, and felt that it was almost impossible to 'move forward in life' in Jamaica and support his girlfriend and young child. Like other Jamaicans, he believed that Jamaicans living 'in foreign' (a term used to describe living overseas) possessed an obligation to take advantage of their opportunities to support their family and friends left behind in Jamaica. Although he called his family overseas on a regular basis, Indian's relatives routinely sent money to his grandmother who redistributed it within the family as she saw fit. Not only did family members abroad see her as the head of the family, but they also believed that she was no longer able to make money herself; from their perspective, young people like Indian could always find work, which meant that Indian received relatively little in the way of direct contributions. Over time, Indian began to resent his lowly position within the extended family as well as the attitude that, as a young man, he must be able to find work. Indian often described how women and the older generation were more likely to garner sympathy and thereby found it easier to get support when paid work was unavailable.

Channelling his frustration, Indian decided to cultivate relationships more actively with his male 'links' from his community, high school and extended family who had moved to the USA. Every two weeks, Indian called his relatives living in Brooklyn and New Jersey. The frequency of calls resulted in an extra $US20 or $US30 every few weeks, an amount that comprised a sizeable portion of his monthly income. While these amounts were small compared with the funds sent to his grandmother, they were sent directly to him from his male brother and other cousins who were more sympathetic with his struggle. In addition to phone calls, Indian leveraged his ability to maintain the links by keeping them connected to everyday life in Jamaica, including local happenings and the music scene. When his relatives returned to Jamaica to visit at Christmas or other holidays, Indian would locate a local mobile phone or SIM card for them to use, arrange for a car or taxi driver, locate mangoes, ackee, coconuts and other Jamaican delicacies or take them to dancehall sessions, shows, bars and other places where they could experience being at home in Jamaica. Most of these activities would still be funded by the visiting relations and friends given Indian's tenuous economic situation, but this process of keeping people abroad connected to authentic Jamaican culture while they were home – tasting ackee, jerk pork, smoke ganja, drink over-proof rum and so on – facilitated the experience of coming home and of making those visiting from abroad return home in style and with status, 'like a big man'. This, in turn, provided Indian with his own sense of status and opportunity, transforming Indian into a 'big man' during these visits.

In both examples, we see how the mobile phone enters into a broader set of practices of communication involved in conveying emotion and care. In a context such as Jamaica, where economic uncertainty is part of everyday life, the mobile phone was used by Mrs D. effectively to travel emotionally to the UK from Jamaica through voice and sound. For Indian, using his mobile phone remained one of the key ways in which he could maintain his links that helped him to subvert the gendered and generational hierarchy associated with the remittance economy in many Jamaican households. In such cases, it is not so much what the mobile can 'do' or the ease with which it has been appropriated, but rather its usefulness in the creation, maintenance and extension of relationships.

Researching ambient playfulness through *Happy Farm*

In China, three very different but interrelated phenomena have evolved around online gaming communities. First, phenomena such as in-game protesting (Chan 2009; Hjorth and Chan, 2009) have highlighted the role of the Internet as a form of public sphere for political agency which is especially apparent in blogging culture (Qiu, 2009; Wallis, 2013). Second, the locative capability of mobiles exemplified in the rise of gamified Location Based Services such as *Jiepang* where electronic and co-present social spaces are overlaid onto the geographic and physical (Hjorth and Gu, 2012; Hjorth and Richardson, 2014). Third, we see millions of young and old people who now play simple casual, social games such as *Happy Farm* through social media such as Renren and Kaixin. It is this third phenomenon that is of special interest to this chapter on relationships.

In the social media game *Happy Farm*, players acquire, raise and sell farm produce while chatting with neighbours and exchanging gifts and favours. One of the key affordances of the game is the capacity to steal other people's produce when they are offline or not in the game, simulating a real-world scarcity of resources to compensate for the game-world's infinite resources. *Happy Farm* is an example of persistent and ambient play with many millions of players having it open on a browser all day and night while doing something else. Many of the Chinese players interviewed by Hjorth and Arnold (2013) discussed how they enjoyed the ambient quality of *Happy Farm*, having it sitting in the background (of the desktop) so that they could move in and out of the mainframe of their focus. Many *Happy Farm* players keep the game open on their desktop whilst doing other activities (such as work) to avoid being robbed of their virtual produce, and some even set their alarms for late in the night so that they can go online in order to steal when everyone else is asleep. In its omnipresence, players often found it hard to articulate how long they played it each day.

Data collected during fieldwork in Shanghai from 2009 to 2010 at Fudan University provided a perfect snapshot of the rise and fall of *Happy Farm*. Through ethnographic methods such as participant observation with students and their parents, along with focus groups, scenarios of use and interviews, we were able to gain a sense of the ways in which *Happy Farm* was helping students, parents and grandparents overcome geographic distance through co-present ambient playfulness within the fields of *Happy Farm*. For many of these students from predominantly working-class backgrounds, the socioeconomic mobility gained through education is being transferred in unofficial ways to their parents and grandparents through cross-generational media literacy. This is particularly prevalent in the uptake of social media games.

In a curious twist to the usual narratives concerning young people's compulsive media use, some respondents even claimed that their parents were 'addicted' to games, especially parents who had retired and had 'too much time on their hands'. Many respondents also noted that their parents viewed the Internet as a contemporary version of the television in terms of its status as an entertainment medium. We became inquisitive as to whether this 'inappropriate' usage and understanding of new media was a reality or whether it was the subjective perspective of the participants. This, in turn, made us wonder about these new forms of cross-generational media literacy and attendant types of usage.

To reflect on these questions, Larissa Hjorth and Michael Arnold conducted follow-up fieldwork in June and July 2010. This time, in addition to student surveys, focus groups and one-to-one interviews, Hjorth and Arnold interviewed a specific group of students and conducted separate interviews with their parents. Through these conversations, they explored some of the ways in which these students traverse home and away through mobile and Internet technologies. In Shanghai, students often use mobile media to communicate with their parents through a variety of media, including voice calls and social media. For many of the older generation, China's oldest social media, QQ, is synonymous with being online (Figure 5.4).

Figure 5.4   Mobile, yet still in China

Source: Photograph by Larissa Hjorth.

Geographic mobility is increasingly common among the *ba ling hou* (generation y). In this mobility, social media games, played with both friends and family at home and also fellow students, help alleviate the loneliness experienced when absent from home. However, while these games helped people to bond, they were also marked by different usage and etiquette, especially across generations. For example, a 26-year-old female student noted that online games were becoming integral to connecting with friends and family. As she described:

I never used to play games but now I play many (online) games with friends and family. I will play with students whilst we are in a lab waiting for experiments to be finished. I play *Happy Farm* with my mum. She loves stealing my vegetables. I also play it with my roommate and often she will say aloud, 'I'm going to steal your vegetables!' and it makes me laugh.

By the end of 2010, the *ba ling hou* were no longer ambiently playing *Happy Farm* on their PCs. Instead, they were taking up mobile gaming with the rise of smartphones and again teaching their parents and grandparents again to use different multiplayer mobile media games so that they might play together while occupying a co-present gaming space.

In 2009, 3G mobile technologies were introduced, heralding another shift in gaming practices, including the growth of smartphone pirate industries (*shanzhai*) and the movement of gaming and gamification in social media on PCs to its convergence on smartphones. By late 2010, media-rich microblog Sina Weibo (like Twitter, but it allows for embedded video and images) dominated the scene, as, too, did a new breed of gamified location-based services, along with camera phone mobile apps such as Jiepang which began to emerge. In 2010, *Happy Farm* released its second version, but by then everything had 'gone to seed' (Millward, 2012). For the *ba ling hou,* mobile media games are essential in negotiating place and co-presence as they traverse the distance between home and away. In a negotiation of older social media like QQ and new mobile games, *ba ling hou* are continuing to teach, and be taught by, their parents and grandparents.

Understanding the rise and fall of *Happy Farm* in China helps us to appreciate the particular ways in which social media gaming has been embraced by different generations. It also provides insight into the ebbs and flows of games as part of popular culture imaginaries. *Happy Farm* highlights the rise and fall of social media games, but within a different cultural context. *Happy Farm* was the precursor to one of the first social media game successes in English-speaking contexts, Zynga's *FarmVille*. *FarmVille* helped to define Zynga's importance in the newly developing area of social games and apps and assisted Zonga's colonisation of Facebook games. Launched in the summer of 2008, *Happy Farm* soon boasted 23 million users across three social media platforms: Renren, Kaixin and QZone (Millward, 2012). By 2009, millions of parents in China were playing *Happy Farm* day and night with their young adult children who had moved away from home to study or work. *Happy Farm*, through its ambient play, afforded a type of omnipresent co-presence between family members separated by physical distance. Like having a family member in the background, *Happy Farm* helped to ease much of the loneliness on the part of both parents and their children studying away from home (Hjorth and Arnold, 2013).

This study provided insight into the cross-generational media practices being used in Shanghai to connect geographically distinct children and their parents.

Ba ling hou often taught their parents how to use the new media and were surprised by their sometimes passionate uptake. The cross-generational usage demonstrates the ways in which the often tacit etiquette and vernacular around mobile media differs across the generations. Moreover, this study highlights how intimacy and co-presence are culturally specific with many of the mundane practices particular to the cultural and linguistic history of China, while others speak more generally to shifting relationships to, and within, mobile media.

REFLECTING ON RELATIONSHIPS AS A CATEGORY OF DIGITAL ETHNOGRAPHY RESEARCH

The three examples in this chapter explored how digital ethnography enables researchers to understand how relationships are formed in, through and with digital media and technology, and the different forms of co-presence which are central to relationships. As we illustrated, the particular ways in which co-presence becomes meaningful is shaped by different cultural contexts, norms around the ways in which intimacy is expressed, gendered forms of behaviour and expectations, particularly across different generations.

The first two examples highlight some of the transformations in the practices of co-presence that have come with the introduction of the mobile phone. As the first examples demonstrate, mobile phones entwine the material and immaterial dimensions of relationships both in terms of representation and maintenance. We saw how Hello Kitties attached to a phone can help to emotionally 'locate' the phone through personalisation practices. However, in each different cultural context we see how the media can be 'located' and made meaningful by entangling personalisation practices across platforms, media and contexts. In both cases, the mobile phone becomes a repository for fleeting moments of intimacy both in terms of the co-presence they enable but also the 'records' of calls archived into the mobile phone which Horst and her colleagues used to review phone calls. It became evident in Hjorth and Horst's respective studies that if someone's mobile phone was lost or stolen, the messages and images would not necessarily be decipherable. They are fleeting contingencies of the moment, representing what we have been describing as intimate co-presence. These messages and images – shared across online and offline software and hardware spaces – are indexes of the contemporary life and its movements across temporality and liveness, immediacy and intimacy.

The second two examples work together to highlight the importance of mobile phones and social media in mediating a sense of co-presence and intimacy across different national scales. In the example of a grandmother in Jamaica worrying about her children and grandchildren in England, we see how the mobile phone becomes a way through which she copes with a family crisis where, if present, she would have played a central role as the female head of the family in keeping the family together. Through her affordable mobile phone connection, she works to find ways to stay connected and to care for and support her children and grandchildren. Listening to voices and sounds become central to this process. In the example of *Happy Farm*, we see Chinese young people using a gaming platform to create the sense of being together to maintain the close ties with parents when they move away from their hometown for study or work. However, in their case, the sense of co-presence comes through the creation of a sense of being together in a mundane, but playful fashion – almost as if they were gathered around the television together in their home.

We also see broader issues of power being negotiated in all three examples. In the first example of a girlfriend inscribing her eye as a screen saver on a mobile phone, the screen saver is not only a reminder of her, but is also a reminder about the proper way to behave as a boyfriend in Korea. The second example, in Jamaica, highlights the ways in which the mobile phone can be at once an object through which norms around grandmothering can be maintained, but is also the same object through which young men in Jamaica work to counteract the economic marginalisation that many young men feel in Jamaica. Finally, the cross-generational relationships developed through the use of *Happy Farm* among Chinese families challenges the myth that all members of Generation Y are 'digital natives' (Crawford and Robinson, 2013; Gasser and Palfrey, 2008). In this case, parents were often heavier media users than the younger generation. In all these examples, the mobile phone is neither a 'good' nor a 'bad' device which brings about change or transformation; it is the agency and contexts for their use that determine their meaning and, in turn, their capacity to empower, survey or reinforce the structures of power in a given setting.

As noted in the first ethnographic example, the mobile phone has been a particularly fruitful device through which to understand digitally mediated relationships and a great deal of the early mobile media and communication literature pushed the boundaries of what could be understood and studied through the mobile phone. However, and as we see in the case of *Happy Farm*, the mobile phone is often a route into other digital media practices. As digital and online media become more mobile, the ways in which we can research, produce knowledge with, analyse and disseminate research findings are shifting. The potential uses of mobile and locative media in these contexts are expanding as these technologies are part of the lives of participants in research, as well as forming part of research practice. Researchers are diversifying their methods in order to carry out more nuanced studies and identify different scenarios of media use. How do we study a phenomenon as dynamic as relationships across multiple forms of co-presence and co-location? What are some of the ways in which the messiness of media can be engaged as a lens to understand the messiness of social relationships?

Interviews, often in which mobile and locative media technologies and video are used, still form an important part of the way that we as researchers can be with people as they play out their social, embodied and sensory and technological relationships with and through these technologies. Participant observation in this context becomes a tool of communication and research, as personal locative and mobile media are used as part of a research process, both within our relationships with participants and as parts of people's relationships with others that we wish to observe unfold. Additionally, scenarios of use, and re-enactments as participants use and show us how they use various platforms and applications, can enable us to consider the types of performativity and etiquette (tacit and phatic) that are part of the ways that social relationships are constituted through the material and immaterial dimensions of the ways that people use and experience digital media. Finally, the mobile itself emerged as a personal archive of relationships, communication patterns and the emotional landscapes of individuals and families. Continued innovations in digital ethnographic methods will enable us to understand these intimacies and relationships.

SUMMING UP

In this chapter, we explored the various ways in which digital ethnography can provide insight into understanding relationships. From customisation outside the phone to the use of mobile phones for calls and playing games, this chapter has sought to demonstrate the multiple ways in which the digital – as both a material culture and a set of media practices – is overlaid and entwined in our maintenance of relationships. By focusing on the importance of co-presence in maintaining relationships, we have sought to demonstrate a variety of ways through which digital media and technologies can be used to create a sense of presence over space and time – whether the distances to be bridged are temporary moments of not being together as a couple or distance created through migration and transnational livelihoods. The quality of the sense of co-presence properties are intricately tied to the affordances of particular digital media and technologies – text, voice, archiving, synchronous and asynchronous communication and so on.

A particular focus of the chapter revolves around the importance of social and cultural context in defining how digital media and technologies are taken up in relationships. Throughout our ethnographic examples, the focus on mobile phones and transformation acknowledges the importance of understanding mobile phone use in the context of relationships, rather than the mobile phones' 'impact on' people in different cultural contexts; it is the relationship dynamics that determine how mobile phones – of different types, basic phones, smartphones and mobile media – are taken up in each cultural, social and relationship context.

Researching Social Worlds

CHAPTER CONTENTS

INTRODUCTION

This chapter examines how digital ethnographers research social worlds. We first introduce how social worlds, broadly defined, have figured in social research histori-cally as a central concern of anthropologists and sociologists. The study of social worlds has been a focal element for ethnographers since the inception of these disciplines and has also been important to related interdisciplinary fields of study, including media studies and media anthropology. The concept of social worlds has been debated across a range of different theoretical perspectives. Some of these debates downplay its relevance; others place it at the centre of the analysis. In a digital context, some researchers have debated to what extent social worlds that involve digital elements are reducing, increasing or changing social life and its consequences. In this chapter, we assess these debates and outline how ethnographic research can inform them. Focusing on three ethnographic examples – a Malaysian online forum, a Spanish protest movement and cosplay ('costume play') in Australia – we outline the methods that have been employed to study socio-digital worlds and the different forms of knowledge these methods produce.

WHAT IS THE CONCEPT OF SOCIAL WORLDS?

The concept of social worlds – unlike others discussed in this book such as practices, social things or events – does not have a trajectory of use in the social sciences as a defining theory. Instead, in this chapter, we use the notion of social worlds as a heuristic device, that is, as an open-ended way of exploring a question. By social worlds, we mean those relatively bounded – but never airtight – domains of social life. Ethnographers typically immerse themselves in these worlds by spending long periods of time with their research participants. The potential variation of these worlds is as vast of that of human sociocultural diversity. They can range widely from the worlds inhabited by bikers, surfers, farmers, nuns or herders, to those of online poker players, 3D virtual environments, Facebook groups or Weibo users.

Yet, in the messiness of ethnographic practice, grasping the notion of social worlds can be elusive. We tend to refer to these worlds in ways that are related to the experiences we are having, opting for an almost infinite set of notions that tend to be specific to each field project: a longhouse in Sarawak (Postill, 2006), the bullfighting 'scene' in southern Spain (Pink, 1997), or a group of community activists or environmentalists in Melbourne (Lewis, 2015). Immersing oneself through participant observation in a new social world ethnographically is a process. It can be awkward at times, and usually involves a steep learning curve about the inhabitants of that world and their everyday lives. Immersion, participant observation and 'the everyday' are three ideas that are bound up with how we study social worlds. However, one problem that complicates the apparently neat immersion metaphor is that social worlds are never sealed off from other social worlds, or indeed from the rest of humankind in our massively interconnected world. Unlike most swimming pools, to continue with the immersion metaphor, social worlds are not usually walled off or separated from other pools. In fact, they tend to intersect with other worlds, with their boundaries neither fixed nor always clear to insiders or outsiders. People come and go, and the worlds wax and wane over time. For example, Internet activists might move between different 'groups' while remaining activists, or they might re-focus their politics from for example resistance to taking up a political position (Postill, 2010). That said, we shouldn't be too hasty to abandon the idea that there *are* social worlds, or uncritically buy into the image of unboundedness. The degree and quality of boundedness, access, openness and porosity of any given social world cannot be assumed, but needs to be established through empirical research. For example, a Freemason's lodge is likely to be a more closed social world, 'by invitation only', than a popular public park in a town centre.

How, then, have social science and humanities scholars tried to understand and define social worlds? We focus on a set of key concepts that have been, and in some cases continue to be, influential across academic disciplines. We first look at how the concepts of 'community' and 'network' have been used in what we might characterise as pre-digital sociology and anthropology in order to try to understand social worlds and how they were structured, connected and bound together. We next discuss how these were then adapted to the Internet. Joining other contemporary scholars, we take a critical view of these concepts to suggest that some of the gaps they leave can be filled with the plural concept of 'socialities' (so long as we regard this concept as a handy research tool, not as a theoretical panacea). Indeed, as we later suggest, the types of social world that we might work with as digital ethnographers in a digital–material environment of social media platforms and mobile and locative technologies would be hard to squeeze into the frameworks of either community or network because they were developed in conventional studies during the twentieth century.

HOW HAVE SOCIAL WORLDS BEEN STUDIED?

Various concepts have been used to understand and research social worlds. In the past, these have sought to account for the specific cultures associated with social groups or collectives. In the earlier parts of the twentieth century, a 'culture' was generally assumed to coincide with a group of people who lived together in one place. This idea was undermined by the critical literature of the 1980s and onwards that disassociated culture from place (e.g., Gupta and Ferguson, 1997) and shifted focus towards the multi-sitedness of culture and the need, therefore, to do ethnography that stretches across multiple sites (Marcus, 1995). In sociology and cultural studies, this urge to associate social groups with cultural boundedness and internal similarity led to concepts such as that of 'subculture' (Gelder, 2007; Hebdige, 1995) and 'ethnic groups'. These classifications had a similar effect of dividing social worlds into sets of discrete entities.

The concept of community also played a dominant role in describing social groupings through much of the twentieth century. Community studies were a key unit of analysis for both anthropologists and sociologists particularly around the middle of the century. The concept of community creates a 'feel good' sense of human togetherness, evoking a social world that is warm and supportive. As an academic concept, however, it is limited in its empirical application to describing social formations (Amit and Rapport, 2002; Creed, 2006; Pahl, 2005; Pink, 2008). As Vered Amit summarises: 'Invocations of community do not present analysts with clear-cut groupings so much as signal fields of complex processes through which sociality is sought, rejected, argued over, realized, interpreted, exploited or enforced' (2002: 14). Amit identifies a slippage between the ideas of community as an actual social group and as an imagined category (ibid.: 18).

Indeed, according to some scholars, by the end of the twentieth century, the concept of community had little use as an analytical category (discussed in Pink, 2008). However, it remained important as a category that could be explored with participants because it had local meanings as well as academic significance. The concept of community thus fostered greater understanding of people's perceptions of social relationships and the political implications of collective terms. For example, Pink's interviews with Slow City activists in England included exploring their definitions of 'community'. They often told her that the term was a policy category that they needed to use, but that it was also for them quite meaningless beyond it referring, in policy terms, to a specific geographically located group of people (Pink, 2008). Other academic uses of the term 'community' have reconceptualised it in ways that are more useful than the original formulation, including concepts such as 'communities of practice' (Wenger, 1998) that refers to the 'doing' of community through active participation in sets of shared practices that bind people together (Lave and Wenger, 1991). We will refer to this conceptualisation again later in this chapter.

The concept of the 'network' has also played a key role in the development of social research in the twentieth century. This concept was particularly important in the work of the anthropologists in the 1950s and 1960s, who sought new ways of understanding the relationships between the way society was structured and the ways in which social relationships and activities come together (Postill, 2011). In part, the idea of researching social networks also depended on the specific methods used in ethnographic research, in that these anthropologists, who were largely working in urban settings such as in African cities, began to follow 'individuals across social fields' in the hope that these observations would 'be able to capture the open-ended nature of much social life' (Postill, 2011; and see Mitchell, 1969; and Amit, 2007). For anthropologists, however, this approach became increasingly redundant because it was not applicable to the type of work that often characterises anthropology, especially the practice of focusing on smaller groups. As a result, it was little used by the 1970s (Postill, 2011).

Outside of anthropology, this theoretical strand survived in the social sciences. At the same time, what was known as 'social network analysis' (SNA) became popular amongst sociologists and economists, especially since computers were now becoming mainstream tools in the work of social scientists (Freeman, 2007; Postill, 2011).

Granovetter's work in the USA demonstrated how Boston jobseekers found that their 'weak' connections, meaning their connections with friends of friends, helped them more in their job-seeking than their 'strong' connections with family and close friends. Granovetter's (1973) famous thesis of the 'strength of weak ties' is a landmark study in this area and continues to be influential in contemporary studies of the Internet (Wellman et al., 2003), mobile communication (Ling, 2004) and communication studies broadly (Haythornthwaite, 1996). More recently, anthropologists have also re-engaged with the concept of social networks, which, importantly for the question of digital ethnography theory and practice, has meant that it has been used in dialogue with ethnographic research (Freeman, 2007; Postill, 2011). This has become particularly relevant for the study of social activism (which, as we also show in this book, is a field of practice that is often highly implicated in the use of digital and social media) (e.g., Juris, 2008). Yet, at the same time, there have been a good number of anthropologists who have critically engaged with the concept of social networks and sought to rethink its assumptions (e.g., Amit, 2007; Horst and Miller, 2006; Moeran, 2002; Postill, 2011; Pink, 2012).

EXISTING CONCEPTS AND UNDERSTANDING OF DIGITAL SOCIAL WORLDS

The ongoing boom in Internet sites and mobile technologies centred around *individuals* and their own personal networks has been a fertile ground for the application of SNA and network theory to sociological research into the Internet. In part, this has involved the use of SNA amongst Internet researchers (e.g., Chiu et al., 2011; Trusov et al., 2010). However, there have been other influential scholars in this field who have advanced our understanding of networks in new directions. One of the most influential works in this is by the sociologist Manuel Castells, who developed the theory of the network society (published in his trilogy of books between 1996 and 1998). Castells argues that fluid, transnational networks are the dominant social formations of our age, replacing earlier formations such as communities or associations. Related to Castell's work and also following a sociological approach, other influential scholars have linked this trend to the global rise of 'networked individualism' (e.g., Wellman et al., 2003). For Wellman, the local neighbourhood (see Chapter 7) is no longer a key site for social relationships in North Amercia (Wellman and Leighton, 1979). Instead, he proposes that communities have come to exist in the form of 'geographically dispersed "personal communities"', which are personal networks of the type written about by the sociologist Ray Pahl (cf. Pahl, 2005) (Postill, 2011: 12). For these authors, the Internet 'merely reinforces a global trend towards networked individualism that was already well under way' (Postill, 2011: 12). In such a world, 'communities' have not disappeared but have been reconfigured around individuals' personal networks. Therefore, while it was argued by sociologists such Anthony Giddens that 'community' as it existed in its traditional pre-modern form shifted in modernity (1990), the notion of 'networked individualism' accommodated the idea that there was a reconfiguration of social relations away from the collective forms that predominated in the past (families, villages, associations, firms) and towards 'me-centred' formations.

More recently, the notion of community has also been revived in Internet ethnography. A key example for our discussion here is Rob Kozinets' 'netnography' approach (2010). Netnography has become fast established and discussed by ethnographers working online and offers a useful framework for some types of analysis. One of the key concepts that underpins netnography is that of community, along with the idea that communities can be found, and studied, online. Kozinets defines online communities as having both online (virtual) and offline (face-to-face) elements (ibid.: 15). He mobilises the term community in a specific way in that he suggests that it should be used 'to refer to a group of people who share social interaction, social ties, and a common interactional format, location or "space" – albeit, in this case, a computer-mediated or virtual "cyberspace"'. He further proposes using a 'continuum of participation' to define 'community membership', involving 'self-identification as a member, repeat contact, reciprocal familiarity, shared knowledge of some rituals and customs, some sense of obligation, and participation' (ibid.: 10).

The community and network approaches have not been without their critics, particularly from anthropological and ethnographic quarters. However, in evaluating these specific developments of the concept of network, it is also important to be mindful of the disciplinary differences in interest and focus they represent between anthropologists and sociologists. Indeed, we would not want to suggest that anthropologists and ethnographers are not interested in understanding digital worlds through the concepts of community or network. Yet, as often happens, in-depth ethnographic research has tended to question some of the universalising tendencies of such theories. For example, Horst and Miller (2005, 2006) question the idea that there is empirically such a thing as a 'network society' spreading from the metropolitan north to the rest of the world. Following their ethnographic research into the uses of mobile phones in Jamaica, they found that low-income Jamaicans have their own vernacular forms of networking, which they call 'link up'. These networks have deep roots in the country's cultural history. Mobile phones did not turn Jamaicans into networked individuals. Rather, they were appropriated into local forms of sociality, relationships and the reciprocity, becoming for some people a lifeline in times of economic hardship.

The plural concept of 'socialities' shows promise as a more ethnographically informed way to understand Internet use and its relationship to everyday materialities.

For a number of years, anthropologists who have found these existing concepts to be limited for understanding the specificity and detail of ethnographic work have been developing concepts of sociality as a possible alternative (Amrit, 2002; Pink, 2008; Postill, 2008, 2011). The concept of socialities refers, not to a specific type of social relationship per se, but rather to the qualities of social relationships. It is an open concept that enables us to recognise that social relations between people are multiple, can be fluid, and change at different rates. Hence, it also allows us to conceptualise how the ways in which people become related or 'connected' to each other through and with digital technologies might be similarly changing.

Across the humanities and social sciences, the concept of sociality has often been used in rather general terms. For instance, the sociologist Andreas Wittel (2001) has distinguished two main forms of sociality, namely 'community sociality' versus 'network sociality'. For this author, community sociality is the slow, locality-based form of social intercourse that has characterised the human species for most of our cultural history. By contrast, network sociality captures the fast-paced, fleeting, trans-local nature of today's urban, post-industrial lifestyles. Wittel fleshes out the latter form of sociality by drawing from his late 1990s research into London's 'new media' sector (Postill, 2011).

One problem with this dichotomy is that it may prevent us from exploring the diverse range of *socialities* – in the plural – that are likely to coexist within a given field site, in this case the world of London-based new media workers. It is logical to assume, for instance, that the sociality of a speed-dating event in London will be markedly different from that of a pub quiz night, a media lab or a board meeting. A second problem with this binary is that it relies on an odd pairing of vague notions ('community' and 'network') that have bedevilled digital media studies for years, as discussed above, hindering our collective understanding of the shifting socio-technical terrains that most of us inhabit today (Postill, 2011).

RESEARCHING SOCIAL WORLDS THROUGH DIGITAL ETHNOGRAPHY

In the previous sections, we explored how selected concepts that were developed in the pre-digital era of researching social worlds have been engaged by scholars attending to the Internet, digital platforms, technologies and the social and political relationships that within which these are entangled. Concepts of community, network and sociality have played a role in scholarship that has sought to theorise and research the Internet and digital media more generally. In our three ethnographic examples, we look at how these debates have been advanced through contemporary ethnographic research, including studies of Web forums.

An ethnographic investigation of the 'thread sociality' of a Malaysian Web forum

One of the strengths of ethnography is that it can help us to expand our conceptual repertoires as researchers, including those related to the study of digitally mediated social worlds, enabling us to develop finer-grained distinctions (Postill, 2012a). The notion of 'sociality' just discussed is a case in point. There are many definitions of this term, but here we can provisionally define it as the unique social quality that characterises a given shared practice or interaction, such as playing tennis, attending a wedding, riding on a bus or having a Skype conversation.

During John Postill's (2008, 2011) work on the Internet in the Kuala Lumpur suburb of Subang Jaya (Malaysia), the concept of sociality offered a route into understanding how social worlds are formed in relation to online and offline activity. In this locality, Postill did not find a single 'community sociality' (Wittell, 2001), but rather a diversity of residential socialities around practices such as shopping in a mall, playing basketball, attending local committee meetings, patrolling the streets or interacting on a local Web forum. Thus, the quality of social intercourse and technological mediation found while patrolling a neighbourhood is notably distinct from that of a committee meeting or a Web forum. Thus, while pairs of volunteer patrollers walk side by side, carrying torches, batons and mobile phones, committee members face one another around a table equipped with pens, paper and the occasional laptop. Meanwhile, forum users engage in remote, computer-mediated communication. It would be very odd, indeed, to treat a committee meeting as if it were a street patrol, or to conflate the feel and ambiance of a Web forum with that of an offline meeting. Like all other skilled social beings, digital ethnographers doing fieldwork must learn how to navigate different social settings, responding to their social cues, making appropriate use of media technologies in context.

Take, for instance, Subang Jaya's main Web forum, USJ.com.my. The website was founded in 1999 by the local businessman and activist Jeff Ooi, who later went on to achieve national fame as a political blogger and Opposition MP (Postill, 2014a). This online forum soon became an important meeting point for Subang Jaya residents wishing to keep informed about local issues or simply to converse with like-minded people from across the municipality (and beyond). Although some of the posts are written in Malay, Mandarin and other languages, by far the most commonly used language on the forum is the country's middle-class lingua franca: Malaysian English. The forum is open to any topic, although participants must exercise care when broaching 'sensitive' matters such as race and religion in a country where Malay Muslims enjoy constitutional privileges that are not extended to non-Muslims. The combination of a large critical mass of users with the freedom to choose almost any topic results in a highly dynamic environment in which participants compete to attract conversational partners to their own threads, thereby gaining visibility and social capital.

The forum sustains what we might call 'threaded sociality', a generic form of sociality commonly found across the Internet (including mailings lists, Web forums, blogs and personal network sites) but with unique local or subcultural characteristics. As the discussion below shows, threaded sociality in Subang Jaya exhibits seven main features: it is polylogical, sequential, asynchronous, emoticonic, publicly intimate, online/offline and political.

First, Web forum discourse is mostly *polylogical*, that is, it is neither a monologue nor a dialogue, but rather involves three or more conversational partners. Postill learned this lesson the hard way when he created a thread about his fieldwork and invited feedback from other forum users. This was an ill-fated effort at making his ethnographic research more participatory. At an offline gathering, one of the more popular 'forumers' (as they are called) nicknamed Orchi, asked John whether he felt that he was talking to himself on that thread. John had to agree with Orchi, as the thread had not attracted much attention. The implications were clear: the forum fostered a type of suburban sociality based on group conversations, not soliloquies.

Second, in contrast with general theories of Web sociality as being inherently hypertextual and non-linear (e.g., Castells, 2001), thread sociality is intra-textual and *sequential* (or serial). In other words, thread posts succeed one another within the bounded domain of the forum platform. Although it is true that Subang Jaya forumers will often share hyperlinks to other websites, participants are still bound in their discursive agency by the linear logic of threads if they wish to sustain a meaningful conversation (which most regulars do). Unlike the overlaps and indeterminacies typical of an offline group conversation – particularly in a noisy place such a bar or a pub – thread posts are non-overlapping speech acts.

Third, as shown by Mesch and Levanon (2003) for suburban Israeli listservs, the Web forum's *asynchronicity* allows busy Subang Jaya residents to stay connected to fellow residents at their own leisure. Because messages are automatically archived, latecomers can scroll up and down a thread in order to join the conversation either as silent listeners (lurkers) or as posters. Participation is aided by the option of receiving emailed alerts each time a new post is added to a thread. It is highly significant that forum users subscribe, not to the forum as a whole, but to threads. To paraphrase a Twitter marketing slogan, this pre-Twitter site allows local residents to 'follow their interests'.

Fourth, in contradistinction, moreover, to gesturally rich offline practices such as local committee meetings, Subang Jaya forum users must rely on *emoticons* to compensate for the relative poverty of online bodily cues (*pace* Hine, 2000: 14–27). The following exchange captures the use of a smiling emoticon by one of the forum's micro-celebrities, the aforementioned Orchi. In the manner typical of Malaysian English, this user code-mixes more than one language – in this case English, Malay and Hokkien – ending his digital intervention with a smiley. The topic was *teh tarik* (TT), a tea beverage popular in Peninsular Malaysia:

Err ... met up with a couple of seasoned forumers last night for the regular cuppa TT ... as **Orchi** got there earlier ... it was late n **Orchi** felt a tinch of sleepiness ... so **Orchi** ordered a glass of kopi-o ice ... which was rare thing to happen ... n the mamak looked at **Orchi** one kind ... Then the first thing when the boyz came ... one of them noticed that **Orchi** was drinking kopi-o ice instead ... so they started firing **Orchi** what ... '**Orchi** takut mati kar ... kia si ar?' ... ☺ ['Are you afraid of dying, Orchi?']

Fifth, forum thread sociality is characterised by what we might call *public intimacy*. Because of the narrow-cast, quasi-oral nature of online threads, participants may feel as if they are sharing a conversation with an intimate group of conversational partners. At the same time, forumers are aware that potentially anyone in the World Wide Web could be lurking in the shadows.

Sixth, although the forum's dominant sociality is Web-based, some of the longer threads undergo *offline phases* throughout their life courses. One of the oldest and lengthiest threads on USJ.com.my is devoted to arranging monthly *teh tarik* meetings like the one just mentioned. This thread had clocked 889 posts and close to 35,000 viewings as of 3 April 2006. By 24 January 2011, the thread had 2837 posts, over 125,000 viewings and 190 pages! These sessions take place on the first Friday of every month and attract some ten to fifteen enthusiasts. This may not seem like a large number, but it does constitute a hard core of forum supporters vital to its long-term sustainability. Such face-to-face encounters have their own polylogical character, albeit of the offline variety: utterances overlap, unmoderated topics and sub-topics break off rapidly, and the group splinters into subgroups.

Finally, in the specific case of the Subang Jaya e-Community forum, thread sociality can be seen as *political* because it is marked by the conflicting priorities of the forum administrators on the one hand, and the majority of regular users on the other. For the management team led by the activist Jeff Ooi (at least until he became occupied with extra-local matters), the forum was an experimental means towards an end, namely to strengthen local governance. For most users, however, the forum is primarily a source of local information, entertainment and conviviality: one of Oldenburg's (1989) 'third places', venues where suburbanites can socialise outside the home and the workplace, such as in pubs, bowling clubs and post offices. When a critical issue that affects them directly emerges on the forum, many will join the campaigning, but during peaceful periods most will remain uninvolved.

How applicable is the notion of threaded sociality to social worlds beyond the specificities of this unique Malaysian suburb? Further research would be required to answer this question, yet recent research elsewhere (Postill and Pink, 2012; see next example) and our everyday experience as users suggests that this notion could shed light on the social dynamics found on digital platforms as diverse as mailing lists, Twitter, Weibo, Facebook or WhatsApp. The terminology and syntax will vary from one platform to another ('thread', 'hashtag', 'trending topic', 'comments', 'chat' and so on), but all these sites organise their conversations through discrete series of bounded posts, that is, through threads. It is reasonable to assume, then, that myriad variants of threaded sociality have emerged worldwide in recent years, variants that are ripe for comparative ethnographic research.

The birth of a new social world: An ethnographic approach to understanding the Indignados

The Malaysian example just presented concerns a social world that remained fairly stable throughout the main period of fieldwork. However, digital ethnographers will sometimes find that the social worlds they are researching will experience dramatic changes over a short period of time. In some cases, they may even witness the birth of a new social world while in the field. This is precisely what happened to Postill whilst conducting fieldwork among Internet activists in Barcelona, Spain. In mid-May 2011, with little prior warning, the small Internet activism scene he had been researching for ten months was swept up by a tidal wave of popular indignation involving millions of Spanish citizens who took to the streets and squares demanding 'real democracy now' (Postill, 2014a; Postill and Pink, 2012). This 'wave' soon came to be known as the *indignados* (outraged) or 15-M movement – a new, gigantic social world demanding urgent investigation.

Here is a rough outline of the events. When some forty anti-austerity protesters decided to stage a sit-in at Madrid's main square, Puerta del Sol, in the early hours of 16 May 2011, they could not have anticipated the repercussions of their spontaneous action. After calling for reinforcements via Twitter and other social media, their numbers grew into the hundreds during the day. Yet, it was only when they were removed from the square by the police on 17 May that their plight 'went viral'. This led to the retaking of the square, only now by thousands upon thousands of protesters from all walks of life – an action that was soon replicated in dozens of other squares up and down the country. What started on 15 May as a series of peaceful marches had turned within 48 hours into the Tahrir Square, Cairo-inspired occupation of countless squares across Spain. The fledgling protests had morphed into a mass social movement, a social media phenomenon and a global media event. Within days, millions of Spaniards were exchanging a huge volume of 15-M digital contents through email, Facebook, Twitter, Tuenti, blogs and countless other platforms, both on desktop computers and handheld devices (Rodríguez, 2011).

Since those eventful days, Postill has sought to conceptualise the 15-M social world in a number of different ways. We could regard these efforts as diachronic, 'multitimed' versions (Postill, 2012b) of the influential 'follow the' approach to multi-sited ethnographic research proposed by Marcus (1995). Here, we briefly review some of them, namely following: (a) the viral contents; (b) the digital technologies; (c) the digital technolo*gists*; (d) the field of contention; and (e) the protest temporalities.

With regards to virality, Postill (2014a) has recently argued that we are entering a new age of 'viral reality' in which media amateurs and professionals are co-defining what constitutes a newsworthy story through citizens' increased ability to choose which digital contents to share – or not – with their personal networks. These 'hybrid media systems' (Chadwick, 2013) or 'convergence cultures' (Jenkins, 2006a) pose formidable challenges to ethnographers, and require new conceptual tools and approaches. In this vein, Postill (2014a) outlines a new research programme that he terms 'media epidemiography'. This concept blends Sperber's (1996) 'epidemiology of representations' with the ethnography of digital media. By analogy with medical epidemiology, its remit is to track the endemic and epidemic distribution of digital contents (or 'representations') across a given population – in this case, 15-M contents across Spain – through ethnographic means. For a protest movement like 15-M, Postill (2014a: 56–62) proposes four working types of viral form: campaign virals (i.e., campaign contents that 'go viral'); viral campaigns (the whole campaign goes viral); niche virals (digital contents shared within a specific demographic, e.g. law students in Barcelona); and sustainable virals (contents that become endemic within a whole population, e.g. the slogan 'Real democracy now!' across Spain). Given the speed with which digital contents will sometimes spread, media epidemiographers will have to develop new digital forensics techniques to investigate them retrospectively, such as through interviews with activists involved in creating campaign memes, Twitter trending topics and the like.

A second avenue open to the digital ethnographer is to 'follow' one or more technologies as they traverse different social contexts (Marcus, 1995; Spitulnik, 2002). For instance, Monterde and Postill (2014) tracked the uses of mobile phones by 15-M participants during the first semester of the movement's existence, through both qualitative and quantitative data. They found a great deal of variation from one event or action to another, coining the notion 'mobile ensembles' to refer to the unique mix of digital media, participants and issues found in each instance. This term is derived from the earlier notion of 'media ensembles' that was introduced by the media theorist Bausinger (1984) to refer to the combination of radio, TV and print media typically found in a Western home in the early 1980s.

Another option available to the digital ethnographer is to follow, not the technolo*gies*, but rather the technolo*gists*. For instance, Postill has followed a specific subcategory of political actor he calls 'freedom technologists', that is, those people who are passionately interested in the limits and possibilities of new digital technologies for progressive political change (e.g., bloggers, vloggers, hackers, geeks, online journalists, civil rights lawyers). In this context, 'following' does not necessarily entail physically shadowing participants in real time. Digital ethnographers will often retrace the steps of key participants after the fact, by means of interviews, Web archives, social media platforms, field notes and other materials. Thus, Postill has translated and edited a series of transcripts of YouTube interviews with Spanish freedom technologists available on a 15-M website (Figure 6.1). The interviews were neither commissioned nor conducted by the ethnographer, but rather by a collective of freedom technologists. He then shared these 'para-ethnographic' materials (Holmes and Marcus, 2008) on his research blog. In turn, these posts have been recirculated via Twitter and other sites by the research participants, thereby reaching non-academic audiences. As digital technologies and free/open ideals and practices continue to spread, such intersections between the work of ethnographers, activists, and other political actors will become more habitual – and potentially rewarding.

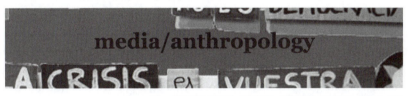

Figure 6.1 Postill follows the participants in his research online, and writes about this on his blog, thus participating as an ethnographer in a social media world

Source: Image copyright of John Postill.

The 15-M social world can also be conceptualised as a field (Postill, 2015). More specifically, as a movement-field or field of contention, that is, a highly dynamic political domain in which variously positioned field agents (activists, hackers, journalists, politicians, celebrities and so on) struggle over a small set of pressing issues and rewards, often through digital media. By contrast with more institutionalised fields such as art, sociology or journalism studied by Bourdieu and his colleagues, a movement-field (particularly in the digital age) is characterised by its mercurial dynamism, that is, by the swiftness and unpredictability with which it can expand, contract, mutate and migrate (Postill, 2011). Rather than a 'community of practice' (see above) with its shared membership, the 15-M field resembles the 'affinity space' of a massively multiplayer online game (Gee, 2005). This is an open, inclusive socio-technical world in which 'players' can find highly diverse routes to participation and accomplishment, regardless of prior qualifications or social identity.

Finally, the digital ethnographer can approach a social world like 15-M genealogically, that is, by teasing out its entangled processual lineages. Eschewing the received notion of non-linear time – popular in anthropology since the 1980s – Postill (forthcoming) opts instead for the idea of multi-linearity. Reworking a conceptual trinity developed by the historian William Sewell (2005), Postill distinguishes between 15-M events, routines and trends as three distinct forms of temporality with their own unique trajectories (or lineages). He notes that not all 'media events' in Dayan and Katz's (1992) classic formulation qualify as 15-M events in the Sewellian sense of the term. To qualify as such, they must *transform* the movement-field. For example, when 15-M participants throughout Spain abandoned the occupied squares in June 2011 to relocate to local neighbourhoods, this move had a profound effect on the movement, marking a new stage in its evolution. Events such as this will have a direct impact on a social world's web of routines: whilst some square routines survived the relocation (e.g., holding assemblies), others perished in the process. Finally, trends are of interest, not only to the diachronic ethnographer, but also to movement-field participants themselves. Perceived trends push 15-M collective action towards traits regarded as desirable (e.g., non-violence) and away from those seen as undesirable by most participants (e.g., a turn towards violent 'direct action').

Ethnography of the games industry in Australia: Alternative routes for gender performativity

As gaming becomes increasingly part of mainstream culture, we are beginning to see other modes of gaming subcultures, including what is called 'cosplay'. Cosplay is short for 'costume play' and cosplayers take their inspiration from games, manga (comics), anime (animation) and movies. As a subcultural movement, various forms of cosplayers can be found both within Japan and around the world. Cosplaying provides new avenues for fans to express their interest in Japanese popular culture creatively; in turn, cosplay also provides a great example of how new types of fan agency and professionalization of player genres (like e-sports) are occurring around games as they become progressively synonymous with contemporary popular culture and thus part of emergent social worlds.

Figure 6.2 'Cosplayers' are inspired by various forms of popular culture, such as games, manga (comics), anime (animation), and movies

Source: Image copyright Larissa Hjorth.

In particular, cosplay's role as a vehicle of transition is significant in the rites of passage for many young females as they enter into the traditionally male-centred gaming worlds – thus moving from being game players, to co-producers/produsers (producing consumer), and then to game designers/producers. It is this transition from *player* to *produser* and *producer* that is pivotal in emerging forms of female engagement and agency in an industry (games) that is largely dominated by men. Phenomena such as cosplay reassert Japan's central role in the imaginings of digital popular culture circuits in the region. For many, rites of passage into gaming in locations such as Australia and Taiwan involve a disavowal of USA 'mainstream' games in exchange for 'subcultural' and 'cool' Japanese games. This is an alternative entrance into global gaming that unites players across transnational borders, while reorienting Japan as the alternative centre for popular culture. But this is not a mere mirroring of Japanisation with Americanisation, as homogeneous definitions of globalisation would have it.

Rather, forms of localisation emerge as gaming shifts from the periphery to the centre of twenty-first-century media cultures. As Craig Norris (2007) has discussed, there is a trend for Australian fans to use anime and manga to explore gendered and racial identities that produce different forms of cultural capital and identity.

While there is a growing body of scholarly research on cosplayers in locations such as Japan, Hong Kong, Taiwan and South Korea (Ito et al., 2012), in Australia there has been comparatively little research done, despite the existence of conventions such as Animania that are dedicated to the 'key' event, the cosplay competition. As Patricia Maunder notes in 'Dress Up and Play Cool', cosplay provides a space where 'games meet reality' (2009). One of the first cosplay conventions was held at the Australian Centre for Independent Gaming, Melbourne, in 2000, with the beginnings of the now annual Manifest (Melbourne Anime Festival) convention. In 2002, Animania began in Sydney, expanding to Brisbane and Melbourne. According to cosplayer and manager of Animania, Kenny Travouillon, Australian cosplayers draw from '60% anime and 40% games', with the level of professionalism and commitment excelling each year, so much so that in 2009 an Australian team will attend the Holy Grail for cosplayers (apart from the Tokyo Game Show), the World Cosplay Summit in Nagoya.

Figure 6.3 Cosplay is also part of an events culture

Source: Image copyright Larissa Hjorth.

One of the significant differences in the politics of cosplaying in Australia, as opposed to Taiwan or Hong Kong, is the issue of multiculturalism. In Australia, East, South East (Asia), European and Anglo-Saxon young people can take the guise of a cosplayer, performing a different ethnicity and gender. For Melbourne cosplayers Anna Nguyen and Jeni McCaskill, 'they are not limited to female personas', as many male characters in Japanese pop culture are what Nguyen describes as 'pretty' (cited in Maunder, 2008). In Australia, the consumption of Japanese popular culture provides an alternative avenue for imagining localisation and globalisation. It reorients Australia away from its colonial past and into its geo-ideological proximity in the region, re-imagining Australia as part of the 'Asia-Pacific'. Events such as Manifest provide cosplayers with official occasions to perform. However, for many, much of the time spent being a cosplayer is adapting this performativity within everyday settings. Many of the cosplaying young females whom Hjorth interviewed had enrolled in a games program degree and saw it as an integral part of being involved in the cultural industries whereby entanglements between the online and offline can converge. Indeed, for many cosplayers, this is a full-time passion that runs through their various activities extending beyond periods when in costume. Cosplayers are always looking for inspiration – both online and offline – to make their costume better, often reflecting on potential choices and decisions.

Figure 6.4   Attention to detail in cosplay costumes

Source: Image copyright Larissa Hjorth.

Given Melbourne's relative multiculturalism, the issue of ethnicity further complicates the gendered performativity and re-imagining of Japan evoked by cosplaying. Cosplay provides a space for cross-cultural and intercultural imagining for many of these players.

Cultural, ethnic and gendered performative diversity is celebrated rather than undermined. It is this ethnic diversity in constructing types of femininity around imagining Japan vis-à-vis cosplaying, along with the role of cosplaying in affording young women entrance into the games industry, that is the focus of this example. For example, how does a Hong Kong-born student, studying in a games program in Melbourne, reconfigure her identity within a Melburnian context in order to consume Japan?

Conducted in the latter part of 2007 and early 2008 in Melbourne, a study of fifteen young female cosplayers (aged between 18 and 26 years) was initiated by Larissa Hjorth's experiences as a teacher in a university Games Program and her frequenting events such as the Tokyo Game Show. Many of the cosplayers Hjorth interviewed were studying in games programs and hoping to gain long-term employment in the industry. The study was motivated by a phenomenon that Hjorth began to see as young women shifted from consumers and players to produsers and games designers (see Hjorth and Chan, 2009). Through interviews in which players talked through their creations and their relationship to their social worlds, along with participant observation at both official cosplay and unofficial settings, Hjorth sought to understand the performative elements and how they related to presentations of self, imagining Japan, and the realities of the games industry in Australia.

For many of the research participants, cosplay provided a space to play and explore forms of self-expression as well as articulating and deepening their interest in Japanese culture. Through cosplay they could overcome their shyness and meet new friends. The role of the cute (*kawaii*) featured prominently, so much so that it often seemed self-explanatory. Many had dressed as both male and female characters to attend different events, enjoying the gender flexibility of *kawaii* culture. For games students, cosplay helps further solidify their commitment to games without necessarily surrendering their femininity or succumbing to gender-stereotypical roles. In games programs in Australian universities, where a commitment to Japanese culture is almost a standard rite of passage, we can see how the deployment of cosplay enables young female students in particular to graduate from players and produsers to producers/designers/programmers. For one young Eurasian female student studying towards a games degree, being a cosplayer and a gamer provides her with:

> better connections with people. Although those connections are more based on the fact that we enjoy the Japanese culture and watch anime. Talking about cosplay is just another sub topic of something much larger. (In interview.)

Cosplayers often perform in both official (cosplay conventions) and unofficial (everyday) contexts. This movement between unofficial and official plays an important role in the performative elements. In this example, we will focus on 'Rachel' – a Games student who epitomised the spirit of cosplaying. As Rachel stated:

The thing with cosplay is, when outside a convention or a photo shoot or stuff like that, it's hard to tell who is a cosplayer or not. Sometimes you can tell who is a cosplayer outside of these events, a cosplayer's casual clothing sometimes stands out more then the 'everyday' person's (Let's face it, cosplayers can be attention whores) ... but at the same time, you can't really tell them apart from people who like to dress differently. (Rachel, Melbourne, 20 December 2007)

When Hjorth inquired as to whether she imagined still partaking in cosplay once she graduates and gains employment in the industry, she noted:

I think I'll keep cosplaying till the day where my kids get embarrassed by it and tell me to stop ... but then again I don't think I'd listen to what my kids have to say, um, but really, I think I'll still be cosplaying when I'm working in the industry, the only real difference will be unlike high school and Uni, I just won't cosplay to work ... unless they pay me for it. Cosplay is a hobby; at some point it can become a way of life and it can also be a phase, there is no real age limit to cosplay, because there will always be a character you can relate to and dress up as and act like you really are that person and so forth ... Seeing that I have like one and a half years till I leave Uni and find a (poorly paid) QA (quality assurance) job to start my climb to the top, I'm pretty sure I'll be still cosplaying. (Rachel, Melbourne, 20 December 2007)

Seven years later, the same participant still enjoyed cosplaying and had a job in a games-related industry. It will, indeed, be interesting to watch this phenomenon evolve as female cosplayers graduate from their games degrees and enter the ever-changing field of the games industry. As these respondents have demonstrated, cosplaying functions on various levels, including imagining Japan, gaming and gender. This transition from (cos)player to produser to producer for many young females offers hope for the increasing diversity and relevance of the games industry in an age of participatory media and the commercialisation and professionalisation of players (Taylor, 2012).

For some of the female students enrolled in games degrees, cosplay can be a way not only to connect with others who enjoy consuming 'Japan' but also provide avenues for gendered performativity and empowerment. As the young female student noted above, the fact that most cosplayers are female afforded her with a space to build strong female relationships in an industry still attempting to address its gender inequalities. In the case of these young women's entrance into the games industry, the gender performativity of cosplay provided a bridge between players, produsers and producer agencies. These social worlds of cosplay move in and out of the digital, creating spaces for reimagining not only Japan but also women in the games industry.

REFLECTING ON SOCIAL WORLDS IN
DIGITAL ETHNOGRAPHY

These three examples of ethnographic research extend previous work into the digital mediation of social worlds by engaging with questions of identity, sociality, boundaries, change and continuity. Taken together, these cases open new methodological and theoretical vistas onto the rich diversity of technological mediations in the (re)construction and maintenance of social worlds.

One insight explored above is the possibility that a given social world may experience dramatic changes during ethnographic fieldwork, sometimes within a matter of days or weeks. As a species spread throughout the planet, our social worlds have always been subject to sudden changes, including internal and external shocks caused by war, famine, natural disasters and so on (Fligstein and McAdam, 2012). What distinguishes the current era is the added element of speed and reach of information enabled by our modern transport and telecommunications networks, and, most recently, by the proliferation of online and mobile digital media. This has profound implications for various social phenomena, including the spread of protests across a national territory, and even across borders, as we witnessed in the wave of protests across the Mediterranean and the North Atlantic in 2011. In the Spanish *indignados* example taken from Postill's work, we saw how a small sit-in in a central Madrid square soon morphed into a new mass movement that took Spain's political class and mainstream media by storm.

With their 'follow the' heuristic (Marcus, 1995), digital ethnographers are well placed to 'follow the protesters' (or their technologies, virals, events and so on) across rapidly changing social and political terrain. There are great opportunities here for ethnographers interested in activism and social movements to develop new epidemiological techniques in partnership with colleagues from quantitative fields. These would enable them to not only study ephemeral 'virals', but also to design new techniques to understand the rate and quality of fluctuations in personnel, issues, actions, slogans and so on, typically experienced by today's protest movements. Eventually, these investigations could be extended to the epidemiographic study of other social worlds, including those that appear to be relatively stable and unchanging by comparison to new protest movements. Indeed, in paying so much attention to high-profile 'media events' such as the Arab Spring or Hong Kong's pro-democracy protests, we could be missing out on more subtle changes taking place outside of the media limelight.

Another insight arising from the examples concerns the problematic status of popular digital media studies metaphors such as 'community' and 'network', discussed in the earlier parts of this chapter. As explained earlier, the concepts of community and network have had a chequered career in the social sciences owing to their vagueness, normativity and overexposure. Each example allowed us to take a peek into a very different – indeed, unique – social world. But why should we be wary of calling Melbourne cosplayers or Subang Jaya residents a 'community', or of regarding Spain's *indignados* movement as a 'network'? Shouldn't people who regard themselves as a community – or as a network – have the right to be called by that name if they so wish? These are difficult questions, for they are prone to conceptual muddles on the part of both authors and readers. To broach them, we need to recall once again the crucial distinction between emic (vernacular) and etic (scholarly) terms. While some terms can function equally well as emic and etic terms, for example the words 'car', 'house' or 'tree', others are inherently problematic as etic concepts, for example 'nation', 'God' or 'community'. This is because the latter type of term refers to an abstract, vague or fictional entity that lies beyond empirical investigation. In other words, the ontological (i.e., empirical) status of God is of an altogether different order from that of a chair, a motorbike or a cosplayer. However, this analytical distinction between emic (vernacular) and etic (academic) understandings of community does not mean that ethnographers can ignore local sensibilities. For instance, the earnestly felt sense among many in Barcelona that Catalonia is a bounded national community with its own distinctive history, language and culture.

At this point, the reader may query the notion of 'social world'. After all, a social world could refer to practically any array of people, practices and artefacts. It is as vague a term as community or network. Are we not practising double standards? Here we must again proceed with caution. While it is true that 'social world' is a highly polysemic concept, it comes with fewer moral or normative strings attached in the ways that long-since established concepts such as 'community' and 'network' do. Unlike community, with its pleasant connotations of warmth and togetherness, or network with its suggestions of horizontality and connectivity, social world is a neutral, heuristic concept that invites empirical investigation and comparative analysis. Moreover, it is not associated with any ideological current, as is the case with community (communitarianism), and network ('networkism'; see Juris, 2008), again allowing the fieldworker to resist the temptation of prematurely labelling the social actualities under investigation.

SUMMING UP

In this chapter, we used the notion of social worlds as a starting point for discussing the various different concepts that social science and humanities scholars have developed and engaged for studying the ways in which people group together and/or understand themselves to be members of groups. We discussed how concepts such as 'community' and 'network' have come to dominate sociological discussions and showed how anthropologists have developed concepts such as sociality as alternatives to these, in order to think about how relationships between people in groups emerge. As scholarly debates, theory and ethnographic practice have shifted their focus towards the digital, concepts that purport to describe social collectives have increasingly been tested out and debated in relation to how people group together and perceive themselves and their relationships to others online. A digital ethnography approach is particularly appreciative of the ways in which people who participate in social worlds come to comprehend them and make meaning of them. This is because the work of the digital ethnographer involves seeking means to gain an appreciation of what it feels like to be part of social worlds that are configured across large geographic distances. Often there is slippage between the terms that people use to refer to their social worlds and those used by academics, which can, if we are not careful, lead to confusion. Part of the work of the digital ethnographer is, therefore, to be aware of these different layers and distinction, and to make the connections between categories and the ways in which participants themselves experience, and make meaning of, their social worlds and the socio-technical relationships that compose them.

SEVEN

Researching Localities

CHAPTER CONTENTS

INTRODUCTION

This chapter examines how digital ethnographers research localities. We first introduce how the concept of locality has emerged in social research through a focus on the work of anthropologists, geographers and sociologists. The locality has been an important site of ethnographic research, along with the affordances of the study of the local, which invite us to think about local knowledge and the relationship between the local and global. Indeed, in a contemporary theoretical and empirical context, the focus on the local and digital means a recognition of the local within its relationality to configurations of scale and place. The local places a question mark over how we might find, distinguish or research online localities and/or how localities spill over between the online/ offline in ways that acknowledge their partial merging. In this chapter, we outline how these issues have been approached in existing work and discuss how an ethnographic approach brings new insights to them. We then outline methods that have been used in research into and in localities. In doing so, we focus on the examples of researching local uses of digital technologies in Malaysia, California's Silicon Valley and in UK Slow Cities.

WHAT IS THE CONCEPT OF LOCALITY

The concept of 'locality' has been used across anthropological and sociological research in a number of ways. A useful starting point for understanding its development as a unit of analysis in social science research is through a consideration of the work of the Chicago School of urban sociology in the 1930s and 1940s. William Foote Whyte's *Street Corner Society* (1943) showed the benefits of undertaking intensive ethnography within an urban microcosm. It focused on a neighbourhood and unpicked the social relationships concentrated in that area. Whyte did not use the term 'locality', but his focus on the local is reflected in the 62 uses of the word 'local' throughout the book. Indeed, during the twentieth century, a focus on community studies in both sociology and anthropology meant that it was commonplace for ethnographers to *go to* particular and often geographically delimited localities, and to *stay in them* for a determined period of time, before leaving them to write up their findings. This approach was later critiqued through the 'reflexive turn' in ethnographic practice that developed from the 1980s onwards, particularly through the claim that many studies were dominated by a masculine narrative and tended to exploit participants rather than collaborate with them. Subsequently, new ways of considering locality have been proposed.

For instance, in his well-known essay 'The Production of Locality' (1995), which emerged as part of the literature 'after' the reflexive turn, the anthropologist Arjun Appadurai introduced some important questions relating to how localities and neighbourhoods might be conceived. He regards locality as 'primarily relational and contextual, rather than as scalar or spatial', that is, 'as a complex phenomenological quality constituted by a series of links between the sense of social immediacy, the technologies of interactivity and the relativity of contexts' (1996: 178). He contrasts this with the concept of neighbourhood, which he describes as the 'actually existing social forms in which locality, as a dimension or value, is variably recognised' (ibid.: 178–9). Appadurai's argument is interesting because he seeks to dislodge the idea of locality from that of a physically grounded and demarcated territory. 'What', he asks, 'can locality mean in a world where spatial localization, quotidian interaction, and social scale are no longer isomorphic?' (1996: 179). This problem, as we see in the next section, has endured throughout recent theoretical attempts to understand the relationship between the tangible physical environment and the experiential, invisible, and mobile elements of everyday life, and has similarly impacted questions discussed in other chapters of this book (particularly Chapters 4 and 6).

Another idea that has gained ground in recent years is that of 'glocality'. Meyrowitz (2005: 23) suggests that we no longer live in localities. Instead, as a result of the new communication and transport technologies, we now inhabit 'glocalities' in which a 'global matrix' of interconnections has overlaid our experience of the local. Although for Meyrowitz each glocality has unique features, all glocalities are now shaped 'by global trends and global consciousness' (ibid.: 23):

> The media-networked glocality also affords the possibility of having multiple, multi-layered, fluid, and endlessly adjustable senses of identity. Rather than needing to choose between local, place-defined identities and more distant ones, we can have them all, not just in rapid sequence but in overlapping experiences. We can attend a local zoning board meeting, embodying the role of local concerned citizen, as we cruise the Internet on a wireless-enabled laptop enacting other, non-local identities. (Ibid.: 28)

As both these perspectives show, the question of locality therefore takes us far beyond physical location, and has continued to be debated.

HOW THE CONCEPT OF LOCALITY HAS BEEN DEVELOPED IN EXISTING RESEARCH

In more recent theoretical discussion, the concept of locality has been slightly differently developed, specifically in relation to concepts of place and space. These terms tend to be used in ways that are inconsistent across different disciplinary and/or theoretically oriented literatures, which can be confusing for readers unfamiliar with the development of these literatures. Here, we concentrate on how concepts of place have begun to be commonly used across literatures in human geography and anthropology. These concepts of place actually offer us a way to define locality so that it can be effectively engaged as a concept that refers to the local but does not restrict the local in the ways already problematised by Appadurai (see above).

One of the most useful distinctions in the recent wave of discussions of place in human geography is developed in the work of Doreen Massey. She sees place as an 'event' or a 'constellation of processes' (Massey, 2005: 141). Massey's theory of place enables us to think beyond the ways in which place has often been defined as bounded in earlier work, towards the notion of place as 'open' and constantly changing through the movements of things (see ibid.). Using this notion of place as a way to consider how different things and processes come together to make place, we can subsequently redefine locality as representing environments as they are inhabited. As Sarah Pink (2012) has argued, place and locality are different. Locality as we use it here refers to an inhabited place. However, this does not necessarily mean that locality is a physical entity or category as it was in the sense of the Chicago School's neighbourhoods. Instead, localities as inhabited places generate particular qualities because they are forged precisely through the close relationships between their different elements. It is this closeness or intensity of their elements that makes them a coherent unit of analysis – in that they are somehow bound together into a unit that can be analysed. This also means that localities are *knowable* by people, in that they are places that are experienced as entities.

To make the concept of locality operational for ethnographers, we also need to consider how we might use it to define how certain things are known and done and experienced, in what we might think of as local 'environments'. A focus on the idea of localities as known or knowable also helps us to consider what to look for as ethnographers when we seek to understand definitions, and the meaning, of localities for the people who inhabit them. For example, the concept of 'local knowledge' (Geertz, 1973) as developed by the anthropologist of development Paul Sillitoe (2007) enables us to understand how knowledge is particular and how expertise can be invested in the ways of knowing of people who inhabit and best know a particular environment. This approach can be applied, not only to ways of knowing in environments that are physically fixed, but indeed also to moving, fragmented and constantly changing environments, like the social, material and weather-world milieus in which construction workers work (Pink et al., 2010).

WHAT ARE THE IMPLICATIONS OF THE 'DIGITAL' FOR THE CONCEPT OF LOCALITY?

In Chapter 6, we discussed the concepts of community and network, how they have been used in digital scholarship and research, and their value for digital ethnography. The development and use of these concepts, especially in relation to their engagement in digital and Internet research, has been closely entangled with the concept of locality. There have been two primary approaches to studying what he has called 'Internet localisation', both of which use the concepts of community and network (Postill, 2011: 11–12) The first of these concepts was developed in the field of applied research called Community Informatics, in which researchers undertake a research and intervention process to identify the technological needs of a specific 'local community' and seek to address them in collaborative, participatory ways that involve local people.

Michael Gurstein, a leading figure in this field, sees such local communities as 'the bedrock of human development' (Gurstein, 2004). This approach also has a political agenda, in that researchers in this field propose that local people need to be in control of community-based information and communication technologies (ICTs) in order to resist the advancement of global corporate capitalism. Without being empowered, Gurstein and his colleagues suggest that such local communities are under threat (Gurstein et al., 2003).

The second concept that is relevant here takes a rather different view to that of community informatics scholars and activists. This is the notion of 'networked individualism' advanced by Barry Wellman and introduced in our discussion of social worlds in Chapter 6. This concept questions the very existence of locality-based communities, arguing that they are becoming obsolete. Therefore, according to Hampton and Wellman, whereas 'communities had "streets and alleys", Internet researchers are now imagining communities bound "by bits and bytes"' (see also in Postill, 2011: 12).

If we take the argument seriously that we now live in an world in which the digital and material domains of our lives are not separate from each other but part of the same lives and world, this has consequences for how we think about localities beyond the idea of them being material and physically apparent elements of places that are knowable and that can be known, referred to and identified. In this sense, we are arguing for going beyond both the community informatics idea that local communities exist 'on the ground' and need to be connected to IT for their own empowerment, and the idea that local communities do not even exist at all in a networked world. Instead, our argument is that localities exist, and can be found all over the world. Localities can be constituted through the technologies themselves and the online–offline are part of the same processes through which localities are produced, experienced and defined. In this sense, certain actual physical-digital related sites can be explored as forms of digital–material locality.

These might include activities and contexts that are thought of in a vernacular language as being related to neighbourhoods, institutions such as schools, and local council wards. An example from everyday life is the UK music-sharing website Last.fm. The site's algorithms distinguish two main categories of significant others, namely 'friends' (i.e., contacts) and 'neighbours' (people with a similar taste in music based on their digital track record, not unlike Amazon's recommendation system). There is even a 'neighbourhood radio' based on the algorithm's 'local knowledge' of taste neighbourhoods. Intuitively, the creators of Last.fm have recognised the crucial difference between two key sociological principles: proximity within a social network and proximity in taste (in this case musical taste). In effect, they have combined an algorithm-driven social network analysis with the correspondence analysis of Bourdieu's theory of taste (see de Nooy, 2003) to create two strong bonds between users and the site.

Last.fm is just one example: there are numerous different ways in which the digital has rearranged the way we think about locality. This has led to a range of different academic ways of rethinking the environments we live in and through. These have been used to describe field sites that interweave the digital and material. In the next section, we outline a set of key examples of these in order to explain how and where the digital ethnographer does her or his research and how research and scholarship in this field has developed.

THE DEVELOPMENT OF ETHNOGRAPHIC DIGITAL LOCALITY STUDIES

In this section, we discuss how the ethnographic study of digital localities has developed, with a main focus on the example of the study of Second Life. Earlier in this book, we have discussed Tom Boellstorff's (2008) ethnographic research in the 3D virtual environment Second Life (http://secondlife.com), in which he provides vivid descriptions of what it was like to actually 'live' and participate in Second Life. Thomas Malaby (2009) has also studied the development of Second Life and the ethos of its openness extensively (Karanovic, 2012). As Kaplan and Haenlein explain, Second Life is a 'three-dimensional virtual world' which 'was founded and managed by the San Francisco-based company Linden Research, Inc.', and describe how 'Similar to other virtual worlds, *Second Life* users – called "residents" – can enter the virtual environment through a downloadable client program in the form of personalized avatars' (Kaplan and Haenlein, 2009: 565).

Boellstorff's discussion of Second Life shows us how the ethnographic study of virtual worlds can shift the way we think about digital localities. He emphasises that there has been a long tradition in mass media studies in which virtual worlds have been seen as the antithesis of place-making. Yet, he argues that virtual worlds are 'new kinds of places', they are 'sets of locations'. Based on his ethnographic research, Boellstorff insists that Second Life users are not 'players', but rather they are 'residents' and as such they have a strong sense of place. For example, when talking about the homes in Second Life, one of his participants would say: 'It's my place: it's mine' (Boellstorff, 2008: 89–117). While we would differ slightly from Boellstorff's use of the term 'place', his points still stand. He and others have developed a notion of virtual worlds as 'sets of locations' (see also Boellstorff et al., 2012) and places where the action happens (see also Nardi, 2010). Indeed, touching on a theme which connects with the interests of the Community Informatics movement, discussed previously, and the forms of locality-based Internet activism which we will discuss in the next section, Boellstorff suggests that there are also forms of neighbourhood activism in Second Life.

Boellstorff argues that Second Life is not a simulation or a virtual reality, and that while it may approximate aspects of reality for purposes of immersion, it does not seek to replicate the actual world. Neither is it a sensational new world. Indeed, more often than not, it is a place where everyday banal forms of interaction occur (Postill, 2011: 22). For instance, it has virtual money that can be exchanged for real money (see also Malaby, 2012). In Second Life, people actually find friends and lovers, attend weddings, buy and sell property: you cannot do that in a TV programme or a novel. This is why an ethnographic and holistic approach has worked well, because virtual worlds are 'robust locations for culture', locations that are bounded but at the same time porous (Boellstorff, 2008: 237–49).

Boellstorff's work focuses specifically on an online platform. Other studies, however, also show how localities are made and experienced between online and offline practices and activities. For example, we discuss in more detail below the example of the formation of what Postill calls a 'field of residential affairs'. This is a specialist domain of practice and action mediated by the Internet, in this particular instance in Subang Jaya, a middle-class suburb of Kuala Lumpur (Malaysia). The concept has been engaged specifically to bypass the issues raised in Chapter 6 regarding the concepts of 'community' and 'network'. A field of residential affairs is there defined as that specialist domain of practice found in every locality in which various kinds of social agents (e.g., politicians, councillors, activists, journalists, religious leaders and so on) and social formations (e.g., parties, lobbies, cliques, factions, residents' groups, mosques) compete and cooperate over matters of concern to local residents, often via the Internet.

In sum, digital technologies and media have played a key role in shaping the nature of the immediate environments in which we live, making our local contexts and our local knowledge shift towards being something that refers, not only to the material physical environment, but also to the digital.

THE IMPLICATIONS OF AN ETHNOGRAPHIC APPROACH TO DIGITAL-MATERIAL LOCALITIES

As our discussion above shows, although the concept of locality has been defined in different ways, and has referred to online and offline contexts, it has often been associated with an ethnographic approach. Indeed, to know the local and to learn how local people know has always been an ethnographic endeavour. The implications of a digital ethnography approach to researching localities is to invite ethnographers to attend to the ways in which what is known by research participants and what is knowable are part of a world that is made up of qualities and affordances. These bring together the digital and material to create new ways of knowing and being.

This includes, for example, asking what ways of knowing and forms of human action are engaged through the relationships between the kind of visuality of the online that Boellstorff and others write about and the visual-material experience of standing in a city street.

A digital ethnography approach might, therefore, encompass online research such as Boellstorff's study of Second Life, which is indeed a landmark study in that particular way of engaging with the digital ethnographically. Yet, following our broader focus on bringing the digital and material together as part of the same 'world', we also invite readers to consider how researching a locality becomes an experience that happens precisely through the relationship between the digital and the non-digital. As the examples developed in the following sections demonstrate, local issues and activisms, ways of representing the experience of locality and ways of coordinating and acting in localities in a contemporary context, happen in ways that weave together digital, material and weather worlds. As ethnographers, we now visit those localities that we wish to come to know online through digital mapping, like Google Maps and Google Streetview. We still engage with localities through these technologies when we are physically moving through them; the local is often *known simultaneously* through our feet moving over the ground below us, and our sensing of a Google map image of that very ground as already photographed (see Pink, 2011a). These new visualisation technologies thus change the ways in which we come to *know* locality and share these ways of knowing with local people. It thus takes navigation and the ways of knowing that are shared with research participants beyond earlier uses of paper maps and verbal directions.

Digital ethnographers have also begun to take into account the diachronic, or historical, dimensions of their research (Postill, 2012b). For instance, the anthropologist and activist Jeff Juris (2012) has studied the uses of social and mobile media during #OccupyBoston. Juris coins the notion of 'logic of aggregation' (see also Monterde, 2011) to distinguish the new form of participation facilitated by social media from earlier forms developed within the anti-corporate globalisation movement in which a 'logic of networks' was prevalent (Juris, 2008). People now attach themselves to a protest or an occupation much more on an individual basis, and not because they have been recruited into a network. This integration of individuals is made easier by the personalisation of media, a trend accelerated by the spread of social media and mobile phones, especially smartphones in more affluent countries. However, although the logic of aggregation was predominant during the first phase of the Occupy movement that began in 2011, the logic of networks became important once again. Together, these two logics helped to transform the protesters' relationship with their locality, to Boston, and especially with its public spaces (see also, Gerbaudo, 2012, on the articulation of the online and offline and their anchoring in the occupied squares).

RESEARCHING LOCALITIES THROUGH DIGITAL ETHNOGRAPHY

As we have shown above, approaches to researching localities have developed in the social sciences and humanities over the last century. Today, they include studies that encompass online and offline worlds to varying extents and degrees. As digital ethnographers, our main interest is in the ways in which we can acknowledge localities as being both online and offline at the same time. This involves both drawing on those studies discussed above, and advancing beyond them in some ways. In the following sections, we outline three examples of how digital–material localities have been researched following a digital ethnography approach. First, we outline the example of how local issues and locality were managed and produced in Subang Jaya, a suburb of Kuala Lumpur in Malaysia, in a context where online services, campaigns and activism were becoming enmeshed with offline activities and issues related to the locality in the early 2000s. Next, we discuss the example of the production of lived spaces in Silicon Valley, in California. Our third example reflects on how the digital and analogue were interwoven in the ways that Slow City activists in the UK and Australia produced locality in their towns.

Researching localities in Malaysia through diachronic ethnography

The municipality of Subang Jaya (see Chapter 6) was created in 1997, coinciding with the South East Asian financial crisis that led to a deep political crisis in Malaysia and to the onset of the *reformasi* movement in 1998. Although Internet penetration was still low in Malaysia at the time, it played an important role in the reform movement as an alternative means of information, opinion and mobilisation, especially among the elites and (sub)urban middle classes (Abbott, 2001; Postill, 2014a).

A year later, in 1999, Subang Jaya residents used the Internet to campaign against a 240 per cent overnight rise in local tax rates. Their campaign successfully reversed the municipal council's decision. That same year, a Yahoo mailing list and a Web forum were created by and for residents as venues for both 'serious' and light-hearted exchanges about local issues, leisure pursuits, national and international affairs and so on. As we saw in the previous chapter, the forum was a huge success, and it soon became Malaysia's most lively local forum.

John Postill (2011) conducted anthropological fieldwork in Subang Jaya in 2003 and 2004. He was part of a team of digital ethnographers studying e-governance initiatives in multiethnic areas of six different countries. The aim of this comparative project was to determine whether the Internet was making any significant difference to local governance policies and practices in those localities. In Postill's case, events on the ground led him to an unplanned focus on Internet activism around local issues and its implications for relationships between the municipal authorities and local residents.

Postill discovered a panoply of digital initiatives in Subang Jaya on both sides of the government–civil society divide, including a trisectoral 'smart township' project aimed at bringing together the public sector, the private sector and the local residents. Malaysia suffered an acute 'democratic deficit' after local elections were banned in the 1960s following race riots that pitted the Malay majority against the Chinese minority (Postill, 2011: 53). Digital initiatives were used in an attempt to solve a range of political issues such as these. Although the 'smart township' project failed, it did contribute to the flourishing of Internet activism and some modest democratic reforms. To Postill's surprise, ethnic identity was not really a major concern among Subang Jaya's activists fighting for better local governance in their largely middle-class, yet overcrowded and underserviced, suburb. The most salient identity marker was, in fact, residentiality, not ethnicity, and a common refrain heard among activists was: 'We are local residents and rate-payers.' The key issue was not so much democracy either (e.g., a campaign to reinstate local elections gained few adherents). It was ensuring that the local authorities used residents' taxes wisely and efficiently to resolve seemingly mundane problems related to traffic, waste disposal, green areas and the like. This is a type of collective action Postill calls 'banal activism' (2011: 18).

On returning from the field, Postill first tried to analyse his empirical materials on Subang Jaya's various local Internet initiatives along a community-network continuum, with communal projects at one end of the spectrum and network-like projects at the other. However, this soon proved to be a dead end that did not do justice to the fluidity and heterogeneity of conditions on the ground. Inspired by the Manchester School of Anthropology's pioneering studies of urbanisation and social change in Central and Southern Africa, where they fashioned new concepts such as field, network or social drama, he developed the notion of 'field of residential affairs' to escape from the analytical constraints of the community/network duo. This term, 'field of residential affairs', refers to a conflict-prone domain of action in which residents, politicians, municipal staff, journalists, entrepreneurs and other social agents compete and cooperate over local issues, often via the Internet (Postill, 2011: xii).

Postill followed up his 2003–04 fieldwork in Subang Jaya (Figure 7.1) with part-time online research in the UK until 2009, as well as online archival research reaching back to 1999. The result was a 'diachronic ethnography' spanning 10 years (Postill, 2012b). Interestingly, during several breaks from 'the field' in the UK, he was often actually able to be a more active participant with a broader range of residents via the lively Web forum than when he was physically in Subang Jaya, where he was busy interviewing people and attending events with narrower segments of the population and the local elites (Figure 7.2). In addition, the broadband connection was faster and more reliable in the UK than in Malaysia. Ironically, Postill felt closer to the local residents when he was 10,000 km away from the township than while physically 'being there' (cf. Geertz, 1988).

Figure 7.1 As a physical locality, Subang Jaya is a residential neighbourhood near Kuala Lumpur, Malaysia

Note: Subang Jaya is place where people participate in local events and activities.

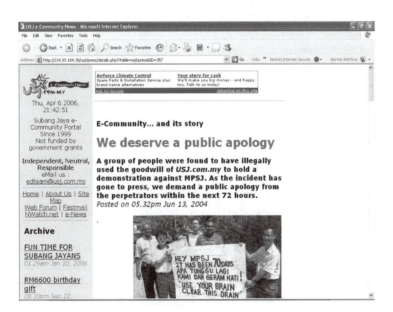

Figure 7.2 Online activity, Subang Jaya, Malaysia

Note: During Postill's research, there was lively online activity focused on Subang Jaya, forming part of that locality, and part of Postill's connection to it.

What are the implications for ethnographers and other qualitative researchers of this increasingly common technological ability to conduct participant observation remotely? Is 'remote ethnography' as valid a mode of inquiry as traditional co-present ethnographic research? After all, 'being there' has been the *sine qua non* of ethnographic research since Malinowski's fieldwork revolution (Geertz, 1988). What does 'being there' mean today, particularly among the (sub)urban middle classes, when ethnographers and their research participants alike have a range of telematic media at their disposal? Does this state of 'polymedia' (Madianou and Miller, 2011) destabilise earlier notions of what counts as ethnographic fieldwork? Where are we when we Skype research participants across two or more locations? Are we in a virtual 'third place' akin to Second Life or in several physical places simultaneously?

We cannot answer all of these questions here in any detail, but clearly the notion of 'being there' requires some unpacking. With the widespread adoption of digital media in recent years, we are now in a position to discern at least four fundamental ways of being in the field. First, one can be there physically, *co-presently*, interacting with research participants face-to-face (or, indeed, side-by-side, back-to-back and so on; see Postill, 2008). Second, the ethnographer can also be there *remotely*, that is, via Skype, streaming, chat, Pads and other telematic media. Third, we can be in the field *virtually*, in a 'third place' that is neither our present location nor that of our interlocutors, for example via a mailing list, a Web forum, a 3D real-time game and so on. Fourth, ethnographers (and their participants) can be elsewhere *imaginatively*, after the fact, through digital stories or images found on blogs, social media, video-sharing sites and so on.

To add another layer of complexity to this heuristic scheme, these modes of being can be combined in potentially infinite ways. For instance, it is common nowadays for ethnographers or their interlocutors to use their mobile devices while in the presence of others, sometimes interrupting the flow of conversation several times in the course of an interaction, or adding a physically absent interlocutor to the conversation through a real-time connection, stored images or video of them, or a combination of these formats. All modes of digitally mediated presence/absence entail a trade-off. Digital ethnographers will typically switch and mix among these modalities in the course of their ethnographic research, often without having the time to pause the process as it unfolds, let alone catalogue and analyse all such instances in the post-fieldwork phase. In other words, this mixing and switching in our ways of being there has become almost fully naturalised.

It follows that we should abandon the received anthropological notion that unmediated physical co-presence is inherently superior to, or more legitimate than, other forms of being there. In fact, there are certain situations in which we can learn more by following a Facebook exchange about a local issue or the live streaming and tweeting of a local event from our homes thousands of miles away than if we had been there at the time, as Postill found when researching the digital practices of activists in

Malaysia and Spain. The crucial point here is triangulation, that is, the ethnographic imperative to gather primary and secondary materials on a given question through as rich a variety of sources as possible, including the ever-expanding ways of being there. Relying solely on physical co-presence, non-digital fieldwork or telematics is still theoretically possible, but in most research settings it would no longer make epistemological sense to do so.

RESEARCHING THE PRODUCTION OF SILICON VALLEY THROUGH GIFT EXCHANGE

'Silicon Valley' has captured the global imagination through its association with technology, innovation and other monikers of the globalisation in late capitalism, namely work, flexibility and discipline. Over the past few decades, economists, political scientists and geographers have researched and theorised the factors that have influenced the development of the region, often identifying the cluster of high-quality scientists and researchers working at educational institutions such as Stanford University and the University of California, Berkeley, the support of the US Defense industry in providing base funding and a series of venture capitalist firms in the Valley and nearby San Francisco. These and other factors have been analysed with an eye towards generating 'models' for the development of other technology and innovation hubs, or 'Silicon Places'. From Silicon Fen in Cambridge, UK, Silicon Hills in Austin, Texas, and Silicon Wadi in Haifa and Tel Aviv, Israel, to Silicon Valley of India (sometimes referred to as Silicon Plateau) in Bangalore, India, and Silicon Cape in Cape Town, South Africa, Silicon Places have largely been analysed as a series of structuring economic and institutional principles that can be localised to particular contexts and heralded by communities and governments as part of their imagination about the future.

Yet, as anthropologist Jan English-Lueck (2002) noted in *Cultures@SiliconValley*, Silicon Valley is as much a lived place produced through daily interactions between engineers in offices as it is between schools engaged in teaching the children of Silicon Valley workers and the parents seeking to raise their children in this technology-centric region. Indeed, English-Lueck (ibid.) discusses the constant presence of phone calls during dinner, programming on the weekend and logging into work for a few hours after putting the kids to bed as a way of life for many of the region's residents. The post-boom era (*c*.2000) further reconfigured this incorporation of the Silicon Valley ethos of work and innovation into domestic life as companies downsized and made their employees redundant, creating a culture of independent contractors and consultants working from home. During her research on young people and informal learning on the Digital Youth Project (see Ito et al., 2009, 2010), Heather Horst used interviews and diary studies (see also Chapter 3 for a more detailed discussion of the diary study) to focus on how the moral economies of technological innovation, and the corporate capitalism which underpins its production, come to dominate everyday life in Silicon Valley (Horst, 2015).

Given widespread aspirations to reproduce and replicate Silicon Valley around the world, Silicon Valley is a particularly important, if not peculiar, place to explore the dimensions of media and technologies in families. As the map in Figure 7.3 – a calendar of businesses and companies who call Silicon Valley home – illustrates, technology and the IT industry that buttresses it are part of Silicon Valley's identity. There is a deep identification among these companies and professional families who work for them (see Figure 7.3). Silicon Valley is more than a geographic space that is centred in places such as Mountain View, Sunnyvale or Cupertino (the home of Apple Computer). Rather, it represents a *geo-cognitive space* in which the ubiquity and ethos of 'technology' dominates the rhythm of life for Silicon Valley's residents.

The persistent presence of a variety of different technologies enable people in the region to view technology as normal and normative, often part of the backdrop of everyday life. Young people in the region often developed quite personal relationships with technology that were facilitated through friends and family members. For example, high school student Melissa describes the direct link between technology and her childhood:

> I did grow up in the tech age, and my dad is in the tech industry so that helped. As a little toddler, I was drawing stuff in Microsoft Paint and I used the Internet probably on our first computer, I think, hooked up to my dad's work like through a dial-up phone line. I mean we still had a phone line, but you couldn't like just get on and surf ... The first time I used the Internet was to do e-mail things, and I was probably like seven and so then shortly after that, I created my own e-mail account.

The creation of this geo-cognitive space also occurred through ritualised exchanges of gifts of technological forms. Indeed, for many of the young people in Horst's study, the personal computer became a symbol through which parents acknowledged that their children were growing up. Iraina, a freshman (or Year 10) high school student, recalled when she received her first computer:

> When I was twelve it was a gift from my grandparents and they continued the tradition so when my brother turned twelve he got one and when my sister turned twelve she got one. And we also have – my dad has a laptop and a PC and he used to have another old MAC. We have a kitchen computer and my mom has her own computer. Part of it was my dad, he worked, when he was still working in an office before he went to consulting, he worked as a computer person so we just always had a lot of computers around.

Figure 7.3 Mapping Corporate Capitalism in Silicon Valley

Source: Photo of calendar by Heather Horst, 2008.

  Alongside computers, digital cameras and video recorders gifted on birthdays, graduations and other significant events were often viewed as the core focus of a range of family activities. As middle school student Evalyn noted:

> My brother just got a digital video camera for his birthday; it was his big present this year … we [used it to film my grandparents] for their anniversary and it was kind of a little documentary thing. Only we forgot to bring a stand that day and my mom let us kids film them. Another thing is daddy, for his birthday just got kind of from himself, kind of from myself; he told everyone he wanted one. He got a professional radio mic [microphone] so we've been playing around with that.

As these examples suggest, access to computing technologies, such as an old computer to play basic kids' games, receiving a laptop computer, iPods, digital cameras and video recorders to 'play around with' represents the first steps in a longer trajectory of a relationship with technology (Horst, 2009, 2010). In Iraina's family, this practice has been ritualised through the gift of a computer at age 12, akin to the bar mitzvahs and other celebrations which the family acknowledge and chronicle on their family's shared website. Similarly, being surrounded by Apple, Yahoo! and Google, shapes not only the political and economic landscape of the region but also the ways in which young people (and adults) relate to and understand the possibilities of technology in their everyday lives. This has the effect of shaping the ways in which young people living in places like Silicon Valley internalise, not only what it means to grow up, but also what it means to grow up to become a 'citizen' or person. Acquiring and using technology becomes a ticket to entry for living in the region such that without digital media and technology full participation does not seem possible. The family effectively becomes one of the key social institutions through which this sense of belonging emerges and, in turn, the production of silicon people and places occur.

Researching Slow Cities as digital–material localities

Sarah Pink has been researching the Slow City movement in the UK, Spain (with Lisa Servon) and Australia (with Kirsten Seale and Tania Lewis) since 2005. During the period of her research, the online presence of the movement has developed considerably (Pink, 2012) and this research has increasingly involved understanding the digital entanglements of being slow. Slow Cities are towns that are accredited as members of the movement, and both demonstrate and commit themselves to working towards a set of principles that are broadly focused towards environmental sustainability, and that are set out in the movement's criteria. The Slow City movement is based in Italy and its central website, www.cittaslow.org/, is associated with the movement's base there. However, it is an international site in many ways, including through its use of multiple languages, although text is dominated by English and Italian. The movement was founded in Italy in 1999, with the aim of extending ideas related to the Slow Food movement to towns, and its membership list in April 2014 stated that it had '187 Cities present in 28 Countries in the World' (www.cittaslow.org/download/DocumentiUfficiali/CITTASLOW_LIST_april_2014_PDF.pdf).

Pink and her colleagues have discussed various aspects of the Slow City movement in existing publications, notably its production of everyday and activist socialities (Pink, 2008; and see also Chapter 6), its sensory and experiential elements and the ways in which these aid the transferability of its framework globally (Pink and Servon, 2013), and how it participates in producing new forms of locality-based resilience (Pink and Lewis, 2014). Pink has also written about the digital elements of Slow Cities, and the relationships between the digital and analogue practices of participants in the movement and in local events (Pink, 2012). Indeed, as Pink has shown, the Slow City movement does not engage digital media in its work in the same ways or to the same extent as do the 'digital culture' oriented groups of activists whom we also discuss in this book, such as the Free Culture Movement (see Chapter 8) and the Indignados (see Chapter 6). However, their work is continually entangled with digital technologies and practices. Therefore, researching how Slow City activism unfolds and grows, specifically in relation to the material and sensory qualities and affordances of physical localities, is also an inevitably digital ethnography process. Indeed, when research is not about the digital per se, digital ethnography enables us to attend to those layers of life that are inevitably and inescapably implicated with digital technologies, experiences and environments and to recognise the importance of these entanglements. In this example, we reflect briefly on two instances in Slow City research where an ethnographic approach brought the digital to the fore in ways that were not necessarily expected: an encounter with photography, digital media and paper at a Slow City carnival; a digital maritime heritage museum; and a campaign relating to a locality that was under way in an area where a Slow City application was being developed.

When Pink was researching the Slow City Movement in the UK, part of her ethnographic fieldwork was in the town of Aylsham in Norfolk. Aylsham had been the second town to gain Slow City status in the UK and had a very active programme of Slow City events and activities. The annual carnival was one of these events, which had been revived specifically in relation to the town's Slow City status and objectives. Another project associated with the work of the Slow City committee in the town was a digital archiving project, which had served to collect and digitalise a good number of local historical photographs and narratives from local people, including photographs of past carnivals. In 2005, this project was integrated into the carnival activities as an exhibition, slide show and interactive paper-based activity in the town hall and surrounding rooms.

Pink researched this event in a number of ways. Participants told her about the archive during a series of interviews that she had undertaken with town leaders, and had also already participated in one Aylsham Carnival as well as other local Slow City events, activities and a carnival-planning committee. Using photography and video as well as audio-recording in her research, she also already had transcripts, written notes, audio and video-recordings of previous carnivals and experience of the way in which photography was used in Slow City events, as digital and material exhibits that documented past activities both in Aylsham and more internationally. At the 2005 carnival, she meandered through the exhibition with her video camera, and when and where she had permission from participants she recorded activities, images and her conversations with people who were participating in the event. This meant that she could collect stories about how and where photographs had been found and what they meant to people. As Pink argues, this exhibition can be seen as part of the work of Slow City activists in making place and locality, and in connecting it to the work of the movement (Pink, 2011b). The digital/analogue relationship was central to this process, as it created an avenue through which the archived photographs moved, first connecting them to the digital archive, and then re-materialising them in printed black and white on A4 sheets. This reconnected them to the locality by asking local people to write notes on them identifying the people featured. As this example shows, the ways in which digital technologies are present in people's visual practices vary in terms of their extents and their visibility.

Indeed, we often find that digital forms imitate the pre-digital, or that they are implicated in processes that might look just the same as analogue practices. Pink was able to learn, through this study, how digital photography and the material elements of its production and dissemination were entangled in the making of the town as a locality. They drew together – in a set of activities that combined digital technologies, analogue photos and paper print-outs – historical and contemporary images and narratives of the local, collecting photographic and narrated memories and investing these into a future oriented digital archive. As such, we can see how the local in this instance was 'made', established through its history and formed part of a vision for the future, which was framed by the principles of the Slow City Movement. In other publications (Pink, 2013; Pink and Servon, 2013), Pink outlines her experience of going to a Maritime Heritage Centre in a Slow City in Northern Spain. The ethnologists Tom O'Dell and Robert Willim (2013) have suggested the metaphor of composition as a route to understanding ethnography and it seems particularly appropriate in this case to consider how the local was constituted. Here again, the Heritage Centre was created through digital and material elements that produced a composition of the local. This included evocative audio and images of stories of the sea, and as she describes elsewhere in more detail, a material boat, which was combined with journey through a digital sea (Figures 7.4 and 7.5). Each different medium, technology and material, sensory or affective strand of these compositions became entangled to create a series of statements about or sensations of the local, while as a whole they created a composition of locality. The task of the digital ethnographer is to unravel such compositions and to recompose them through their ethnographic practice, this time with their interpretive notes and framing ideas woven in.

Slow City leaders in some towns also engage more explicitly with digital media when developing a sense of locality. Another example is based on the work of Pink and Lewis in the Dandenong Ranges, a short drive outside Melbourne in Victoria, Australia. At the time of Pink and Lewis's research (see Pink and Lewis, 2014), a Slow City group was forming in this area as a reaction to an intensive campaign against the building of a global fast food drive-through in one of the area's small towns. As part of this research, they learned about the sense of locality for people who lived in the region in various different ways, which again showed how the digital, memory and imagination can become bound together in the research experience in ways that are mutually meaningful. Even when not explicitly brought together in the narratives of participants, it is sometimes clear that they pertain to similar ways of knowing and being part of a specific locality.

Figure 7.4   The sea itself, Northern Spain

Note: The sea itself and the Maritime Heritage Centre, Northern Spain, where it was represented together created a digital–material locality where the materiality of the physical sea and land and its digital evocation in the Heritage Centre in Figure 7.5 were entangled.

Source: Image copyright Sarah Pink.

Figure 7.5   The Maritime Heritage Centre, Northern Spain

Source: Image copyright Sarah Pink.

Pink and Lewis focus on how the Slow City Movement creates forms of resilience in local contexts (Pink and Lewis, 2014). They discuss two examples that bring to the fore the ways in which local people who were campaigning for their area experienced natural environment of the Dandenong Ranges and what they felt about it. While taking the natural environment as a starting point might seem initially to focus away from the digital, it in fact suggests that the digital and material–physical worlds cannot be separated when we are seeking to understand the meanings of the local. The first research moment in which this emerged was at the beginning of the researchers' work in the area. They attended a rally against the fast food restaurant along with a good number of local people who walked down a stretch of the main road to the school, which was close to the proposed site and where the protest events continued. Before this event, while investigating it online, the researchers found the video *Tecoma Gnomes' Call to March*, which was later to go 'viral' (see also Postill, 2014b, on viral reality). The locally made video featured a group of garden gnomes collecting up litter from McDonald's from their forest, who collectively decide to join the humans at their anti-Maccas (Maccas is often used to refer to McDonald's in Australia) rally. At the rally, the gnomes were individually auctioned to raise money to support the campaign. In the video, the gnomes are particularly concerned with collecting litter from the fast food restaurant and as such with the environment of the forest, which is a typical part of the natural environment of the hills. Hence, for Pink and Lewis, this video brought to the fore the importance of these aspects of locality, and the ways in which local people felt that they needed to ensure that they were protected. A few weeks later on in their research they again encountered the forests, again indirectly, this time when they attended a planning meeting organised by the group that was developing the Slow City membership application. Pink and Lewis describe how

> While seeking a fit between locality and the criteria, the discussion turned to the group's biographical and everyday sensory, embodied and affective experiences of the area. Participants recounted how when you arrive in the Dandenongs the first thing you see and smell is the forest, and that at night you can see the stars through the car windows. Some remembered how when they were younger they used to be able to smell the gum trees and one participant recalled how her mother would always tell them to wind down the car windows as they arrived to appreciate this – an experience now becoming rare as the trees were increasingly felled. They emphasized the importance of the *feeling* of living in the Dandenongs, the way it 'gets into your blood', that they *knew* it was a unique place to live, the importance of being able to express what this means to them, to be able to celebrate that feeling and to be able to 'conserve and protect' what they have. (Pink and Lewis, 2014: 699)

Here, again, the digital and the experiential dimensions of locality were brought together in the research process to create and emphasise particular ethnographic meanings. The viral digital video focused on the specificity of locality and how this could be threatened. It reached international audiences alongside historical memories of the smell of the trees in a pre-digital era. This shows how a digital ethnography approach can be used to understand how digital media and platforms can be used to generate a sense of locality in relation to the material and sensory environment that they are both part of and seeking to connect with and represent in some ways.

REFLECTING ON RESEARCHING LOCALITIES THROUGH DIGITAL ETHNOGRAPHY

Three main themes – the first two ontological, the third epistemological – run through these empirical examples. First, all three localities considered above experienced 'shocks' of various kinds that shaped their respective digitally mediated processes of place-making (on how exogenous shocks shape social fields, see Fligstein and McAdam, 2011). We could call them *formative shocks*. Thus, Subang Jaya residents were appalled when their municipal council raised local taxes overnight by over 200 per cent and they swiftly organised a sophisticated Internet campaign that overturned this decision. As a leading local activist put it:

> We were furious. But before we could take up the matter with the council, we needed to gather and compile supporting evidence. Using the Internet, we set up a residential database to compile data according to the type of houses, the assessment rates residents were paying, their contact numbers and so forth. Within two weeks, 50% of the community responded. The collective effort yielded a 20% reduction across the board. That was one of the milestones that proved how effective the Internet was. (Jeff Ooi, quoted in Postill, 2011: 56)

Similarly, local residents in the picturesque Dandenongs Ranges outside Melbourne, Australia, made creative use of the Internet – in their case, by means of a witty video that became a 'niche viral' (Postill, 2014b) – to oppose the presence of a McDonald's restaurant in their midst. In the Silicon Valley example, there is no mention of local activism but we do gain a glimpse into the profound lifestyle consequences of the Valley's 'dotcom crash' of 2000 when Horst explains how 'companies downsized and made their employees redundant, creating a culture of independent contractors and consultants working from home'. Something similar was experienced after the 1997 Asian financial crash by many Subang Jaya residents dependent on the region's once flourishing IT industry, epitomised by the Malaysian government's ambitious answer to Silicon Valley, the so-called Multimedia Super Corridor.

The second ontological theme explored by the examples is the elusive relationship between digitality and materiality. This forms the focus of Pink's Slow City materials but it is also present in the other two ethnographic examples. In the Slow City case, Pink shows how inseparable the digital, the sensory and the material are in the process of ethnographic research, even in contexts such as the Dandenongs in which the researchers did not set out to study digitally mediated events such as the anti-McDonald's protest. The importance of digital artefacts to technology-oriented families is made clear in Horst's Silicon Valley example, in which digital gifts feature prominently in the annual cycle of birthdays and other ritualised celebrations. In the Subang Jaya case, materiality emerges in yet another guise, namely as the taken-for-granted basis of a great deal of the suburb's banal activism around infrastructural woes such as missing pedestrian crossings, uncollected piles of rubbish or unrepaired playgrounds. These may not be originally digital artefacts, but they are made into techno-political artefacts through the deft use of digital photography, blog posts and emails to the local press to shame the council into action.

Finally, the epistemological implications of a digital ethnographic engagement with the production of localities – a never completed, always precarious achievement (Appadurai, 1995) – are also discussed in all three examples, and particularly in Postill's call for a rethink of what 'being there' may mean in the increasingly digitised localities we study today. Postill's preliminary unpacking of being there into four modes of presence – co-presently, remotely, virtually and imaginatively – is, in fact, enriched in the other two examples. Thus, Pink emphasises the sensory and digital dimensions of the Dandenongs experience of ethnographers and research participants. When participants feel pangs of nostalgia when recalling the smell of gum trees as they were driven through the area as children, they are helping the ethnographers triangulate people's place-making thoughts and actions through both digital and non-digital materials. Together with the viral video of the anti-McDonald's campaign and a wide assortment of other local evidence, these field materials allow digital ethnographers to weave rich accounts of the place of the digital in place-making.

SUMMING UP

This chapter started by reviewing some of the earlier approaches to the study and conceptualisation of locality within the social sciences, notably by the Chicago School of sociology with its pioneering studies on urban neighbourhoods. This implicit conflation between locality and neighbourhood was later challenged by anthropologists and others influenced by the 1980s reflexive turn, including Appadurai (1996), whose landmark essay 'The Production of Locality' (1995) argued for the need to distinguish between these two notions in an age of new communication and transport technologies. A similar argument was put forward by Meyrowitz and other advocates of the idea that we now inhabit 'glocalities', in which the global and the local are deeply implicated in each other. Missing from most of these accounts is the middle level of the nation-state, without which technology-centred regions such as Silicon Valley in the USA or the Multimedia Super Corridor in Malaysia cannot be understood, as we saw in the examples above.

Our inquiry into the digital/ethnographic dimensions of the production of locality took us to the closely related notion of place-making. Drawing from the work of Massey (2005), Pink (2012) and Sillitoe (2007), we suggested that digital technologies are inseparable from the evolution of local forms of knowledge and place-making, and that it makes little sense to separate the digital from the non-digital in our research and theorisation about locality. This emphasis on local knowledge (Geertz, 1973) is closely related to another well-known Geertzian term discussed later in the chapter: 'being there' (Geertz, 1988). As we have just seen, digital ethnographers can be in a local 'field of residential affairs' (Postill, 2011) in many different ways, including remotely, and often we become as proficient as many of our research participants in switching and mixing digital technologies as we strive to retain and deepen our local knowledge while 'keeping in touch'.

But today's localities are not only produced at the intersection of physical locales and 'the digital'. Sometimes, this form of production can take place almost entirely within a virtual environment such as Second Life or a massively multiplayer game. Increasingly, such socio-technical processes are shaped by algorithms over which ordinary users may have little control. For instance, the music-sharing site Last.fm draws from users' digital trails to co-create 'neighbourhoods' that are based, not on geospatial location, but rather on musical taste. With their versatile combination of digital and non-digital research tools, ethnographers are well placed to chart and analyse the ongoing changes and continuities in the (re)production of locality.

EIGHT
Researching Events

CHAPTER CONTENTS

INTRODUCTION

This chapter examines how digital ethnographers research events. First, we discuss the concept of the event by outlining how the notion of the ritual event was appropriated from anthropology by media studies to create the concept of the 'media event'. This connection has created a long-lasting relationship between ethnographic and media studies approaches. However, for a contemporary context, we rethink the event as taking place in the relationship between the online/offline and digital/material. We outline how we might therefore understand the event as a contemporary analytical category. Then we discuss three examples of how contemporary events have been researched by digital ethnographers. We describe the methods that have been used for this and the types of knowledge that they have produced by focusing on: Free Culture events in Barcelona, Spain; digital arts events in Asia; and watching national cooking shows in Australia.

THE EVENT AS A CONCEPT

The concept of the event has historically been a key category in social science research. Its use has in the past included a focus on ritual events (Turner, 1969), spectacles (Beeman, 1993) and traditional public performances (Marvin, 1988; Pink, 1997). In this chapter, we are concerned with how to research contemporary events, which are constituted and experienced through online/offline or digital/material entanglements. The notion of event often implies something that happens in a public context, and indeed here, too, through our interest in the media event, we are concerned with events that have a public dimension, or that involve groups of people who are thought of as 'publics' such as television audiences, people who participate in public art or who are involved in activism. However, when it comes to researching events ethnographically, we need to go beyond the notion of the event as a public entity to consider ways in which it is mediated and how it is engaged within domestic and other non-public environments and contexts. Indeed, the concept 'event' has varied definitions across the social sciences and humanities. Therefore, in order to use the term at all we need to be clear about the definition that we are using.

The idea of the ritual event depended on an understanding of ritual as a structured and symbolically meaningful series of repeated activities. Often in the last century, ritual events were interpreted anthropologically as creating forms of societal transformation and/or affirmation (for an early example, consider the work of Victor Turner, e.g. 1969). We return to this background in the next section in the context of discussing the development of the concept of the media event and subsequent commentaries on this in relation to digital media. However, the concept of the event has more recently been analytically to provide more processual and experiential accounts of the world, which, as we point out later in this chapter, offer us new ways in which to understand how digital media are part of and experience within events.

The anthropologist Michael Jackson has used the concept of the event to account for how happenings are experienced and remembered, and how they are used to imply possible futures. Jackson's point that 'multiple points of view' about what has happened emerge after the event (Jackson, 2005: 12) indeed resonates with the idea that ritual symbols were polysemic, that is, they had multiple meanings (e.g., Turner 1969: 41). However, it in fact takes us in a different analytical direction. Jackson's focus is not on events that are ritually repeated, but instead on an extensively documented example of an event involving election violence in Kampala, Uganda, reported in the

Sierra Leone Web in 2003. He then undertakes an ethnographic archaeology of the event through considering the ways in which participants in his research described this event. Jackson argues that, 'Events quickly and imperceptibly blur into and become stories' (Jackson, 2005: 11), and that in doing so they become what he calls 'a window as it were, onto previous events that are all but forgotten and possible events that are already being anticipated or prepared' (ibid.: 12). He thus suggests for the emergent event a temporality where processes are not seen as cyclical but where 'every event opens up an ethical space in which new directions become possible' (ibid.: 14). This approach therefore enables us to see an empirically identifiable event – such as an instance of election violence in the case of Jackson's work, or as we outline below, an art or activist event – as a research 'window' through which we might begin to investigate processes of societal transformation.

Taking the notion of the event to a further level of abstraction can also enable us to use a similar approach to account for what we might think of as the unspectacular type of event. For instance, as we outline in one of our examples discussed towards the end of this chapter, TV viewing events. The human geographer Doreen Massey has suggested a processual definition of the event when writing about the 'event of place' as a 'constellation of processes' (2005: 41) that changes over time. If we, following Massey, think of the event as a happening in which a series of things and processes, of possibly different qualities and affordances come together, and might subsequently then disperse, it is possible to understand both mundane and spectacular happenings as forms of event.

Therefore, the concept of the event has long since been attractive to social scientists as a way in which to understand identifiable occurrences, whether or not these are previously planned. As we show in the next section, the concept has been of equal appeal to media scholars.

THE DEVELOPMENT OF THE CONCEPT OF THE MEDIA EVENT

The relationship between the public event, media and the contexts for its dissemination and consumption (which are often private or domestic) has been a focus for disciplines that use ethnographic methods since the 1990s. Media scholars Daniel Dayan and Elihu Katz's (1992) landmark discussion of the media event brought together anthropological theories of ritual to understand the ways in which media participate in the world. As a critical response to the media effects approach that dominated at the time, it offered new ways to think about how media are part of public culture and everyday life, and how the two are related. As Eric Rothenbuhler explains, according to a media events approach: 'In ritual, individuals participate in symbolic action according to scripts encoded elsewhere and elsewhen, and with purposes, meanings and implication already mostly set by convention' (2010: 63). He writes that: 'When they [media events] are successful, it is their capacity as ritual that produces the results of enthralling audiences, changing minds and changing history' (2010: 64). Academic discussions of television broadcasting formed the context where the notion of the media event was developed. For scholars of media events, the television audience were 'willing' participants in the ritual (2010: 64).

The concept of the media event was highly influential in bringing media studies and ethnography together in an interdisciplinary approach to understanding the relationship between broadcasting at a public level and individual and collective everyday engagements with media content. Twenty years later, Dayan comments that when he and Katz wrote about media events in 1992, they were concerned with: 'great occasions – mostly occasions of state – that are televised as they take place and transfix a nation or the world' (Dayan and Katz, 1992: 1). They divided these into three categories, 'Contests, Conquests and Coronations'. This could mean studying media events like the Olympics and royal weddings, the televised Spanish Bullfight (Pink, 1997) or rural Iban performances in Malaysian Borneo (Postill, 2007), the TV reality show *Big Brother* (Couldry, 2002), 9/11 in America (Rothenbuhler, 2005), People Power II in the Philippines (Rafael, 2003) and natural disasters such as earthquakes, tsunamis and floods (Murthy and Longwell, 2013). Such media events were, Dayan writes, 'events, we argued, that in effect placed a halo over the television set, thus transforming the viewing experience'. Yet, he acknowledges, 'The world has changed' (Dayan, 2010: 24), and it is with respect to this changed world that we outline a methodology for researching (digital media) events.

However, as we have noted above, new ways of thinking about the event theoretically have also emerged, and in the next section we also argue for a shift away from the notion of event as ritual and towards the more existential (Jackson) and processal (Massey) conceptualisations of event that we have described in the previous section.

THE IMPLICATIONS OF THE DIGITAL FOR THE CONCEPT OF THE MEDIA EVENT

In the context of digital media, events have come to be experienced and produced in new ways. Dayan suggests that this has led to further segmentation of television and the closer interrelation between news and media events whereby, 'Any event can be turned into a media event through an addition of specific features' (Dayan, 2010: 29). He also identifies a power shift, noting that, 'Instead of dominant media organising and conferring a hierarchy on the multiplicity of events, dominant events now serve as the contested ground for a multiplicity of media voices' (Dayan, 2010: 29).

Building on this updating of the original concept, Rothenbuhler focuses away from the dramatic elements of media events to remind us of the possibility of the every-dayness of media events, noting how 'rituals are self-preserving and self-replicating' (2010: 65). He emphasises an understanding of communication as ritual that employs established forms, applying this understanding to the analysis of radio in a way that takes the notion of media events beyond the 'special' event to suggest that they 'might not be so radically unique after all' since even 'special as they are, [they] are still part of the continuity of communicative worlds' (Rothenbuhler, 2010: 72). Hepp and Couldry outline a renewed definition of media events for a 'global age', which borrows Dayan's series of 'core' elements of the original definition of media events: '"emphasis", "performativity", "loyalty" and "shared experience"'. They develop an 'understanding of media cultures as resulting from specific "thicken-ings" of meaning that have links of varying strength with specific territories' (Hepp and Couldry, 2010: 10). They argue that: 'media events are closely related to processes of constructing the "mediated center". As a consequence, they are in general power-related and so must be analysed critically, that is, in terms of *how* they are constructed *as centering*' (Hepp and Couldry, 2010: 12).

These media theorists have engaged understandings of digital media's potential to change how people experience and participate in media events, as well as the poten-tial role of events in the constitution of societal structures and processes. Taking insights from media theorists, we might conceive the media event as being somehow 'special' (Dayan, 2010) but at the same time part of the continuity of communication (Rothenbuhler, 2010) and everyday life (Pink, 2012). It might have a 'centre' of the kind referred to by Hepp and Couldry (2010); but some digital media events, particu-larly digital activist happenings, can be more accurately defined as de-centred.

An ethnographic focus on digital media and its relationship to events has pro-found implications for the way in which we understand events, their making and their mediation. Historically, media events concerned incidents that were entangled in the business or public interests. Today, the shifting basis for media production, consumption and dissemination, along with digital convergence and the growth of mobile and locative media, have altered the ways that media events occur. Changes have occurred in how the mediated and material elements of events are constituted and experienced, how they play out spatially and temporally, and the politics through which these events and the participants in them might intervene in change-making processes in the world. Given these changes, there is a case for re-theorising the media event in order to understand how media technologies, production, consumption and dissemination are proliferated temporally and spatially through the processual theory of place-as-event (e.g., Massey, 2005). Such a re-theorisation allows us to acknowledge how events fit into processes of change, rather than simply seeing them as processes of ritual reaffirmation.

RESEARCHING EVENTS THROUGH DIGITAL ETHNOGRAPHY

Digital ethnography explores the digital–material environments that we inhabit and how human activity and the environments in which it takes place are co-constitutive. The digital ethnographer observes people, things and processes as they engage in activity traversing the online/offline. This facilitates their understanding of the digital, material, affective and social relations of events. In the following section, we give examples of three projects in which media events were researched and defined ethnographically. The first example is a television event in India which connects both the materiality of the television viewing context with online materials; the second concerns how a transient digital arts practice event in Japan was both inspired by participant practices and experiences and inscribed digitally online by a participant; and the third is an example of digital activism which not only brings together different face-to-face and digital elements but also constitutes new ways of thinking about the temporality of events.

Spirited events: Audience ethnographies of everyday household rituals and religious TV in India

As we have noted, media events have conventionally been understood as important public sites of shared ritual and spectacle, such as the screening of the Olympic Games on broadcast television. This conception of media event tends to assume an imagined, often national audience of passive viewers 'consuming' the event in question from the safety of their lounge rooms. The example we offer here – of mass televised yoga events and related personal and domestic rituals in India – complicates this conception of the media event in a number of ways.

In family homes in India, the two key material objects that dominate the lounge room are televisions and small domestic shrines, with the shrine and television occasionally combined together in the TV cabinet. As this juxtaposition suggests, both religion and television are central to everyday life in India. Delhi, India's capital, is regularly brought to a standstill by religious festivals, while famous Bollywood and television actors such as Amitabh Bachchan, the host of India's version of *Who Wants to Be a Millionaire*, have shrines constructed in their honour. With the huge growth of television in India and the rise of electronic media more broadly, time-poor Indians are increasingly practising religious rites within the comfort and convenience of their homes rather than visiting temples or public shrines. Spiritual shows on morning TV, featuring various religious gurus, enable householders to start their day with a religious discourse and prayer ritual or 'puja' while temples now offer people 'just-in-time' live broadcasts of religious ceremonies and pujas via their mobile phones (Lewis et al., forthcoming).

We are interested in what such mediated everyday rituals might suggest for notions of the event. We examine the case of yoga on television, in particular the mass television yoga camps run by the well-known spiritual guru and yoga practitioner Baba Ramdev. Baba Ramdev's mass television yoga camps can be read as a kind of event television for participants and viewers alike. The 'event' here, however, is at once public and privatised (through personalised just-in-time yoga practices), contained and dispersed (via digital TV and YouTube), and linked to embodied practices as much as shared forms of symbolism and meaning. Ethnographic methods offer a way in which to understand how such events are experienced at an ordinary, everyday level by audiences. In focusing on TV yoga in India, we question how the domestication of such 'events' blurs the boundaries between public and private religious rites and practices. It also complicates the notion of a mediated 'event', first as something that occurs in public, and second as a mediated 'moment' bounded by time and space and shared simultaneously by audiences.

As part of a larger study of lifestyle television and shifts in lifestyle, identity and consumption in South East Asia, Tania Lewis and Kiran Mullenhalli conducted ethnographic research in 2011 with twelve households in Mumbai, ranging from poorer households to upper- and lower-middle-class families (Lewis, Martin and Sun, forthcoming). The study examined the ways in which people were using lifestyle advice gleaned from television, a huge and growing industry in India. For instance, they were interested in the role played by televised lifestyle gurus such as Baba Ramdev in advising people how to manage rapidly transforming and often increasingly stressful lives. Negotiating the relentless traffic of Mumbai (it often took considerable lengths of time to travel fairly short distances within the city), the researchers visited households in a range of places, from more middle-class suburbs to poorer slum neighbourhoods on the outskirts of the city. After recruiting households through attendance at a community cultural night, Lewis and Mullenhalli spent significant amounts of time with families (ranging from large extended families to smaller nuclear households) in their homes watching TV with them, often sharing a meal, discussing their media use and talking about their daily patterns of living and consumption. They were interested in seeing how television viewing fitted in with, reflected and was imbricated in, their broader lifestyles and material practices.

The growing speed and complexity of daily life was a recurrent theme in people's lives. Both Sushila, a middle-class professional woman, (Figure 8.1) and her family, for instance, spoke of the speed and stressful nature of modern life and of the changing nature of family life with less stay-at-home housewives. They talked of having no time for holidays and barely enough time to watch TV. The son, a law student and avid TV-watcher, described having to catch up on programming repeats on the weekend or via the Internet (for an example of a website for catch-up programming, see: www.youtube.com/user/channelvindia). When they did watch television, this often occurred fairly late at night, given the long working days and travelling times in Mumbai (with peak-hour viewing often around 9.30 or 10 p.m.). The television was also often on in the background. For example, when Sushila was cooking, she might have a cookery show in the background or have a morning spiritual show on in the background while getting organised to go to work.

Figure 8.1   Watching TV with Sushila's family

Note: The family shrine is behind Sushila, on the left.

Source: Image copyright Kiran Mullenhalli.

Despite being increasingly 'time-poor', many households watched religious television on a regular basis, including spiritual–lifestyle advice shows featuring gurus offering instruction on how live, often with an emphasis on health and wellbeing as much as on spiritualism. Baba Ramdev, for example, was regularly cited by households as a major spiritual and wellbeing guru and families spoke of such figures as providing helpful and ethical life guidance ('you learn to be happy with what you have'), while many people saw religious TV in more general terms as offering a calming respite from the stresses of daily living.

Here, the television seems to have taken on the role of a kind of 'electronic shrine' (Lewis et al., forthcoming); rather than (or at least along side) the family shrine, the TV was often a central focus of 'rituals' (in the form of structured repeated activities), both secular and religious, of daily living, from listening to morning sermons at the start of the day or watching afternoon religious shows, to cooking recipes demonstrated on a daytime show, to gathering in the evening to eat dinner and watch the news as a family. Another key embodied ritual involved practicing yoga; a number of households noted that while many Indians cannot afford to attend Baba Ramdev's yoga camps or go to yoga classes, yoga gurus on television and the Internet have provided the opportunity for the broader population to learn and practice yoga techniques in their homes (see, for example, Baba Ramdev's own YouTube channel at: www.youtube.com/user/babaramdev); that is, to in a sense participate in often communal practices but in a privatised, just-in-time manner. As noted, while it is difficult to speak of event television in the context of India, where there is not one TV market or public but rather a multiplicity of markets and audiences, Baba Ramdev's televised mass yoga camps, in which thousands of Indians gather for yoga instruction, offer a kind of mediated 'event', one that sees the embodied practices of the camp attendees replicated in the privatised practices of household viewers. Led by a miked-up Baba Ramdev on a large stage, the yoga events involve chanting and sermons, followed by extended demonstrations of various asanas (yoga postures), with the audience practicing each asana en masse. Viewers at home can also partake in the spectacle as observers, as Ramdev devotees and as yoga practitioners, their movements at home mirroring the synchronised asanas of the camp attendees.

Patil, a 56-year-old government employee who lived very modestly with his wife on the outskirts of Mumbai and was an avid watcher of religious TV, spoke extensively about the health benefits of the yoga he learned from watching and simultaneously practicing the *asanas* demonstrated by gurus like Baba Ramdev:

In 2004, I had three artery blockages – 72, 67 and 52 per cent and I heard that yoga would be helpful. When I was diagnosed, the doctor at the hospital suggested either angioplasty or bypass surgery. I consulted another doctor and he suggested yoga. And then I saw yoga on TV. I thought, instead of spending money, why not try yoga. I practiced it for three to four months and I started feeling better but could not get in to get a medical check-up. However, after six months, I got examined, and the blockage was under 40 per cent.

India is a linguistically and culturally diverse country with few moments of shared televisual spectacle, cricket and reality shows like *Indian Idol* being perhaps the odd exception (though the 'shared' audience here would still be far from 'national' in scope and scale). Religious rituals and practices on television, however, offer the potential for shared embodied forms of what Joseph Alter calls 'somatic nationalism' (2000). They do so in a way that challenges conventional understandings of the media event as a form of public spectacle. As this ethnography of household televisual practices suggests in India, the 'event-ness' of television can be seen to be as much about the habitual embodied practices and rituals of ordinary people as it is about TV spectacles (Couldry 2002). In a post-broadcast digital era, television is increasingly shaped by the ordinary and articulates with people's domestic practices (from cooking and home renovation shows to health and yoga programming) where the rituals and 'events' on television, whether on *MasterChef India*, which also has an online presence (at: www.starplus.in/masterchef/showhome.aspx?sid=40), or on Baba Ramdev's yoga camps, are coextensive with the private rituals conducted in household settings (Bonner 2003; Lewis, 2008).

Another key insight offered by this ethnographic research is its focus on, and recognition of, the culturally embedded nature and understanding of media events. These are emphasised by our findings regarding the centrality of religion and forms of enchantment in Indian media modernity. This ethnographic audience research in India opens up new ways of thinking about rituals and events in a complex post-broadcast media environment where personal spiritualism, embodiment and digital media are seamlessly interconnected.

Ethnography and art: Researching *Keitai Mizu*, a site-specific mobile game event

Larissa Hjorth's research has combined digital ethnography and arts practice to explore the relationship between climate issues and screen media in Asia. The arts practice project, which involved the development of site-specific mobile game *Keitai Mizu*, that is discussed in this example was inspired by the experience of a gamer and research participant named Toshi, a 25-year-old man who lived in Tokyo at the time of Hjorth's research. Toshi was playing a handheld game during the 2011 Tokyo earthquake and tsunami that is now known as 3/11. Toshi's immersion in the PlayStation Portable (PSP) game was so deep, that he mistook the quake vibrations for the monster's movements in his game. In the moments after the quake, he realised the horror of the real-life event and he desperately tried to contract friends and family. Tragically, his efforts to communicate with his loved ones were to no avail. As Toshi describes:

> When the earthquake occurred, I was alone in my room playing a monster hunter PSP game. Exactly at the time, I was fighting with a monster who makes an earthquake so that I didn't realise that an actual, offline quake had occurred. Only after beating down the monster, I realised something different around me. A fish tank had overflowed and books had fallen down. Initially I was not really shocked by the earthquake itself, but felt frustration with the aftermath – the power failure, panic buying, nuclear accident, and such stuff. During this time I stayed inside with a friend and continued to play the monster hunter game. But the game was no longer entertaining.

In the days after 3/11, and as multiple and conflicting news reports emerged across mass and social media, Toshi and a friend used the game to hide from the pain and confusion. Later, it emerged that the national broadcaster NHK, had deliberately withheld important information about the Fukushima reactor under the instructions of the government. Toshi – like millions of other Japanese – shifted their trust away from broadcast media towards mobile media like Twitter and location-based services such as Foursquare and Instagram. These helped them gain a sense of 'intimate publics' – a form of closeness in a public mediated context – while at the same time, as the example above shows, Toshi sought out a sense of perpetual co-presence with family and friends. Toshi's gameplay is about intentional escapism, particularly when the world is traumatic and confusing. This shift to mobile and social media during 3/11, inspired Hjorth and her colleagues to develop the site-specific mobile game, *Keitai Mizu*, discussed below, specifically to address the question of how researchers/artists can harness Twitter and camera phone apps to make a game that reflected on the environment in new ways.

Hjorth's work was developed within the context of the larger Spatial Dialogues project in which she and her colleagues collaborated with the Japanese Boat People Association in 2013 to develop different artistic ways to map Tokyo sites in terms of the hidden streams. Through a series of video, sound, game and sculptural narratives, their project, Shibuya: Underground Streams, sought to make the general public in Tokyo consider the underground streams making up much of Tokyo. In particular, the project focused on one of the busiest places in the world, Shibuya (Figure 8.2). By putting a shipping container in a park over the month of June 2013, the project explored the idea of cartographies – water, emotional, social, playful, psychological, historical and geographic. Given that Tokyo is made up of numerous little rivers underneath all the trains and roads, the researchers/artists wanted to make audiences aware that they are literally perpetually *walking on water*.

Figure. 8.2 Shibuya: Underground Streams

Source: Image copyright Larissa Hjorth.

In this project, Japanese and Australian artists were asked to make a series of abstract and representational works of water creatures, which were then placed around the park. The project sought to disrupt dichotomies between art and non-art, water and non-water, game and non-game, player and ethnographer. Players had 15 minutes to hunt for, photograph and share online, various *native-only* water-related creatures and objects that have been placed around the site. They then 'captured' the art with their camera phones and shared it online on Twitter or Instagram. Winners only sent pictures of the native species to the *Keitai Mizu* Twitter account (Figure 8.3). The game deployed both old (geo-caching) and new (Twitter and Instagram) media to turn players into ethnographers.

Figure 8.3 *Keitai Mizu* (Mobile Water) game
Source: Image copyright Larissa Hjorth.

The game space was blurred across online and offline, with Instagram and Twitter enabling co-present friends to share the experiences and images. Through the process of game play, participants became more mindful of the local water species as well as being reflective about how the city is made up of numerous little rivers underneath all the trains and roads. In *Keitai Mizu*, the researchers/artists explored the hypervisual omnipresence of camera phone apps to show the multiple ways in which place can be represented, shared and experienced. Far from eroding a relationship between absence and presence, *Keitai Mizu* sought to highlight the importance of ambient co-presence in the construction and experience of place.

Keitai Mizu also attempted to challenge boundaries between official and unofficial game spaces by blurring them with different modes of play (Figure 8.4). In particular, camera phone practices are involved in the creation of new haptic visualities that bring emotional and social dimensions of place and play to the official game play space and drive the motivation for use. By deploying camera phone practices as part of the mobile game, players can develop melodramatic elements – the affective and emotional dimensions – to engage friends into the play of being mobile.

Figure 8.4 *Keitai Mizu* players

Source: Image copyright Larissa Hjorth.

Part of the enjoyment of the project was not only the entanglements between the methods and its transmission, but also how the project lived on in different ways that saw the participants taking the key role. For example, when one student group came through to play, one of the other students took it on herself to document their experiences and responses and turn it into a short film, which she then uploaded onto Vimeo. This video was one of the few artefacts of transmission left after the ephemeral work had ceased. Moreover, traces of the play could be found in the participants' Twitter accounts, creating new nodes for co-present entanglement. The possibility of creating a shared game event challenges the label of 'casual' often used to describe such game events and highlights the point that such a form of participation 'represents an experience that is more flexible with the player's time, more easily incorporated into the player's everyday life' (Keogh, 2014: n.p.).

Through the playful use of Instagram geo-tagging, whereby numerous images of artefacts were assembled upon the website, players were able to see other players' guesses (what they thought were the native animals) and their location through geo-tagging. This created a sense of emplacement, but also of displacement as other players searched for some art objects that were either mistaken for rubbish in the park or too small to see (some artworks, such as Yasuko Toyoshima, were semi-transparent creatures measuring only 5 cm long). The Spatial Dialogues website became a series of emplaced visualities of the park through each of the players' interpretations. The mapping of the park and its underground streams became a series of Instagram clues.

Free Culture Events: Researching digital culture

In 2010–11 in a Web 2.0 context, John Postill and Sarah Pink began a 12-month project on social media and activism in Barcelona. The research spanned both offline and online contexts, including face-to-face interviews, attending events and reviewing them online, and following announcements and events on Facebook, Twitter and other digital platforms. The use of Web-based and digital social media for activism is an increasing phenomenon involving a range of Web platforms. This created a constantly shifting screen-based digital 'landscape' that is composed of a range of (audio)visual and written text. It is also, interestingly, and indeed ironically, a context in which activist and establishment narratives become visually and textually interwoven. Facebook is a good example of this, where activist status posts are viewed alongside the advertisements and personalised items that inhabit the right hand panel of the interface. Thus, we can begin to see how the digital ethnographer, on entering the online world of digital activism, is faced with a complex audiovisual landscape that is constituted through multiple agencies and processes. The digital ethnographer is constantly confronted with a 'constellation of processes' (Massey, 2005).

Simultaneously, as ethnographers become competently mobile in these digital contexts, they develop their own online (research) routines and become actively involved in making the digital ethnographic places that form virtual field sites (Pink, 2015;

Postill and Pink, 2012). Screen-based social media research is part of the material, visual, sensory and social environments that researchers participate in. This point alerts us to the issue that we need to attend to the online–offline relationship on the one hand, but on the other it also reminds us of the materiality of technologies and the need to attend to them. With an increasing range of mobile digital interfaces available, the screen that we are viewing is not necessarily a fixed computer or laptop screen, but might be a mobile phone, tablet or other device. Mobility becomes part of the research process as the participants and the researcher might be involved in moving through various material environments while engaging with social media. The visuality of the screen should, therefore, be contextualised alongside the visuality of the offline world. Given the diversification and mobility of screen-based media, the experience and practice of the visual–virtual ethnographer is shifting beyond the engagements with life online that tend to dominate in the existing literature.

A series of examples from our fieldwork in Barcelona demonstrate how the (audio)visuality of online–offline ethnography might be understood through a theory of place.

The Social Media and Activism project spanned a number of groups who were approached because they were both involved in high-profile campaigns and because they actively used the Internet and social media in their activism. The example we discuss here concerns Free Culture Activism. We have selected this example because it involves a series of audiovisual processes and products that demonstrate rather well how the audiovisuality of Internet ethnography crosses face-to-face and online domains and involves both social media and websites. It is also a movement that, because of its close association with digital culture and the possibilities for sharing created by the Internet, requires the ethnographer to engage with its online activities. While this is not the place to go into the complexities of the history of and debates surrounding Free Culture, the concept is often associated with the work of the legal scholar Lawrence Lessig and his seminal work *Free Culture: The Nature and Future of Creativity* (2004). How 'free culture' might be achieved, however, is widely debated. During our stay in Barcelona, several events associated with Free Culture activism were held, including the annual Free Culture Forum (FCForum) and the oXcars, an arts award event. These events were simultaneously face-to-face, audiovisual, textual and digital. They, therefore, provide interesting examples of how digital ethnographers might engage across different practices and contexts and how a theory of place enables us to understand the relationality between these practices and contexts.

The 2010 Free Culture Forum (FCForum) (http://2010.fcforum.net/) was a three-day event, filled with talks, workshops and group work that presented, debated and examined a series of issues relating to free culture in a digital era. In the words of its website:

Against the powerful lobbies of the copyright industries, the FCForum is a space for the construction of proposals arising from civil society in order to strengthen citizen's positions in the debate around the creation and distribution of art, culture and knowledge in the digital era.

The FCForum was held alongside the oXcars (http://oxcars10.la-ex.net/en). Before and after the FCForum, we interviewed activists who were involved in development, attended several of its events (including the oXcars), and carried out further participant observation in face-to-face and Internet contexts (and in contexts where these were combined). We were able to watch the video-streamed events online and review them at a later date as they remain archived at the above websites, along with photographs and other materials. Conventionally, visual ethnographers might consider their own image production, and the invitation to participants to produce images for the researcher, as part of the research process. Yet, visual and narrative production is already integral to such high-tech events in multiple ways. For example, part of the FCForum was held in a large hall at the University of Barcelona. As the speakers gave their presentations, they were projected directly onto the screen behind them while they spoke, either alone or in combination with a visual slide presentation that they presented. Events were video-streamed online as they happened. This part of the Forum could therefore be viewed globally (http://2010.fcforum.net/day-by-day/). Yet, the flow of media from the event was not only from official event sources whose primary purpose was to project the speakers. Simultaneously, participants seated in the audience were disseminating the event online as it unfolded through microblogging. This created a further online presence during the talks, as participants' microblogging was projected onto another screen in the lecture hall.

The FCForum was concerned with free culture as a characteristic of, or possibility for, a digital era, and it was created not simply as a face-to-face forum but as an event that was simultaneously digital and crossed multiple platforms. As a place, the FCForum, although its speakers had flown to it from all over the world, did not happen only in a material locality, but occurred as a place that encompassed material and electronic digital environments. As such the notion of the 'visual' or visible landscape of such an event – whether as a face-to-face or virtual place – becomes increasingly irrelevant. This is because it requires us to conceptualise an event that is happening partially in a material locality, but which cannot actually be seen from one single perspective because it is not bound or encircled within that locality. Rather, the event is happening in different ways in disparate localities. Following Massey (2005) in thinking of place as open and as something that cannot be encompassed by locality that is not bounded can help us to understand these kinds of events. It enables us to conceptualise both their visuality and their invisibility and to rethink the possibilities for the ethnographer who is aware of the visual as representation, the possibilities of vision in a multisensory context, and the importance of acknowledging and accounting for the *in*visible (the notion that there are always perspectives from which one cannot see everything). Events like the FCForum and the oXcars are clearly hybrid online–offline place events. Indeed, they could be seen as examples par excellence of why, as Ardévol (2012) notes, we often need to do visual Internet research online and offline. They are part of a context where many other public events (including academic conferences) are similarly hybrid, even if on a lesser scale. Indeed, some people's everyday life activities are also characterised by this dispersal, given that we are often connected permanently to the Internet through mobile and other devices.

The presence of online visual materials creates a set of possibilities for analysis and experience. First, the visuality of events that span virtual and face-to-face contexts may be dispersed spatially across the face-to-face event itself (as at the FCForum) and on screens in a number of locations, and temporally as it is multiply reviewed afterwards. We are, therefore, confronted with dual questions of what the visual ethnographer can see in any one moment and to where the images might be travelling. It enhances our understanding of the event that is represented, its composition, narratives and discourses. Yet, this is a rather conventional and limited interpretation of the event, since the place-events that we have described above are neither enclosed spatially nor temporally, but are open as an ongoing digital presence and as extending beyond the locality in which they were performed. Indeed, if we consider that the audience is always part of a performance, then we need to understand how the dispersal of images creates the possibility for the performance to continue as it is reconstituted each time through the engagements of online viewers. In this sense, such place-events are not simply *represented* on websites, but rather they continue on the Web in diverse ways. When viewing video online, it is also important to retain the same principles that we would use to understand the multi-sensorial nature of any ethnographic place for the analysis of online videos. This means considering the phenomenology of the viewing position (both our own and that of other viewers), and in doing so acknowledging that the visual materials are also part of a place that is unbounded.

Elsewhere, Pink (2009) has discussed how, when reviewing researcher-made video clips, the researcher is repositioned in relation to the research subject and locality in a way that is similar to the way she/he was originally positioned. The view on the screen when reviewing footage will be the same one that she/he saw through the viewfinder when originally shooting the footage. This, Pink suggests, offers possibilities to (re)imagine oneself in the place that one occupied during the research encounter and to subsequently activate a series of sensory memories of that event that are not 'shown' in the video. At such digital events as the Free Culture Forum, the same footage that one might see projected (while simultaneously streamed out of the event) is then posted online, allowing the researcher to return to the footage. On one level, this can be seen as a useful way to ensure that one does not 'miss' anything, but, of course, its significance goes beyond this in that it offers the researcher a similar route through which to 'return' to the viewing position that she or he occupied when attending the original Forum. In a way similar to the mode of returning to the research site through reviewing researcher produced video, the evocative potential of such posted video is also important to the process of generating ethnographic knowledge through (audio)visual media after the (face-to-face) event.

REFLECTING ON RESEARCHING EVENTS THROUGH DIGITAL ETHNOGRAPHY

The three examples which we have offered in this chapter describe a set of different but complementary versions of how we might define and research a media event through a digital ethnography approach. They highlight the ways in which digital media have now become a central facet of the media event, whether it is through de-centred activist networks that use digital media to both create and maintain a sense of community and commitment or the development of a media event by artists who integrate everyday media, such as casual games, into the city, effectively transforming the mundane into an event through which the city can be experienced differently. In such examples, a media event is always possible.

Our first example initially takes the concept of the media event in a more tradi-tional media studies direction. In this sense, the example of spirited events is more conventional in its relationship with the notion of the media event as a televised moment, which is understood as a form of ritual, and connects the experience of the viewer with the feeling of nation. Yet, as the example unfolds, we see how the shifting of the field site to India, the attention to researching media events as they unfolded in people's living rooms brings a new set of insights into the nature of religious and familial practices in India, such as the shift of the television as a familial device to a shrine for individual family members.

The example of *Keitai Mizu* created a different relationship between digital ethnography research and public art as both intervention and ethnographic site. In this example, we see how the researchers were able to produce an understanding of the relationship between online gaming, digital screen culture and technologies, climate and the notion of environment through their research with young gamers. Yet, the project did not stop at simply gaining an understanding but used this as a way to inform the generation of an environmentally engaged game in Tokyo, which like-wise brought the digital, material, technological and natural environments together in ways that were inspiring and sometimes ambiguous for participants. By documenting the game using digital video, the researchers were able to create a new layer of explo-ration and learn about how the participants in the game were able to understand the installation they had created in public space.

The Free Culture events involved researchers attending and participating in face-to-face and online events as well as having the possibility to analyse the online materials, including videos that create the ongoingness of these activities as well as archiving them. These activities and resources offer researchers of media events a rich and publicly available archive of materials. In combination with the people who are involved in generating, documenting and sharing a lived reality with these events and their meanings, they create a research site which is at once online and offline, and that requires different but relational forms of engagement with the stories embodied in participants and materials.

SUMMING UP

The media event is a long-established focus of research for scholars across the social sciences and humanities. In this chapter, we argued that the field is of renewed interest to scholars. This is because, as the examples that we have discussed demonstrate, there is a certain inseparability of media and events in contemporary contexts as they are interwoven in multiple ways: digital media are part of how the events are conceptualised, made, and experienced by participants, viewers and users. Yet, as we have also shown, in the context of a digital–material environment and the types of relationships, technologies and meanings that are generated, the media event concept also needs to be revised to accommodate an increasingly decentred media culture and power base, as well as the new socialities and ways of experiencing that are emerging with this.

In this chapter, we outlined the history and development of the concept of the media event and explored how the concept has been impacted on by theoretical and technological change since the twentieth century. We have argued that the notion of the media event still offers us a coherent and fascinating unit or category for ethnographic research and analysis in a digital context. However, as we have stressed, the infrastructural, social, technological, experiential and affective elements of the media event shift into new configurations. This necessitates a rethinking of how we might both conceptualise the media event as part of this digital materiality of the contemporary everyday and how we might go about researching it through the very technologies by which it is made.

References

Abbott, J.P. (2001) 'Democracy@ internet. asia? The challenges to the emancipatory potential of the net: Lessons from China and Malaysia', *Third World Quarterly*, 22 (1): 99–114.

Abu-Lughod, L. (2004) *Dramas of Nationhood: The Politics of Television in Egypt*. Chicago, IL: University of Chicago Press.

Adorno, T. with M. Horkheimer (2002) *Dialectic of Enlightenment*, trans. by Edmund Jephcott, Stanford: Stanford University Press,

Aguado, J.M. and Martinez, I.J. (2014) 'Feeding digital omnivores: The impact of mobile media in digital entertainment', in G. Goggin and L. Hjorth (eds), *Routledge Companion to Mobile Media*. New York: Routledge, pp. 181–93.

Ahearn, L. (2001) *Invitations to Love: Literacy, Love Letters, and Social Change in Nepal*. Ann Arbor, MI: University of Michigan Press.

Ahmed, S. (2004) *The Cultural Politics of Emotion*. London: Routledge.

Allison, A. (2003) 'Portable monsters and commodity cuteness: *Pokémon* as Japan's new global power', *Postcolonial Studies*, 6 (3): 381–98.

Alter, J. S. (2000) *Gandhi's Body: Sex, Diet, and the Politics of Nationalism*. Philadelphia: University of Pennsylvania.

Amit, V. (2002) 'Anthropology and community: Some opening notes', in V. Amit and N. Rapport (eds), *The Trouble with Community*. London: Pluto Press, pp. 13–25.

Amit, V. (2007) 'Globalization through "weak ties": A study of transnational networks among mobile professionals', in V. Amit (ed.), *Going First Class? New Approaches to Privileged Travel and Movement*. Oxford and New York: Berghahn, pp. 53–71.

Amit, V. and Rapport, N. (2002) *The Trouble with Community: Anthropological Reflections on Movement, Identity and Collectivity*. London: Pluto Press.

Ang, I. (1985) *Watching Dallas: Soap Opera and the Melodramatic Imagination*. London and New York: Routledge.

Appadurai, A. (ed.) (1986) *The Social Life of Things: Commodities in Cultural Perspective*. Cambridge: Cambridge University Press.

Appadurai, A. (1995) 'The production of locality', in R. Fardon (ed.), *Counterworks: Managing the Diversity of Knowledge*. London and New York: Routledge, pp. 204–25.

Appadurai, A. (1996) *Modernity at Large: Cultural Dimensions of Globalization*, Vol. 1. Minneapolis, MN: Public Works Publications.

Ardévol, E. (2012) 'Virtual/visual ethnography: Methodological crossroads at the intersection of visual and Internet research', in S. Pink (ed.) *Advances in Visual Methodology*. London: Sage, pp. 74–94.

Askew, K. and Wilk, R.R. (eds) (2002) *The Anthropology of Media Reader*. Malden, MA: Blackwell.

Augelli, J.P. (1980) 'Nationalization of the Dominican borderlands', *Geographical Review*, 70: 19–35.

Bakardjieva, M. (2005) *Internet Society: The Internet in Everyday Life*. London: Sage.

Banks, M. (2001) *Visual Methods in Social Research*. London: Sage.

Baptiste, E., Horst, H. and Taylor, E.B. (2010) 'Haitian Monetary Ecologies and Repertoires: A Qualitative Snapshot of Money Transfer and Savings'. *Submitted to the Institute for Money, Technology and Financial Inclusion, 16*.

Barendregt, B. (2012) 'Diverse digital worlds', in H.A. Horst and D. Miller (eds), *Digital Anthropology*. Oxford and New York: Berg, pp. 203–24.

Barth, F. (1969) *Ethnic Groups and Boundaries: The Social Organization of Culture Difference*. Oslo: Universitetsforlage.

Bartlett, L., Jayaram, K. and Bonhomme, G. (2011) 'State literacies and inequality: Managing Haitian immigrants in the Dominican Republic', *International Journal of Educational Development*, 31: 587–95.

Bauman, R. and Sherzer, J. (1975) 'The ethnography of speaking', *Annual Review of Anthropology*, 4: 95–119.

Bausinger, H. (1984) 'Media, technology and daily life', *Media Culture & Society*, 6 (4): 343–51.

Baym, N.K. (1999) *Tune In, Log Out: Soaps, Fandom, and Online Community*. Thousand Oaks, CA: Sage.

Baym, N. (2010) *Personal Connections in the Digital Age*. Cambridge: Polity.

Beaulieu, A. (2010) 'Research note: From co-location to co-presence: Shifts in the use of ethnography for the study of knowledge', *Social Studies of Science*, 40: 453–70.

Beeman, W.O. (1993) 'The anthropology of theater and spectacle', *Annual Review of Anthropology*, 22: 369–93.

Behar, R. (1996) *The Vulnerable Observer: Anthropology That Breaks Your Heart*. Boston: Beacon Press.

Behar, B., Gordon, D.A. (1985) (eds.) *Women Writing Culture*. Berkeley: University of California Press.

Bell, G. (2005) 'The age of the thumb: A cultural reading of mobile technologies from Asia', in P. Glotz and S. Bertschi (eds), *Thumb Culture: Social Trends and Mobile Phone Use*. Bielefeld: Transcript Verlag, pp. 67–87.

Bell, G. and Dourish, P. (2012) *Divining a Digital Future*. Cambridge, MA: MIT Press.

Bell, D., Caplan, P. and Karim, W-J. B. (1993) *Gendered Fields: Women, Men and Ethnography*. London: Routledge.

Benjamin, W. (2008 [1936]) *The Work of Art in the Age of Mechanical Reproduction*. New York: Penguin.

Benítez, J.L. (2006) 'Transnational dimensions of the digital divide among Salvadoran immigrants in the Washington, DC, metropolitan area', *Global Networks*, 6 (2): 181–99.

Berlant, L. (1998) 'Intimacy: A special issue', *Critical Inquiry*, 24 (2): 281–8.

Bhabha, H.K. (1990) *Nation and Narration*. London and New York: Routledge.

Bhabha, H.K. (1994) *The Location of Culture*. London and New York: Routledge.

Bijker, W. E., Thomas P. Hughes, Trevor Pinch (1987) (eds) *The Social Construction of Technological Systems: New Directions in the Sociology and History of Technology*. Cambridge, MA: MIT Press.

Bijsterveld, K (2008) Mechanical Sound: Technology, Culture, and Public Problems of Noise in the Twentieth Century (Inside Technology). Cambridge, MA: MIT Press.

Blumer, H. (1962) 'Society as symbolic interaction', in A. M. Rose (ed.), *Human Behavior and Social Process: An Interactionist Approach*. Houghton-Mifflin, pp. 179–92.

Boellstorff, T. (2008) *Coming of Age in Second Life: An Anthropologist Explores the Virtually Human*. Princeton, NJ: Princeton University Press.

Boellstorff, T. (2012) 'Rethinking Digital Anthropology' in D. Miller and H. Horst (eds), *Digital Anthropology*. Oxford: Berg, pp. 39–60.

Boellstorff, T., Nardi, B., Pearce, C. and Taylor, T.L. (2012) *Ethnography and Virtual Worlds: A Handbook of Method*. Princeton, NJ: Princeton University Press.

Bolter, G. and Grusin, R. (2000) *Remediation: Understanding New Media*. Cambridge, MA: MIT Press.

Bonner, F. (2003) *Ordinary Television: Analyzing Popular TV*. London, Thousand Oaks, New Delhi: Sage.

Born, G. (2013) *Music, Sound and Space: Transformations of Public and Private Experience*. Cambridge: Cambridge University Press.

Bourdieu, P. (1977) *Outline of a Theory of Practice*. Cambridge: Cambridge University Press.

Bourdieu, P. (1984) *Distinction: A Social Critique of the Judgment of Taste*. Cambridge, MA: Harvard University Press.

Bovill, M. and Livingstone, S.M. (2001) 'Bedroom culture and the privatization of media use', in S. Livingstone and M. Bovill (eds), *Children and Their Changing Media Environment: A European Comparative Study*. London and New York: Routledge, pp. 179–200.

boyd, D. (2008) 'Why youth (heart) social network sites: The role of networked publics in teenage social life', in D. Buckingham (ed.), *Youth, Identity, and Digital Media*. Cambridge, MA: MIT Press, pp. 119–42.

boyd, D. (2014) *'It's Complicated': The Social Lives of Networked Teens*. New Haven, CT: Yale University Press.

Bräuchler, B. and Postill, J. (eds) (2010) *Theorising Media and Practice*. Oxford and New York: Berghahn.

Broadbent, S. (2012) 'Approaches to personal communication', in H.A. Horst and D. Miller (eds), *Digital Anthropology*. London: Berg Publications.

Brunner, C. (2002) 'The feminization of technology', in N. Yelland and A. Rubin (eds), *Ghosts in the Machine: Women's Voices in Research with Technology*. New York: Peter Lang, pp. 71–96.

Bruns, A. (2006) 'Towards produsage: Futures for user-led content production', in F. Sudweeks, H. Hrachovec and C. Ess (eds), *Proceedings of Cultural Attitudes Towards Communication and Technology 2006*, Tartu, Estonia, 28 June–1 July, pp. 275–84.

Buchli, V. (ed.) (2002) *The Material Culture Reader*. Oxford and New York: Berg.

Buckingham, D., Willett, R. and Pini, E. (2011) *Home Truths? Video Production and Domestic Life*. Ann Arbor, MI: University of Michigan Press.

Bull, M. (2000) *Sounding out the City: Personal Stereos and the Management of Everyday Life*. Oxford and New York: Berg.

Bull, M. (2008) *Sound Moves: iPod Culture and Urban Experience*. London and New York: Routledge.

Burrell, J. (2012) *Invisible Users: Youth in the Internet Cafés of Urban Ghana*. Cambridge, MA: MIT Press.

Burrell, J. (forthcoming) '"Through a screen darkly": On remote, collaborative fieldwork in the digital age', in R. Sanjek and S. Tratner (eds), *eFieldnotes: The Makings of Anthropology in the Digital World*. Philadelphia, PA: University of Pennsylvania Press.

Carter, S. and Mankoff, J. (2005) 'When participants do the capturing: The role of media in diary studies', in *Proceedings of the Conference on Human Factors in Computing Systems (CHI)*. 2–7 April, Portland, OR, USA, pp. 899–908.

Carter, S., Mankoff, J. and Heer, J. (2007) 'Momento: Support for Situated Ubicomp Experimentation', *Proceedings of the Conference on Human Factors in Computing Systems (CHI)*. 28 April–3 May, San Jose, CA, USA, pp. 125–34.

Castells, M. (1996) *The Rise of the Network Society*, Vol. 1: *The Information Age: Economy, Society and Culture*. Oxford: Blackwell

Castells, M. (1997). *The Power of Identity*, Vol. 2: *The Information Age: Economy, Society and Culture*. Oxford: Blackwell

Castells, M (1998). *End of Millennium,* Vol. 3: *The Information Age: Economy, Society and Culture.* Oxford: Blackwell.

Castells, M. (2001) *The Internet Galaxy.* Oxford: Oxford University Press.

Castells, M., Fernandez-Ardevol, M., Qiu, J. and Sey, A. (2006) *Mobile Communication and Society.* Cambridge, MA: MIT Press.

Centre for Contemporary Cultural Studies (1982) *The Empire Strikes Back: Race and Racism in 70s Britain.* London: Hutchinson/Centre for Contemporary Cultural Studies.

Chadwick, A. (2013) *The Hybrid Media System: Politics and Power.* Oxford: Oxford University Press.

Chan (2009) 'Beyond the "Great Firewall": The Case of In-Game Protests in China', in L. Hjorth and D. Chan (eds), *Gaming Cultures and Place in Asia-Pacific* (Routledge studies in New Media and Cyberculture; 5), New York: Routledge, pp. 141–57.

Chandola, T. (2010) 'Listening in to others: In between noise and silence'. PhD thesis, Queensland University of Technology, Brisbane.

Chandola, T. (2012a) 'Listening into others: Moralising the soundscapes in Delhi', *International Development Planning Review,* 34 (4): 391–408.

Chandola, T. (2012b) 'Listening in to water routes: Soundscapes as cultural systems', *International Journal of Cultural Studies,* 16 (1): 55–69.

Chandola, T. (2014) 'I wail, therefore I am', in M. Gandy and B. Nilsen (eds), *The Acoustic City.* Berlin: Jovis Verlag, pp. 212–17.

Chiu, C., Ku, Y., Lie, T., and Chen, Y. (2011) 'Internet auction fraud detection using social network analysis and classification tree approaches', *International Journal of Electronic Commerce,* 15 (3): 123–47.

Clarke E. (1999 [1957]) *My Mother who Fathered Me: A Study of the Families in Three Selected Communities of Jamaica.* Kingston: University of the West Indies Press.

Classen, C. (1993) *Worlds of Sense: Exploring the Senses in History and Across Cultures.* London: Routledge.

Classen, C., Howes, D. and Synott, A. (1994) *Aroma: The Cultural History of Smell.* London: Routledge.

Clifford, J, and Marcus, G.E. (1986) *Writing Culture: The Poetics and Politics of Ethnography: A School of American Research advanced seminar,* Berkeley, CA: University of California Press.

Clough, P.T. (2009) 'The new empiricism affect and sociological method', *European Journal of Social Theory,* 12 (1): 43–61.

Coleman, G. (2010) 'Ethnographic approaches to digital media', *Annual Review of Anthropology,* 39: 487–505.

Coleman, E. (2012) *Coding Freedom: The Ethics and Aesthetics of Hacking.* Princeton: Princeton University Press.

Cooley (1922) *Human Nature and the Social Order.* New York: Charles Scribner's Sons.

Correll, S. (1995) 'The ethnography of an electronic bar', *Journal of Contemporary Ethnography*, 24 (3): 270–98.

Couldry, N. (2002) 'Playing for celebrity: *Big Brother* as ritual event', *Television & New Media*, 3 (3): 283–93.

Couldry, N. (2003) *Media Rituals: A Critical Approach*. London and New York: Routledge.

Couldry, N. (2004) 'Theorising media as practice', *Social Semiotics*, 14 (2): 115–32.

Couldry, N. (2006) *Listening Beyond the Echoes: Media, Ethics, and Agency in an Uncertain World*. London: Paradigm.

Couldry, N. (2010) 'Theorising media as practice', in B. Bräuchler and J. Postill (eds), *Theorising Media and Practice*. Oxford and New York: Berghahn, pp. 35–54.

Couldry, N. (2012) *Media, Society, World: Social Theory and Digital Media Practice*. Cambridge, UK, and Malden, MA: Polity Press.

Couldry, N. and Markham, T. (2008) 'Troubled closeness or satisfied distance? Researching media consumption and public orientation', *Media, Culture & Society*, 30 (1): 5–21.

Couldry, N., Hepp, A. and Krotz, F. (eds) (2010) *Media Events in a Global Age*. Abingdon: Routledge.

Crapanzano, V. (2004) *Imaginative Horizons: An Essay in Literary-Philosophical Anthropology*. Chicago, IL: University of Chicago press.

Crawford, K. and Robinson, P. (2013) 'Beyond generations and new media', in J. Hartley, K. Burgess and A. Bruns (eds), *A Companion to New Media Dynamics*. London: Wiley/Blackwell, pp. 472–9.

Creed, G.W. (ed.) (2006) *The Seductions of Community: Emancipations, Oppressions, Quandaries*. Martlesham: James Currey Publishers.

Csordas, T.J. (ed.) (1994) *Embodiment and Experience: The Existential Ground of Culture and Self*. Cambridge: Cambridge University Press.

Davidson, M. (2008) *Concerto for the Left Hand: Disability and the Defamiliar Body*. Ann Arbor, MI: University of Michigan Press.

Dayan, D. (1994) *Media Events*. Cambridge, MA: Harvard University Press.

Dayan, D. (2010) 'Beyond media events: Disenchantment, derailment, disruption', in N. Couldry, A. Hepp and F. Krotz (eds), *Media Events in a Global Age*. Oxford and New York: Routledge, pp. 23–31.

Dayan, D. and Katz, E. (1992) *Media Events: The Live Broadcasting of History*. Cambridge, MA: Harvard University Press.

de Certeau, M. (1984) *The Practice of Everyday Life*. Berkeley, CA: University of California Press.

de Nooy, W. (2003) 'Fields and networks: Correspondence analysis and social network analysis in the framework of field theory', *Poetics*, 31: 305–27.

Deger, J. (2005) *Shimmering Screens: Making Media in an Aboriginal Community*. Minneapolis, MN: University of Minnesota Press.

Delamont, S. (2007) 'Ethnography and participant observation', in Clive Seale, David Silverman, Jaber F. Gubrium, Giampietro Gobo (eds), *Qualitative Research Practice: Concise Paperback Edition.* London: Sage, pp. 205–17.

Derby, L. (1994) 'Haitians, magic and money: Raza and society in the Haitian–Dominican borderlands, 1900–1937', *Comparative Studies in Society and History*, 36 (3): 488–526.

Derby, L. and Turits, R. (1993) 'Historias de terror y los terrores de la historia: La masacre haitiana de 1937 en la República Dominicana', *Estudios Sociales*, 26 (92): 65–76.

Detmer, D. (2013) *Phenomenology Explained: From Experience to Insight.* Vol. 9. Chicago, IL: Open Court.

DeNicola, L. (2012) 'Geomedia: The Reassertion within Digital Culture', in H.A. Horst and D. Miller (eds), *Digital Anthropology.* London: Berg, pp. 80–98.

Dewey, J. (2005 [1934]) *Art as Experience.* New York: Penguin.

Dicks, B. et al. (2005) *Qualitative Research and Hypermedia: Ethnography for the Digital Age.* London: Sage.

Donner, J. (2004) 'Microentrepreneurs and mobiles: An exploration of the uses of mobile phones by small business owners in Rwanda', *Information Technologies and International Development*, 2 (1): 1–21.

Donner, J. (2008) 'Research approaches to mobile use in the developing world: A review of the literature', *Information Society*, 24 (3): 140–59.

Dourish, P. and Bell, G. (2007) 'The infrastructure of experience and the experience of infrastructure: Meaning and structure in everyday encounters with space', *Environment and Planning B: Planning and Design*, 34 (3): 414–30.

Dourish, P. and Bell, G. (2011) *Divining a Digital Future: Mess and Mythology in Ubiquitous Computing.* Cambridge, MA: MIT Press.

Drazin, A. (2012) 'Design Anthropology: Working on, with and for Digital Technologies', in D. Miller and H. Horst (eds), *Digital Anthropology.* Oxford: Berg, pp. 245–65.

du Gay, P., Hall, S., Janes, L., Mackay, H. and Negus, K. (1997) *Doing Cultural Studies: The Story of the Sony Walkman.* London: Sage.

Dumont, L. (1980 [1957]) *Homo Hierarchicus: The Caste System and its Implications.* Chicago, IL: University of Chicago Press.

Duranti, A. (1994) *From Grammar to Politics,* Berkeley, CA.:University of California Press.

Edmond, Y.M., Randolph, S.M. and Richard, G.L. (2007) 'The lakou system: A cultural, ecological analysis of mothering in rural Haiti', *Journal of Pan African Studies*, 2 (1): 19–32.

Ellis, K. and Kent, M. (2011) *Disability and New Media.* London and New York: Routledge.

English-Lueck, J. (2002) *Cultures@SiliconValley.* Stanford, CA: Stanford University Press.

Escobar, A. (1994) 'Welcome to Cyberia: Notes on the Anthropology of Cyberculture, *Current Anthropology,* 35 (3): 211–31.

Feld, S. (1990) *Sound and Sentiment: Birds, Weeping, Poetics and Song in Kaluli Expression.* Philadelphia. UPP.

Fischer, C. (2002) *America Calling: A Social History of the Telephone to 1940*. Berkeley, CA: University of California Press.

Fligstein, N. and McAdam, D. (2011) 'Toward a general theory of strategic action fields', *Sociological Theory*, 29 (1): 1–26.

Fligstein, N. and McAdam, D. (2012) *A Theory of Fields*. Oxford: Oxford University Press.

Fortes, M. (1953) 'The structure of unilineal descent groups', *American Anthropologist*, 55 (1): 17–41.

Fortunati, L. (2002) 'Italy: Stereotypes, true and false', in J.E. Katz and M. Aakhus (eds), *Perpetual Contact: Mobile Communications, Private Talk, Public Performance*. Cambridge: Cambridge University Press, pp. 42–62.

Frazer, J.G. (1957) *The Golden Bough: A Study in Magic and Religion*. London: Macmillan.

Freeman, L. (2007) 'The study of social networks', International Network for Social Network Analysis (INSNA), available at: www.insna.org/INSNA/na_inf.html (accessed 15 October 2014).

Gasser, U. and J. Palfrey (2008) *Born Digital: Understanding the First Generation of Digital Natives*. NY: Basic Books.

Gee, J. (2005) 'Semiotic social spaces and affinity spaces', in D. Barton and K. Tusting (eds), *Beyond Communities of Practice: Language, Power and Social Context*. Cambridge: Cambridge University Press, pp. 214–32.

Geertz, C. (1973) *The Interpretation of Cultures: Selected Essays*. New York: Basic Books.

Geertz, C. (1986) 'Making experiences, authoring selves', in V.W. Turner and E.M. Bruner (eds), *The Anthropology of Experience*. Chicago, IL: University of Illinois Press, pp. 373–80.

Geertz, C. (1988) *Works and Lives: The Anthropologist as Author*. Stanford, CA: Stanford University Press.

Geismar, H. (2013) *Treasured Possessions: Indigenous Interventions into Cultural and Intellectual Property*. Durham: Duke University Press.

Geismar, H. (2012) 'Museums + digital = ?', in D. Miller and H. Horst (eds), *Digital Anthropology*. Oxford: Berg, pp. 266–87.

Gelder, K. (2007) *Subcultures: Cultural Histories and Social Practice*. London: Routledge.

Gerbaudo, P. (2012) *Tweets and the Streets: Social Media and Contemporary Activism*. London: Pluto Press.

Gergen, K. (2002) 'The challenge of absent presence', in J. Katz and M. Aakhus (eds), *Perpetual Contact*. Cambridge: Cambridge University Press, pp. 227–81.

Gershon, I. (2010) *The Breakup 2.0: Disconnecting Over New Media*. Ithaca, NY: Cornell University Press.

Geurts, K.L. (2002) *Culture and the Senses: Bodily Ways of Knowing in an African Community*. Berkeley, CA: University of California Press.

Giddens, A. (1984) *The Constitution of Society: Outline of the Theory of Structuration*. Berkeley, CA: University of California Press.

Giddens, A. (1990) *The Consequences of Modernity*. Cambridge: Polity.

Giddens, A. (1991) *Modernity and Self-Identity: Self and Society in the Late Modern Age*. Cambridge: Polity.

Giddens, A. (1992) *Transformation of Intimacy: Sexuality, Love And Eroticism in Modern Societies*. Cambridge: Polity Press.

Gilroy, P. (1987) *There Ain't No Black in the Union Jack: The Cultural Politics of Race and Nation*. London: Hutchinson.

Gilroy, P. (1993) *The Black Atlantic: Modernity and Double Consciousness*. London: Verso.

Ginsburg, F. (1993) 'Embedded aesthetics: Creating a discursive space for indigenous media', *Cultural Anthropology*, 9 (2): 365–82.

Ginsburg, F. (2002) 'Screen memories: Resignifying the traditional in indigenous media', in F. Ginsburg, L. Abu-Lughod and B. Larkin (eds), *Media Worlds: Anthropology on New Terrain*. Berkeley, CA: University of California Press, pp. 39–57.

Ginsburg, F. (2007) 'Found in translation', *Media Res: A MediaCommons Project*, available at: http://mediacommons.futureofthebook.org/imr/2007/03/28/found-in-translation (accessed 30 September 2014).

Ginsburg, F. (2008) 'Rethinking the Digital Age', in P. Wilson and M. Stewart (eds), *Global Indigenous Media: Cultures, Poetics, and Politics*. Durham: Duke University Press, pp. 287–306.

Ginsburg, F. (2012) 'Disability in the digital age', in H.A. Horst and D. Miller (eds), *Digital Anthropology*. Oxford and New York: Berg, pp. 101–26.

Ginsburg, F., Abu-Lughod, L. and Larkin, B. (2002) *Media Worlds: Anthropology on New Terrain*. Berkeley, CA: University of California Press.

Gitlin, T. (1983) *Inside Prime Time*. New York: Pantheon Books.

Gluckman, M. (1963) 'Papers in Honor of Melville J. Herskovits: Gossip and Scandal', *Current Anthropology*, 4 (3), 307–16.

Goffman, E. (1959) *The Presentation of Self in Everyday Life*. New York: Double Day.

Goffman, E. (1963) *Behavior in Public Places*. New York: Free Press.

Goggin, G. (2011) *Global Mobile Media*. London and New York: Routledge.

Goggin, G. and Newell, C. (2003) *Digital Disability: The Social Construction of Disability in New Media*. Lanham, MD: Rowman & Littlefield.

Goggin, G. and Hjorth, L. (eds) (2009) *Mobile Technologies*. New York: Routledge.

Goggin, G. and Hjorth, L. (eds) (2014) *The Routledge Companion to Mobile Media*. London: Routledge.

Gómez Cruz, E. (2012) *Sobre la fotografía digital: una etnografía*. Editorial UOC, Barcelona.

Granovetter, M. (1973) 'The strength of weak ties', *American Journal of Sociology*, 78 (6): 1360–80.

Grasseni, C. (ed.) (2007) *Skilled Visions: Between Apprenticeship and Standards*. Oxford and New York: Berghahn.

Gray, C. and Driscoll M. (1992) 'What's real about virtual reality? Anthropology of, and in cyberspace', *Visual Anthropology Review*, 8 (2): 39–49.

Gregg, M. (2011) *Work's Intimacy*. Cambridge, UK, and Malden, MA: Polity Press.

Gunn, W. and J. Donovan (2012) 'Design anthropology: an introduction', in W. Gunn and J. Donovan (eds) *Design and Anthropology*. Farnham, UK: Ashgate.

Gupta, A. and Ferguson, J. (1997) 'Culture, power, place: Ethnography at the end of an era', in A. Gupta and J. Ferguson (eds), *Culture, Power, Place: Explorations in Critical Anthropology*. Durham, NC: Duke University Press, pp. 1–29.

Gumperz, J. J. (1971) *Language in Social Groups* (Vol. 3), Stanford, CA: Stanford University Press.

Gurstein, M. (2004) 'Editorial: Welcome to the Journal of Community Informatics', *Journal of Community Informatics* 1(1), available at: http:// ci-journal.net/index. php/ciej/article/view/193/14 (accessed July 2015).

Gurstein, M., Menou, M.J. and Stafeev, S. (eds) (2003) *Community Networking and Community Informatics: Prospects, Approaches, Instruments*. St Petersburg: Centre of Community Networking and Information Policy Studies.

Haddon, L. and Silverstone, R. (1995) 'Telework and the changing relationship of home and work', in N. Heap, R. Thomas, G. Einon, R. Mason and H. Mackay (eds), *Information Technology and Society: A Reader*. London: Sage, pp. 400–12.

Hakken, D. (1999) *Cyborgs@Cyberspace: An Anthropologist Looks to the Future*. New York, Routledge.

Hall, S. (1973) *Encoding and Decoding in the Television Discourse*. Birmingham: Centre for Contemporary Cultural Studies.

Hall, S. (1980) 'Encoding/decoding', in S. Hall, D. Hobson, A. Lowe and P. Willis (eds), *Culture, Media, Language: Working Papers in Cultural Studies, 1972–79*. London: Hutchinson, pp. 128–38.

Hall, S. (1997) *Representation: Cultural Representations and Signifying Practices*. London and Thousand Oaks, CA: Sage.

Hall, S. and Jefferson, T. (eds) (1976) *Resistance Through Rituals: Youth Subcultures in Post-War Britain*. London: Hutchinson.

Hampton, K. and Wellman, B. (2003) 'Neighboring in Netville: How the Internet supports community and social capital in a wired suburb', *City & Community*, 2 (4): 277–311.

Harris, M. (ed.) (2007) *Ways of Knowing: Anthropological Approaches to Crafting Experience and Knowledge*. Oxford and New York: Berghahn.

Haraway, D. (1991) *Simians, Cyborgs and Women: The Reinvention of Nature*, New York: Routledge.

Hayes-Conroy, A. (2010) 'Feeling slow food: Visceral fieldwork and empathetic research relations in the alternative food movement', *Geoforum*, 41 (5): 734–42.

Hayes-Conroy, A. and Martin, D.G. (2010) 'Mobilising bodies: visceral identification in the Slow Food movement', *Transactions of the Institute of British Geographers*, 35 (2): 269–81.

Haythornthwaite, C. (1996) 'Social network analysis: An approach and technique for the study of information exchange', *Library & Information Science Research*, 18 (4): 323–42.

Heath, C., Hindmarsh, J. and Luff, P. (2011) *Video in Qualitative Research*. London: Sage.

Hearn, G. N., and Foth, M. (2007) 'Communicative Ecologies: Editorial Preface', *Electronic Journal of Communication*, 17: 1–2.

Hebdige, D. (1979) *Subculture: The Meaning of Style*. London and New York: Routledge.

Hebdige, D. (1987) *Cut 'n' Mix: Culture, Identity and Caribbean Music*. London: Methuen.

Hebdige, D. (1995) 'Subculture: The meaning of style', *Critical Quarterly*, 37 (2): 120–4.

Heidegger, M. (1962) *Being and Time*, trans. J. McQuarrie and E. Robinson. New York: Harper.

Helmreich, S. (2007) 'An anthropologist underwater: Immersive soundscapes, submarine cyborgs, and transductive ethnography', *American Ethnologist*, 34 (4): 621–41.

Hepp, A. and Couldry, N. (2010) 'Introduction: Media events in globalized media cultures', in N. Couldry, A. Hepp and F. Krotz (eds), *Media Events in a Global Age*. London: Routledge, pp. 1–20.

Herzfeld, M. (1997) *Cultural Intimacy: Social Poetics in the Nation-State*. London: Routledge.

Hesmondhalgh, D. (2010) 'Media industry studies, media production studies', in J. Curran (ed.), *Media and Society*. London: Bloomsbury Academic, pp. 145–63.

Hindmarsh, J. and Tutt, D. (2012) 'Video in analytic Practice', in S. Pink (ed.), *Advances in Visual Methodology*. London: Sage, pp. 57–73.

Hine, C. (2000) *Virtual Ethnography*. London: Sage.

Hine, C. (2015) *Ethnography for the Internet: Embedded, Embodied and Everyday*. London: Bloomsbury.

Hjorth, L. (2003) 'Kawaii@Keitai', in N. Gottlieb and M. McLelland (eds), *Japanese Cybercultures*. New York: Routledge, pp. 50–9.

Hjorth, L. (2005a) 'Locating mobility: Practices of co-presence and the persistence of the postal metaphor in SMS/MMS mobile phone customization in Melbourne', *Fibreculture Journal*, 6, available at: http://journal.fibreculture.org/issue6/issue6_hjorth.html (accessed 9 July 2015)

Hjorth, L. (2005b) 'Odours of mobility: Japanese cute customization in the Asia-Pacific region', *Journal of Intercultural Studies*, 26: 39–55.

Hjorth, L. (2005c) 'Postal presence: the persistence of the post metaphor in current SMS/MMS practices', in *Fibreculture Journal*, 6: Mobilities, New Social Intensities and the Coordinates of Digital Networks, available at: http://journal.fibreculture.org/issue6/

Hjorth, L. (2007) 'Snapshots of almost contact: The rise of camera phone practices and a case study in Seoul, Korea', *Continuum: Journal of Media & Cultural Studies*, 21 (2): 227–38.

Hjorth, L. (2008) 'Waiting for immediacy: The convergent inertia of mobility and immobility', in K. Nyíri (ed.), *Towards a Philosophy of Telecommunications*. Vienna: Passagen Verlag, pp. 189–96.

Hjorth, L. (2008) 'The Game of Being Mobile: One Media History of Gaming and Mobile Technologies in Asia-Pacific', *Convergence: The International Journal of Research into New Media Technologies* Games issue, edited by J. Wilson and H. Kennedy, 13 (4): 369–81.

Hjorth, L. (2009) *Mobile Media in the Asia-Pacific: Gender and the Art of Being Mobile*. London and New York: Routledge.

Hjorth, L. (2011) *Games and Gaming: An Introduction to New Media*. Oxford and New York: Berg.

Hjorth, L. and Arnold, M. (2013) *Online@AsiaPacific: Mobile, Social and Locative Media in the Asia-Pacific*. New York: Routledge.

Hjorth, L. and Chan, D. (eds) (2009) *Gaming Cultures and Place in Asia-Pacific*. London and New York: Routledge.

Hjorth, L. and Gu, K. (2012) 'The place of emplaced visualities: A case study of smart-phone visuality and location-based social media in Shanghai, China', *Continuum: Journal of Media and Cultural Studies*, 26 (5): 699–713.

Hjorth, L. and Kim, K.Y. (2011) The mourning after: A case study of social media in the 3.11 earthquake disaster in Japan', *Television & New Media*, 12 (6): 552–9.

Hjorth, L. and Pink, S. (2014) 'New visualities and the digital wayfarer: Reconceptualizing camera phone photography and locative media', *Mobile Media & Communication*, 2 (1): 40–57.

Hjorth, L. and Richardson, I. (2014) *Gaming in Social, Locative and Mobile Media*. London: Palgrave Macmillan.

Hoggart, R. (1957) *The Uses of Literacy: Aspects of Working Class Life*. London: Chatto and Windus.

Holmes, D.R. and Marcus, G.E. (2008) 'Para-ethnography'. *SAGE Encyclopedia of Qualitative Research Methods*. London: Sage, pp. 595–7.

Holmgren D. (2002) *Permaculture: Principles & Pathways Beyond Sustainability*. Australia: Holmgren Design Services.

Horst, H. (2006a) 'The blessings and burdens of communication: Cell phones in Jamaican transnational social fields', *Global Networks*, (2): 143–59.

Horst, H.A. (2006b) 'Building home: Being and becoming a returned resident', in F. Henry and D. Plaza (eds), *Returning to the Source: The Final Stage of the Caribbean Migration Circuit*. Mona, Jamaica: University of the West Indies Press, pp. 123–44.

Horst, H.A. (2007) '"You can't be two places at once": Rethinking transnationalism through Jamaican return migration', *Identities: Global Studies in Culture and Power*, 14 (1–2): 63–83.

Horst, H. (2009) 'Aesthetics of the self: Digital mediations', in D. Miller (ed.), *Anthropology and the Individual: A Material Culture Perspective*. Oxford and New York: Berg, pp. 99–113.

Horst, H. (2010) 'Families', in M. Ito et al. (eds), *Hanging Out, Messing Around and Geeking Out: Living and Learning with New Media*. Cambridge, MA: MIT Press. pp. 149–194.

Horst, H.A. (2011) 'Reclaiming place: The architecture of home, family and migration', *Anthropologica: Journal of the Canadian Anthropological Society*, 53 (1): 29–39.

Horst, H.A. (2012) 'New media technologies in everyday life', in H.A. Horst and D. Miller (eds), *Digital Anthropology*. New York: Berg Publications, pp. 61–79.

Horst, H. (2013) 'The infrastructures of mobile media: Towards a future research agenda', *Mobile Media & Communication*, 1 (1): 147–52.

Horst, H. (2015) 'Cultivating the Cosmopolitan Child in Silicon Valley', *Identities: Global Studies in Culture & Power,* 1–16.

Horst, H. (2015) 'Being in fieldwork: Collaboration, digital media and ethnographic practice', in R. Sanjek and S. Tratner (eds), *eFieldnotes*. Philadelphia, PA: University of Pennsylvania Press.

Horst, H. and Hjorth, L. (2013) 'Engaging Practices: Doing Personalised Media', in S. Price, C. Jewitt and B. Brown (eds),*The SAGE Handbook of Digital Technology Research*, London: SAGE Publications. pp. 87–102.

Horst, H. and Miller, D. (2005) 'From kinship to link-up: Cell phones and social networking in Jamaica', *Current Anthropology*, 46 (5): 755–78.

Horst, H. and Miller, D. (2006) *The Cell Phone: An Anthropology of Communication*. New York and London: Berg.

Horst, H. and Miller, D. (2012a) 'Normativity and Materiality: A view from Digital Anthropology', *Media International Australia, Incorporating Culture & Policy*, 145: 103–11.

Horst, H.A. and Miller, D. (eds) (2012b) *Digital Anthropology*. New York and London: Berg.

Horst, H. and Taylor, E.B. (2014) 'The role of mobile phones in the mediation of border crossings: A study of Haiti and the Dominican Republic', *Australian Journal of Anthropology*, 25 (2): 155–70.

Horst, H., Herr-Stephenson, B. and Robinson, L. (2010) 'Media ecologies', in M. Ito et al. (eds), *Hanging Out, Messing Around and Geeking Out: Living and Learning with New Media*. Cambridge, MA: MIT Press, pp. 29–78.

Horst, H., Hjorth, L. and Tacchi, J. (2012) 'Rethinking Ethnography: An Introduction', *Media International Australia, Incorporating Culture and Policy*, 145: 86–93.

Howes, D. (2003) *Sensual Relations: Engaging the Senses in Culture and Social Theory*. Ann Arbor, MI: University of Michigan Press.

Howes, D. and Classen, C. (1991) 'Sounding sensory profiles', in D. Howe (ed.), *The Varieties of Sensory Experience: A Sourcebook in the Anthropology of the Senses*. Toronto: University of Toronto Press, pp. 257–88.

Howes, D. and Classen, C. (2013) *Ways of Sensing: Understanding the Senses in Society*. London and New York: Routledge.

Humphrey, C. (2009) 'The Mask and the Face: Imagination and Social Life in Russian Chat Rooms and Beyond', *Ethnos*, 74 (1): 31–50.

Husserl, E. (1966) *The Phenomenology of Internal Time-Consciousness*. Bloomington, IN: Indiana University Press.

Hymes, D. (1962) 'The ethnography of speaking', *Anthropology and Human Behavior*, 13 (53): 11–74.

Hymes, D. (1964) *Language in Culture and Society: A Reader in Linguistics and Anthropology*, New York: Harper and Row.

Illouz, E. (2007) *Cold Intimacies: The Making of Emotional Capitalism*. Cambridge: Polity.

Ingold, T. (2000) *The Perception of the Environment: Essays on Livelihood, Dwelling and Skill*. London and New York: Routledge.

Ingold, T. (2008), 'Ethnography is not anthropology', *Proceedings of the British Academy*, 154: 69–92.

Ingold, T. (2011) *Being Alive: Essays on Movement, Knowledge and Description*. London and New York: Routledge.

Ingold, T. (2012) 'Introduction: the perception of the user–producer', in W. Gunn and J. Donovan (eds), *Design and Anthropology*. Ashgate. pp. 19–33.

Ito, M. (1997) 'Virtually embodied: The reality of fantasy in a multiuser dungeon', in D. Porter, (ed.), *Internet Culture*. London: Routledge, pp. 87–109.

Ito, M. (2002) 'Mobiles and the appropriation of place', Vodafone *Receiver Magazine 08*.

Ito, M. (2010) *Engineering Play: Children's Software and the Productions of Everyday Life*. Cambridge, MA: MIT Press.

Ito, M. and Okabe, D. (2005) 'Intimate connections: Contextualizing Japanese youth and mobile messaging', in R. Harper, L. Palen and A. Taylor (eds), *The Inside Text: Social, Cultural and Design Perspectives on SMS*. Dorddrecht: Springer, pp. 127–45.

Ito, M., Okabe, D. and Anderson, K. (2009) 'Portable objects in three global cities: The personalization of urban places', in R. Ling and S. Campbell (eds), *The Mobile Communication Research Annual*, Vol. 1: *The Reconstruction of Space and Time through Mobile Communication Practices*. New Brunswick, NJ: Transaction Books, pp. 67–88.

Ito, M., Okabe, D. and Matsuda, M. (2005) *Personal, Portable, Pedestrian: The Mobile Phone in Japanese Life*. Cambridge, MA: MIT Press.

Ito, M., Okabe, D. and Tsuji, I. (eds) (2012) *Fandom Unbound: Otaku Culture in a Connected World*. New Haven, CT: Yale University Press.

Ito, M. et al. (2010) *Hanging Out, Messing Around and Geeking Out: Kids Living and Learning with New Media*. Cambridge, MA: MIT Press.

Jackson, M. (2005) *Existential Anthropology: Events, Exigencies and Effects*. Oxford and New York: Berghahn.

James, A., Hockey, J. and Dawson, A. (1997) *After Writing Culture: Epistemology and Praxis in Contemporary Anthropology*. London: Routledge.

Jamieson, L. (1998) *Intimacy: Personal Relationships in Modern Societies*. Cambridge: Polity Press.

Jenkins, H. (1992) *Textual Poachers: Television Fans and Participatory Culture*. London and New York: Routledge.

Jenkins, H. (2006a) *Convergence Culture: Where Old and New Media Collide*. New York: New York University Press.

Jenkins, H. (2006b) *Fans, Bloggers, and Gamers: Exploring Participatory Culture*. New York: New York University Press.

Jenkins, H. with Purushotma, R., Weigel, M., Clinton, K. and Robison, A.J. (2009) *Confronting the Challenges of Participatory Culture: Media Education for the 21st Century*, Digital Media and Learning Series. Cambridge, MA: MIT Press.

Jensen, R. (2007) 'The digital provide: Information (technology), market performance, and welfare in the South Indian fisheries sector', *Quarterly Journal of Economics*, 122 (3): 879–924.

Juris, J.S. (2008) *Networking Futures: The Movements Against Corporate Globalization*. Durham, NC: Duke University Press.

Juris, J. S. (2012) Reflections on #Occupy Everywhere: Social media, public space, and emerging logics of aggregation. *American Ethnologist*, 39(2), 259–279.

Kaplan, A.M. and Haenlein, M. (2009) 'The fairyland of Second Life: Virtual social worlds and how to use them', *Business Horizons*, 52 (6): 563–72.

Karanovic, J. (2012) 'Free software and the politics of sharing', in H.A. Horst and D. Miller (eds), *Digital Anthropology*. London: Berg Publications, pp. 185–202

Katz, J.E. and Aakhus, M. (eds) (2002) *Perpetual Contact: Mobile Communication, Private Talk, Public Performance*. Cambridge: Cambridge University Press.

Keightly, E. (2012) 'Introduction: Time, media, modernity', in E. Keightly (ed.), *Time, Media and Modernity*. Basingstoke: Palgrave Macmillan, pp. 1–24.

Keightley, E. and Pickering, M. (2012) *The Mnemonic Imagination: Remembering as Creative Practice*. Basingstoke: Palgrave Macmillan.

Kelty, C. (2008) *Two Bits: The Cultural Significance of Free Software*, Durham: Duke University Press.

Kendall, L. (2002) *Hanging Out in the Virtual Pub: Masculinities and Relationships Online*. Berkeley, CA: University of California Press.

Kendall, J., Machoka, P., Veniard, C. and Maurer, B. (2012) 'An emerging platform: From money transfer system to mobile money ecosystem', *Innovations*, 6 (4): 49–64.

Keogh, B. (2014) 'Paying attention to *Angry Birds*: Rearticulating hybrid worlds and embodied play through casual iPhone games', in G. Goggin and L. Hjorth (eds), *The Companion to Mobile Media*. New York: Routledge, pp. 267–75.

Kinsella, S. (1995) 'Cuties in Japan', in L. Skov and B. Moeran (eds), *Women, Media and Consumption in Japan*. Richmond: Curzon Press, pp. 220–54.

Kopytoff, I. (1986) 'The cultural biography of things', in A. Appadurai (ed.), *The Social Life of Things: Commodities in Cultural Perspective*. Cambridge: Cambridge University Press, pp. 64–91.

Kozinets, R.V. (2010) *Netnography: Doing Ethnographic Research Online*. London: Sage Publications.

Kraemer, J. (forthcoming) 'Doing fieldwork, BRB: Locating the field on and with emerging Media', in R. Sanjek and S. Tratner (eds), *eFieldnotes: The Makings of Anthropology in the Digital World*. Philadelphia, PA: University of Pennsylvania Press.

Lahlou, S. (2011) 'How can we capture the subject's perspective? An evidence-based approach for the social scientist', *Social Science Information*, 50 (34): 607–55.

Lally, E. (2002) *At Home with Computers*. Oxford and New York: Berg.

Lange, P.G. (2014) *Kids on YouTube: Technical Identities and Digital Literacies*. Walnut Creek, CA: Left Coast Press.

Lange, P. and Ito, M. (2010) 'Creative production', in M. Ito et al., *Hanging Out, Messing Around and Geeking Out: Kids Living and Learning with New Media*. Cambridge, MA: MIT Press, pp. 243–94.

Larkin, B. (2008) *Signal and Noise: Media, Infrastructure, and Urban Culture in Nigeria*. Durham, NC: Duke University Press.

Lasén, A. (2004) 'Affective technologies: Emotions and mobile phones', *Receiver 11*, available at: www.receiver.vodafone.com (accessed 11 July 2012).

Latour, B. (1992) 'Where are the missing masses? The sociology of a few mundane artifacts', in W.E. Bijker and J. La (eds), *Shaping Technology/Building Society: Studies in Sociotechnical Change*. Cambridge, MA: MIT Press, pp. 225–58.

Latour, B. (2005) *Reassembling the Social: An Introduction to Actor-Network-Theory*. Oxford: OUP Oxford.

Lave, J. and Wenger, E. (1991) *Situated Learning: Legitimate Peripheral Participation*. Cambridge: Cambridge University Press.

Leach, E.R. (1951) 'The structural implications of matrilateral cross-cousin marriage', *Journal of the Royal Anthropological Institute of Great Britain and Ireland*, 81 (1): 23–55.

Leder Mackley, K. and Pink, S. (2013) 'From emplaced knowing to interdisciplinary knowledge: Sensory ethnography in energy research', *Senses and Society*, 8 (3): 335–53.

Lennie, J. and Tacchi, J. (2013) *Evaluating Communication for Development: A Framework for Social Change*. Milton Park, Abingdon, Oxon; New York: Routledge.

Lessig, L. (2004) 'Lawrence Lessig and his seminal work', *Free Culture: The Nature and Future of Creativity*. New York: Penguin.

Lewis, T. (2008) *Smart Living: Lifestyle Media and Popular Expertise*. New York: Peter Lang.

Lewis, T. (2015) 'One city block at a time: Researching and cultivating green transformations', *International Journal of Cultural Studies*, 18 (3): 347–63.

Lewis, T., Martin, F. and Sun, W. (forthcoming) *Telemodernities: Television and Transforming Lives in Asia*. Durham, NC: Duke University Press.

Lewis, T., Wilken, R., Allan, M. and Arcari, P. 'Cultural Economies of Hard Rubbish', (Australia Policy Online: 2014) apo.org.au/research/cultural-economies-hard-rubbish

Licoppe, C. (2004) '"Connected" presence: The emergence of a new repertoire for managing social relationships in a changing communication technoscape', *Environment and Planning D: Society and Space*, 22 (1): 135–56.

Lim, S. S. (2005) 'From Cultural to Information Revolution: ICT Domestication by Middle-Class Chinese families', in T. Berker, *Domestication of Media and Technology*, Maidenhead: Open University Press. pp. 185–204.

Lindlof, T.R. and Shatzer, M.J. (1998) 'Media Ethnography in Virtual Space: Strategies, limits, and possibilities', *Journal of Broadcasting and Electronic Media*, 42 (2): 170–89.

Ling, R. (2004) *The Mobile Connection: The Cell Phone's Impact on Society*. Burlington, MA: Morgan Kaufmann.

Ling, R.S. (2012) *Taken for Grantedness: The Embedding of Mobile Communication into Society*. Cambridge, MA: MIT Press.

Ling, R. and Campbell, S. (eds) (2011) *The Mobile Communication Research Series*, Vol. 2: *Mobile Communication: Bringing Us Together or Tearing Us Apart?* Edison, NJ: Transaction Books.

Ling, R. and Donner, J. (2009) *Mobile Phones and Mobile Communication*. Cambridge: Polity.

Ling, R. and Horst, H. (2011) 'Mobile Communication in the Global South', *New Media & Society,* 13 (3): 363–74.

Livingstone, S. (2004) 'The challenge of changing audiences: Or, what is the researcher to do in the age of the Internet?', *European Journal of Communication*, 19 (1): 75–86.

Livingstone, S. (2008) 'Taking risky opportunities in youthful content creation: Teenagers' use of social networking sites for intimacy, privacy, and self-expression', *New Media & Society*, 10 (3): 393–411.

Lorimer, H. (2008) 'Cultural geography: Non-representational conditions and concerns', *Progress in Human Geography*, 32 (4): 551–9.

Lupton, D. (2014) *Digital Sociology*, London; New York: Routledge.

Lyman, P. and Wakeford, N. (1999) 'Going into the (virtual) field', *American Behavioral Scientist*, 43 (3): 359–76.

MacKenzie, D. and Wajcman, J. (1999) 'Introductory essay and general issues', in D. MacKenzie and J. Wajcman (eds), *The Social Shaping of Technology*. Buckingham and Philadelphia: Open University Press, pp. 3–27.

Madianou, M. and Miller, D. (2011) *New Media and Migration: Transnational Families and Polymedia*. Cambridge: Polity Press.

Madianou, M and Miller, D. (2012) *Migration and New Media Transnational Families and Polymedia*. Abingdon, Oxon; New York: Routledge.

Mahler, S.J. and Pessar, P. (2001) 'Gendered geographies of power: Analyzing gender across transnational spaces', *Identities*, 7: 441–59.

Malaby, T.M. (2009) *Making Virtual Worlds: Linden Lab and Second Life*. Ithaca, NY: Cornell University Press.

Malaby, T. (2012) 'Digital gaming, game design and its precursors', in H.A. Horst and D. Miller (eds), *Digital Anthropology*. London: Berg, pp. 288–306.

Malinowski, B. (1923) 'The problem of meaning in primitive languages', in C.K. Ogden and I.A. Richards (eds), *The Meaning of Meaning*. London: Routledge, pp. 146–52.

Malinowski, B. (2002 [1925]) *Argonauts of the Western Pacific: An Account of Native Enterprise and Adventure in the Archipelagoes of Melanesian New Guinea*. London: Routledge.

Malinowski, B. (1954 [1925]) *Magic, Science and Religion*. Garden City, New York: Doubleday.

Malinowski, B. (2013 [1926/1999]) *Crime and Custom in Savage Society*. New Brunswick, NJ: Transaction Publishers.

Mankekar, P. (1999) *Screening Culture, Viewing Politics: An Ethnography of Television, Womanhood, and Nation in Postcolonial India*. Chapel Hill, NC: Duke University Press.

Mantovani, G. and Riva, G. (1998) '"Real" presence: How different ontologies generate different criteria for presence, telepresence and virtual presence', *Presence: Teleoperators and Virtual Environments*, 1 (1): 540–50.

Marcus, G.E. (1995) 'Ethnography in/of the world system: The emergence of multi-sited ethnography', *Annual Review of Anthropology*, 24: 95–117.

Marcus, G. (2008) 'The end(s) of ethnography: Social/cultural anthropology's signature form of producing knowledge in transition', *Cultural Anthropology*, 23: 1–14.

Marcus, G. (2012) 'Foreword', in T. Boellstorff, B. Nardi, C. Pearce and T.L. Taylor, *Ethnography and Virtual Worlds: A Handbook of Method*. Princeton, NJ: Princeton University Press, pp. xiii–xvii.

Marcus, G.E. and Myers, F. R. (1995) *The Traffic in Culture: Refiguring Art and Anthropology*. Berkeley: University of California Press.

Markham, T. (2011) 'Hunched over their laptops: Phenomenological perspectives on citizen journalism', *Review of Contemporary Philosophy*, 10: 150–64.

Markham, T. and Couldry, N. (2007) 'Tracking the reflexivity of the (dis)engaged citizen: Some methodological reflections', *Qualitative Inquiry*, 13 (5): 675–95.

Marres, N. (2013) 'What is digital sociology?' *CSISP Online*, available at: http://www.csisponline.net/2013/01/21/what-is-digital-sociology (accessed 17 November 2014).

Martínez, S. (1995) *Peripheral Migrants: Haitians and Dominican Republic Sugar Plantations*. Knoxville, TN: University of Tennessee Press.

Martínez, S. (1999) 'From hidden hand to heavy hand: Sugar, the state, and migrant labor in Haiti and the Dominican Republic', *Latin American Research Review*, 34: 57–84.

Marvin, G. (1988) *Bullfight*. Oxford: Basil Blackwell.

Massey, D. (2005) *For Space*. London: Sage.

Masten, D.L. and Plowman, T.M.P. (2003) 'Digital ethnography: The next wave in understanding the consumer experience', *Design Management Journal*, 14 (2): 75–81.

Maunder, P. (2008) 'Dress up and play cool', *The Age Green Guide*, 17 April, p. 23.

Maurer, B. (2004) 'Cyberspatial properties: Taxing questions and proprietary regimes', in K. Verdery and C. Humphrey (eds), *Property in Question: Value Transformation in the Global Economy*. Oxford and New York: Berg, pp. 297–318.

Maurer, B. (2012) 'Mobile money: Communication, consumption and change in the payments space', *Journal of Development Studies*, 48 (5): 589–604.

Mauss, M. (1990 [1950]) *The Gift: The Form and Reason for Exchange in Archaic Societies*. New York and London: W.W. Norton.

McRobbie, A. (1991) 'Settling accounts with subculture: A feminist critique', in A. McRobbie, *Feminism and Youth Culture*. New York: Routledge, pp. 37–49.

McVeigh, B. (2000) 'How "Hello Kitty" commodifies the cute, cool and camp: "Consumutopia" versus "control" in Japan', *Journal of Material Culture*, 5 (2): 291–312.

Mead, M. (1954) *Coming of Age in Samoa: A Study of Adolescence and Sex in Primitive Societies*. New York: Penguin Books.

Mead, G.H, (1934/1962) *Mind, Self & Society From the Standpoint of a Social Behaviorist*, Chicago: The University of Chicago Press.

Merleau-Ponty, M. (1996) *Phenomenology of Perception*. Delhi: Motilal Banarsidass Publisher.

Mesch, G.S. and Levanon, Y. (2003) 'Community networking and locally based social ties in two suburban locations', *City and Community*, 2: 335–52.

Meyrowitz, J. (2005) 'The rise of glocality: New senses of place and identity in the global village', in K. Nyiri (ed.), *A Sense of Place: The Global and the Local in Mobile Communication*. Vienna: Passagen, pp. 21–30.

Miller, D. (1988) *Material Culture and Mass Consumption*. London: Wiley-Blackwell.

Miller, D. (2001) *Home Possessions: Material Culture Behind Closed Doors*. Oxford: Berg.

Miller, D. (2009) *Stuff*. Cambridge: Polity.

Miller, D. (2011) *Tales From Facebook*. Cambridge, UK; Malden, MA: Polity Press.

Miller, D. (2012) 'Social Networking Sites', in D. Miller and H. Horst (eds), *Digital Anthropology*. Oxford: Berg, pp. 146–61.

Miller, D. and Horst, H. (2012) 'The digital and the human: A prospectus for digital anthropology', in H.A. Horst and M. Miller (eds), *Digital Anthropology*. New York and London: Berg, pp. 31–8.

Miller, D, and J. Sinanan (2014) *Webcam*. Cambridge: Polity Press.

Miller, D. and Slater, D. (2000) *The Internet: An Ethnographic Approach*. Oxford and New York: Berg.

Miller, D., Skuse, A., Slater, D., Tacchi, J., Chandola, T., Cousins, T., Horst, H. and Kwami, J. (2005) 'Information society: Emergent technologies and development communities in the South', *Report*, Information Society Research Group, London, June.

Millward, S. (2012) 'The rise and fall of China's first hit social game (the one Zynga ripped off as FarmVille)', *Tech in Asia*, 28 December, available at: www.techinasia. com/rise-fall-china-happy-farm-social-game-2012/ (accessed 13 January 2013).

Milne, E. (2010) *Letters, Postcards, Email: Technologies of Presence*. New York: Routledge.

Mintz, S.W. (1962) 'Living fences in the Fond-des-Nègres region, Haiti', *Economic Botany*, 16 (2): 101–5.

Mitchell, J.C. (ed.) (1969) *Social Networks in Urban Situations*. Manchester: Manchester University Press.

Moeran, B. (2002) 'Fields, networks and frames: Advertising social organization in Japan', *Global Networks*, 16: 371–86.

Mollison B. (1988). *Permaculture: A Designer's Manual*. Australia: Tagari Publications.

Mollison, B. and Holmgren, D. (1978) *Permaculture One*. Australia: Transworld Publishers.

Molony, T. (2008) 'Running out of credit: The limitations of mobile telephony in a Tanzanian agricultural marketing system', *Journal of Modern African Studies*, 46 (4): 637–58.

Molony, T. (2009) 'Trading places in Tanzania: Mobility and marginalisation in a time of travel-saving technologies', in M. De Bruijn, F. Nyamnjoh and I. Brinkman (eds), *Mobile Phones: The New Talking Drums of Everyday Africa*. Camaroon and Leiden: Langaa and Africa Studies Centre, pp. 92–109.

Monterde, A. (2011) 'Moviments moleculars a la ciutat-xarxa, producció de noves subjectivitats connectades i emergència dels commons: un preludi del 15M'. MA thesis, Open University of Catalonia, Barcelona, Spain.

Monterde, A. and Postill, J. (2014) 'Mobile ensembles: The uses of mobile phones for social protest by Spain's indignados', in G. Goggin and L. Hjorth (eds), *Routledge Companion to Mobile Media*. London: Routledge, pp. 429–38.

Moores, S. (2006) 'Media uses and everyday environmental experiences: A positive critique of phenomenological geography', *Particip@tions*, 3 (2): (no page numbers).

Moores, S. (2012) *Media, Place and Mobility*. London and New York: Palgrave Macmillan.

Morley, D. (1980) *The Nationwide Audience: Structure and Decoding*. London: British Film Institute.

Morley, D. (1986) *Family Television: Cultural Power and Domestic Leisure*. London: Comedia.

Morley, D. (2000) *Home Territories: Media, Mobility and Identity*. London and New York: Routledge.

Morley, D. (2007) *Media. Modernity and Technology: The Geography of the New*. Oxford: Routledge.

Morley, D. (2009) 'For a materialist, non-media-centric media studies', *Television & New Media*, 10: 114–16.

Murthy, D. (2008) 'Digital ethnography: An examination of the use of new technologies for social research', *Sociology*, 42 (5): 837–55.

Murthy, D. (2011) 'Emergent digital ethnographic methods for social research', in S.N. Hesse-Biber (ed.) *Handbook of Emergent Technologies in Social Research*. Oxford: Oxford University Press, pp. 158–79.

Murthy, D. and Longwell, S.A. (2013) 'Twitter and disasters: The uses of Twitter during the 2010 Pakistan floods', *Information, Communication & Society*, 16 (6): 837–55.

Myers, F. (ed.) (2001) *The Empire of Things: Regimes of Value and Material Culture*. Santa Fe, NM: (School for Advanced Research) SAR Press.

Nardi, B. (2010) *My Life as a Night Elf Priest: An Anthropological Account of World of Warcraft*. Ann Arbor, MI: University of Michigan Press.

Norris, C. (2005) 'Cyborg girls and shape-shifters: The discovery of difference by Anime and Manga Fans in Australia', *Refractory*, October 2005, available at: http://blogs.arts.unimelb.edu.au/refractory/2005/10/14/cyborg-girls-and-shape-shifters-the-discovery-of-difference-by-anime-and-manga-fans-in-australia-craig-norris/ (accessed 20 July 2008).

Norris, CJ, (2007) 'Girl Power: The Female Cyborg in Japanese Anime', in W. Haslem, A. Ndalianis and C. Mackie (eds), *Super/Heroes: From Hercules to Superman*. Washington: New Academia Publishing, pp. 347–61.

O'Dell, T. and Willim, R. (2013) 'Transcription and the senses: Cultural analysis when it entails more than words', *Senses and Society*, 8 (3): 314–34.

Okabe, D. and Ito, M. (2006) 'Everyday contexts of camera phone use: Steps toward technosocial ethnographic frameworks', in J.R. Höflich and M. Hartmann (eds), *Mobile Communication in Everyday Life: Ethnographic Views, Observations and Reflections*. Berlin: Frank & Timme, pp. 79–102.

Oldenburg, R. (1989) *The Great Good Place: Cafes, Coffee Shops, Community Centers, Beauty Parlors, General Stores, Bars, Hangouts, and How they Get you through the Day*. New York: Paragon House.

Ong, W.J. (1991) 'The shifting sensorium', in D. Howes (ed.), *The Varieties of Sensory Experience*. Toronto: University of Toronto Press, pp. 47–60.

O'Reilly, K. (2005) *Ethnographic Methods*. London: Routledge.

Ortner, S.B. (1984) 'Theory in anthropology since the sixties', *Comparative Studies in Society and History*, 26 (1): 126–66.

Orton-Johnson, K. and Prior, N. (eds) (2013) *Digital Sociology: Critical Perspectives*. Houndmills: Palgrave Macmillan.

Pahl, R. (2000) *On Friendship*. Oxford: Wiley.

Pahl, R. (2005) 'Are all communities communities in the mind?', *Sociological Review*, 53 (4): 621–40.

Pahl, J.M. and Pahl, R.E. (1972) *Managers and their Wives: A Study of Career and Family Relationships in the Middle Class*. New York: Penguin.

Palfrey, J. and Gasser, U. (2008) *Born Digital: Understanding the First Generation of Digital Natives*. New York: Basic Books.

Panagakos, A.N. and Horst, H.A. (2006) 'Return to Cyberia: technology and the social worlds of transnational migrants', *Global Networks*, 6 (2): 109–24.

Panhofer, H. and Payne, H. (2011) 'Languaging the embodied experience', *Body, Movement and Dance in Psychotherapy*, 6 (3): 215–32.

Paragas, F. (2005) 'Migrant mobiles: Cellular telephony, transnational spaces, and the Filipino diaspora', in K. Nyiri (ed.), *A Sense of Place: The Global and the Local in Mobile Communication*. Vienna: Passagen Verlag, pp. 241–50.

Parsons, T. (1953) 'Some comments on the state of the general theory of action', *American Sociological Review*, 18 (6): 618–31.

Paterson, M. (2007) *The Senses of Touch: Haptics, Affects and Technologies*. Oxford and New York: Berg.

Paterson, M. (2009) 'Haptic geographies: Ethnography, haptic knowledges and sensuous dispositions', *Progress in Human Geography*, 33 (6): 766–88.

Pearce, C., Boellstorff, T. and Nardi, B.A. (2011) *Communities of Play: Emergent Cultures in Multiplayer Games and Virtual Worlds*. Cambridge, MA: MIT Press.

Pertierra, R. (2006) *Transforming Technologies: Altered Selves*. Manilla: De La Salle University Press.

Pertierra, A. (2009) 'Private Pleasures: Watching Videos in Post-Soviet Cuba', *International Journal of Cultural Studies,* 12 (2): 113–30.

Pessar, P. and Mahler, S.J. (2003) 'Transnational migration: Bringing gender in', *International Migration Review*, 37 (3): 812–46.

Pickering, M. (1997) *History, Experience and Cultural Studies*. Basingstoke: Macmillan.

Pickering, M. (2012) 'Sonic horizons: Phonographic aesthetics and the experience of time', in E. Keightly (ed.), *Time, Media and Modernity*. Basingstoke: Palgrave Macmillan, pp. 25–44.

Pinch, T. and Bijsterveld, K. (2004) 'Sound studies: New technologies and music', *Social Studies of Science*, 34 (5): 635–48.

Pink, S. (1997) *Women and Bullfighting: Gender, Sex and the Consumption of Tradition*. Oxford and New York: Berg.

Pink, S. (2001) *Doing Visual Ethnography*. London: Sage

Pink, S. (2004) *Home Truths: Gender, Domestic Objects and Everyday Life*. Oxford and New York: Berg.

Pink, S. (2006) *The Future of Visual Anthropology: Engaging the Senses*. Abingdon and New York: Routledge.

Pink, S. (2008) 'An urban tour: The sensory sociality of ethnographic place-making', *Ethnography*, 9 (2): 175–96.

Pink, S. (2009) *Doing Sensory Ethnography*. London: Sage.

Pink, S. (2011a) 'Sensory digital photography: re-thinking "moving" and the image' *Visual Studies*, 26 (1): 4–13

Pink, S. (2011b) 'Amateur Documents?: amateur photographic practice, collective representation and the constitution of place in UK slow cities', *Visual Studies*, 26 (2): 92–101.

Pink, S. (2012) *Situating Everyday Life: Practices and Places*. London: Sage.

Pink, S. (2013) *Doing Visual Ethnography*. London: Sage.

Pink, S. (2014) 'Digital–visual–sensory-design anthropology: Ethnography, imagination and intervention', *Arts and Humanities in Higher Education*, 13 (4): 412–27.

Pink, S. (2015) *Doing Sensory Ethnography*, 2nd edn. London: Sage.

Pink, S. and Abram, S. (eds) (2015) *Media, Anthropology and Public Engagement*. Oxford and New York: Berghahn.

Pink, S. and Hjorth, L. (2012) 'Emplaced cartographies: Reconceptualising camera phone practices in an age of locative media', *Media International Australia, Incorporating Culture & Policy*, 145: 145–55.

Pink, S. and Leder Mackley, K. (2012) 'Video and a sense of the invisible: Approaching domestic energy consumption through the sensory home', *Sociological Research*, 17 (1), available at: http://www.socresonline.org.uk/17/1/3.html (accessed 9 July 2015).

Pink, S. and Leder Mackley, K. (2013) 'Saturated and situated: Expanding the meaning of media in the routines of everyday life', *Media, Culture & Society*, 35 (6): 677–91.

Pink, S. and Leder Mackley, K. (2014) 'Re-enactment methodologies for everyday life research: Art therapy insights for video ethnography', *Visual Studies*, 29 (2): 146–54.

Pink, S. and Lewis, T. (2014) 'Making resilience: Everyday affect and global affiliation in Australian Slow Cities', *Cultural Geographies*, 21 (4) 695–710.

Pink, S. and Morgan, J. (2013) 'Short-term ethnography: Intense routes to knowing', *Symbolic Interaction*, 36 (3): 351–61.

Pink, S. and Servon, L. (2013) 'Sensory Global Towns: An experiential approach to the growth of the Slow City movement', *Environment and Planning A*, 45 (2): 451–66.

Pink, S., Tutt, D., Dainty, A. and Gibb, A. (2010) 'Ethnographic methodologies for construction research: Knowing, practice and interventions', *Building Research & Information*, 38 (6): 647–59.

Pink, S., Leder Mackley, K., Mitchell, V., Hanratty ,M., Escobar-Tello, C., Bhamra, T. and Morosanu, R. (2013) 'Applying the lens of sensory ethnography to sustainable HCI', *ACM Transactions on Computer-Human Interaction*, 20 (4): 1–18.

Pitt–Rivers, J. (1958) 'Section Of Anthropology: Ritual Kinship in Spain', *Transactions of the New York Academy of Sciences*, 20 (5 Series II): 424–31.

Pitt-Rivers, J. (1967) 'Race, color, and class in Central America and the Andes', *Daedalus: Proceedings of the American Academy of Arts and Sciences*, 96 (2): 542–59.

Plaza, D. (2000) 'Transnational grannies: The changing family responsibilities of elderly African Caribbean-born women resident in Britain', *Social Indicators Research*, 51 (1): 75–105.

Postill, J. (2006) *Media and Nation Building: How the Iban Became Malaysian*. Oxford and New York: Berghahn.

Postill, J. (2007) 'Field theory and the political process black box: Analysing Internet activism in a Kuala Lumpur suburb', available at: www.antropologi.info/blog/anthropology/html/Postill-Field_Theory.html (accessed 14 July 2015).

Postill, J. (2008) 'Localising the Internet beyond communities and networks', *New Media and Society*, 10 (3): 413–31.

Postill, J. (2010) 'Researching the Internet', *Journal of the Royal Anthropological Institute*, 16 (3): 646–50.

Postill, J. (2011) *Localizing the Internet: An Anthropological Account*. Oxford: Berghahn.

Postill, J. (2012a) 'Digital politics and political engagement', in H.A. Horst and D. Miller (eds), *Digital Anthropology*. Oxford: Berg, pp. 165–84.

Postill, J. (2012b) 'Media and social changing since 1979: Towards a diachronic ethnography of media and actual social changes', Paper presented at the European Association of Social Anthropologists (EASA) 12th Biennial Conference, Nanterre, France, 10–13 July.

Postill, J. (2014a) 'A critical history of Internet activism and social protest in Malaysia, 1998–2011', *Asiascape: Digital Asia Journal*, 1–2: 78–103.

Postill, J. (2014b) 'Democracy in an age of viral reality: A media epidemiography of Spain's indignados movement', *Ethnography*, 15 (1): 50–68.

Postill, J. (2015) 'Fields: Dynamic configurations of practices, games, and socialities', in V. Amit (ed.), *Thinking Through Sociality: An Anthropological Interrogation of Key Concepts*. Oxford: Berghahn. pp. 47–68.

Postill, J. (forthcoming) 'The multilinearity of protest: Understanding new social movements through their events, trends and routines', in O. Alexandrakis (ed.), *Method Acting: The Anthropology of New Social Movements*. Cambridge, MA: Zone Books (MIT Press).

Postill, J. and Pink, S. (2012) 'Social media ethnography: The digital researcher in a messy Web', *Media International Australia*, 145: 123–34.

Qiu, J.L. (2009) *Working-Class Network Society: Communication Technology and the Information Have-Less in Urban China*. Cambridge, MA: MIT Press.

Radcliffe-Brown, A.R. (1940) 'On social structure', *Journal of the Royal Anthropological Institute of Great Britain and Ireland*, 70 (1): 1–12.

Rafael, V.L. (2003) 'The cell phone and the crowd: Messianic politics in the contemporary Philippines', *Philippine Political Science Journal*, 24 (47): 3–36.

Reckwitz, A. (2002) 'Toward a theory of social practices: A development in culturalist theorizing', *European Journal of Social Theory*, 5 (2): 243–63.

Richardson, I. (2011) 'The hybrid ontology of mobile gaming', *Convergence: The International Journal of Research into New Media Technologies*, 17 (4): 419–30.

Richman, K.E. (2005) *Migration and Vodou*. Gainsville, FL: University Press of Florida.

Robinson, L. (2007) 'The Cyberself: The Self-ing Project Goes Online, Symbolic Interaction in the Digital Age', *New Media & Society,* 9 (1): 93–110.

Robinson, L. and Halle, D. (2002) 'Digitization, the Internet, and the Arts: eBay, Napster, SAG, and e-Books', *Qualitative Sociology*, 25 (3): 359–83.

Rodríguez, D. (2011) 'Los virales de la #spanishrevolution'. *Trending Topics*, 19 May, available at: http://blogs.elpais.com/trending-topics/2011/05/los-virales-de-spanish revolution.html (accessed 15 May 2015).

Rothenbuhler, E. W. (2005) 'Ground zero, the firemen, and the symbolics of touch on 9/11 and after' in E. W. Rothenbuhler and M. Coman (eds), *Media Anthropology*. Newbury Park, CA: Sage, pp 176–87.

Rothenbuhler, E. (2009) 'From media events to ritual to communicative form', in N. Couldry, A. Hepp and F. Krotz (eds), *Media Events in a Global Age*. London and New York: Routledge, pp. 61–75.

Rothenbuhler, E.W. (2010) 'Media events in the age of terrorism and the Internet', *Revista Romana de Jurnalism si Comunicare – Romanian Journal of Journalism and Communication*, 2: 34–41.

Rothenbuhler, E.W. and Coman, M. (eds) (2005) *Media Anthropology*. London: Sage.

Sands RR. (1999) 'Experiential ethnography: playing with the boys', *Anthropology, Sport, and Culture*. Westport, CT: Bergin & Garvey.

Savage, R. (2011) *900,000 Frames between Us*, documentary video, available at: www.docwest.co.uk/projects/rebecca-savage/ (accessed 4 November 2014).

Schatzki, T.R. (2001) 'Introduction: Practice theory', in T.R. Schatzki, K. Knorr Cetina and E. Von Savigny (eds), *The Practice Turn in Contemporary Theory*. London and New York: Routledge, pp. 1–14.

Schatzki, T.R., Knorr Cetina, K. and Von Savigny, E. (eds) (2001) *The Practice Turn in Contemporary Theory*. London and New York: Routledge.

Serres, M. (2008) *The Five Senses: A Philosophy of Mingled Bodies*. London and New York: Continuum.

Sewell, Jr., W.H. (2005) *Logics of History: Social Theory and Social Transformation*. Chicago, IL: University of Chicago Press.

Sheller, M. (2009) 'The new Caribbean complexity: Mobility systems, tourism and the re-scaling of development', *Singapore Journal of Tropical Geography*, 30: 189–203.

Sheller, M. (2012) 'The islanding effect: Post-disaster mobility systems and humanitarian logistics in Haiti', *Cultural Geographies*, 20 (2): 185–204.

Sheller, M. and Urry, J. (2006) 'The new mobilities paradigm', *Environment and Planning A*, 38 (2): 207–26.

Sillitoe, P. (ed.) (2007) *Local Science vs. Global Science: Approaches to Indigenous Knowledge in International Development*. Oxford and New York: Berghahn.

Silverstone, R. (1995) 'Media, communication, information and the "revolution" of everyday life', in S. Emmot (ed.), *Information Superhighways: Multimedia Users and Futures*. London: Academic Press, pp. 61–78.

Silverstone, R. and Hirsch, E. (eds) (1992) *Consuming Technologies: Media and Information in Domestic Spaces*. London and New York: Routledge.

Silverstone, R., Hirsch, E. and Morley, D. (1991) 'Listening to a long conversation: An ethnographic approach to the study of information and communication technologies in the home', *Cultural Studies*, 5 (2): 204–27.

Silverstone, R., Hirsch, E. and Morley, D. (1992) 'Information and communication technologies and the moral economy of the household', in R. Silverstone and E. Hirsch (eds), *Consuming Technologies: Media and Information in Domestic Spaces*. London and New York: Routledge, pp. 15–31.

Skuse, A. (2005) 'Enlivened objects: The social life, death and rebirth of radio as commodity in Afghanistan', *Journal of Material Culture*, 10: 123–37.

Slater, D. (2013) *New Media, Development and Globalization: Making Connections in the Global South*. Cambridge, UK and Malden, MA: Polity.

Smith, D.E. (1992) 'Sociology from women's experience: A reaffirmation', *Sociological Theory*, 10 (1): 88–98.

Smith, R. (1996) *The Matrifocal Family: Power, Pluralism and Politics*. London: Routledge.

Sparkes, A.C. (2009) 'Ethnography and the senses: Challenges and possibilities', *Qualitative Research in Sport and Exercise*, 1: 21–35.

Spencer, L. and Pahl, R. (2006) *Rethinking Friendship: Hidden Solidarities Today*. Princeton, NJ: Princeton University Press.

Sperber, D. (1996) *Explaining Culture*. Oxford: Blackwell.

Spigel, L. (1992) *Make Room for TV: Television and the Family Ideal in Postwar America*. Chicago, IL: University of Chicago Press.

Spigel, L. (2001) *Welcome to the Dreamhouse: Popular Media and Postwar Suburbs*. Durham, NC: Duke University Press.

Spitulnik, D. (2002) 'Mobile machines and fluid audiences: Rethinking reception through Zambian radio culture', in F.D. Ginsburg, L. Abu-Lughod and B. Larkin (eds), *Media Worlds: Anthropology on New Terrain*. Berkeley, CA: University of California Press, pp. 337–54.

Star, S. (1999) 'The ethnography of infrastructure', *American Behavioral Scientist*, 43 (3): 377–91.

Stoller, P. (1989) *The Taste of Ethnographic Things: The Senses in Anthropology*. Philadelphia, PA: University of Pennsylvania Press.

Stoller, P. (1997) *Sensuous Scholarship*. Philadelphia, PA: University of Pennsylvania Press.

Strengers, Y. and Maller, C. (2012) 'Materialising energy and water resources in everyday practices: Insights for securing supply systems', *Global Environmental Change*, 22 (3): 754–63.

Sunderland, P. and Denny, R.M. (2009) *Doing Anthropology in Consumer Research*. Walnut Creek, CA: Left Coast Press.

Tacchi, J. (1998) 'Radio texture: between self and others'. In D. Miller (ed.) *Material Cultures: Why Some Things Matter*. Chicago: University of Chicago Press. pp. 25–46.

Tacchi, J. (2000) 'The need for radio theory in the digital age', *International Journal of Cultural Studies*, 3 (2): 289–98.

Tacchi, J. (2001) 'Who listens to radio: The role of industrial audience research', in M. Bromley (ed.), *No News is Bad News: Radio, Television and the Public*. London: Longman, pp. 137–56.

Tacchi, J. (2002) 'Radio texture: between self and others', in K. Askew and R.R. Wilk (eds), *The Anthropology of Media: A Reader*. Malden, MA: Blackwell, pp. 241–57.

Tacchi, J. (2003) 'Nostalgia and radio sound'. In M. Bull and L. Back (eds), *The Auditory Culture Reader*. Oxford: Berg, pp. 281–95.

Tacchi, J. (2006) 'Studying communicative ecologies: An ethnographic approach to information and communication technologies (ICTs)', Paper presented at the 56th Annual Conference of the International Communication Association, Dresden, Germany, 19–23 June.

Tacchi, J. (2009) 'Radio and affective rhythm in the everyday', *The Radio Journal: International Studies in Broadcast and Audio Media*, 7 (2): 171–83.

Tacchi, J. (2012) 'Radio in the (i)Home: Changing experiences of domestic audio technologies in Britain', in L. Bessier and D. Fisher (eds), *Radio Fields: Anthropology and Wireless Sound in the 21st Century*. New York: New York University Press, pp. 233–49.

Tacchi, J. (2014) 'Being meaningfully mobile: Mobile phones and development', in J. Servaes (ed.), *Technological Determinism and Communication for Sustainable Social Change*. Lanham, MD: Lexington Books, pp 105–24.

Tacchi, J. and Chandola, T. (2015) 'Complicating connectivity: Women's negotiations with smartphones in an Indian slum', in L. Hjorth and O. Khoo (eds), *Routledge Handbook of New Media in Asia*. Abingdon: Routledge.

Tacchi, J., Fildes, J., Martin, K., Mulenahalli, K., Baulch, E. and Skuse, A. (2007) *Ethnographic Action Research: Trainers Handbook*. Delhi: United Nations Educational, Scientific, and Cultural Organization (UNESCO), available at: ear.findingavoice.org (accessed 19 July 2015).

Tacchi J., Kitner K and Crawford K. (2012) Meaningful mobility: gender, development and mobile phones', *Feminist Media Studies* 12(4): 528–37.

Taylor, E.B. (2013) *Materializing Poverty: How the Poor Transform their Lives*. Lanham, MD: AltaMira.

Taylor, E.B. and Horst, H.A. (2014) 'The aesthetics of mobile money platforms in Haiti', in G. Goggin and H. Hjorth (eds), *Routledge Companion to Mobile Media*. Abingdon and New York: Routledge, pp. 462–71.

Taylor, T.L. (2002) 'Living digitally: Embodiment in virtual worlds', in R. Schroeder (ed), *The Social Life of Avatars: Presence and Interaction in Shared Virtual Environments*. London: Springer, pp. 40–62.

Taylor, T. (2006) *Play Between Worlds: Exploring Online Game Culture*. Cambridge, MA, USA: MIT Press.

Taylor, T.L. (2009) *Play between Worlds*. Cambridge, MA: MIT Press.

Taylor, T.L. (2012) *Raising the Stakes*. Cambridge, MA: MIT Press.

Thornham, H., and Weissmann, E. (eds) (2013) *Renewing Feminisms: Radical Narratives, Fantasies and Futures in Media Studies*. London: I.B. Tauris.

Thrift, N. (2007) *Non-Representational Theory: Space, Politics, Affect*. Oxford: Routeldge.

Throop, C.J. (2003) 'Articulating experience', *Anthropological Theory*, 3 (2): 219–41.

Tilley, C., Keane, W., Kuchler, S., Rowlands, M. and Spyer, P. (eds) (2006) *Handbook of Material Culture*. London: Sage.

Trusov, M., Bodapati, A.V. and Bucklin, R.E. (2010) 'Determining influential users in Internet social networks', *Journal of Marketing Research*, 47 (4): 643–58.

Tsing, A.L. (2005) *Friction: An Ethnography of Global Connection*. Princeton, NJ: Princeton University Press.

Tucker, R.C. (1978) *The Marx-Engels Reader*, 2nd edn. New York: W.W. Norton & Company.

Turits, R.L. (2002) 'A world destroyed, a nation imposed: The 1937 Haitian massacre in the Dominican Republic', *Hispanic American Historical Review*, 82 (3): 589–635.

Turkle, S. (2005) *The Second Self: Computers and the Human Spirit* (20th anniversary ed.). Cambridge, MA: MIT Press.

Turkle, S. (2011) *Alone Together: Why we Expect More from Technology and Less from Each Other*. New York: Basic Books.

Turner, T. (1992) 'Defiant images: The Kayapo appropriation of video', *Anthropology Today*, 8: 5–15.

Turner, V. (1969) *The Ritual Process: Structure and Anti-Structure*. Piscataway, NJ: Aldine Transaction.

Turner, V. W. (1986) 'Dewey, Dilthey, and Drama: an essay in the anthropology of experience' in V.W. Turner and E.M. Bruner (eds), *The Anthropology of Experience*. Chicago, IL: University of Illinois Press. pp. 33–44.

Turner, V.W. and Bruner, E.M. (eds) (1986) *The Anthropology of Experience*. Chicago, IL: University of Illinois Press.

Tylor, E.B. (1958) *Primitive Culture: The Origins of Culture*. New York: Harper & Row.

Vannini, P., Waskul, D. and Gotschalk, S. (2012) *The Senses in Self, Culture, and Society*. Oxford and New York: Routledge.

Vincent, J. and Fortunati, L. (2009) *Electronic Emotion: The Mediation of Emotion via Information and Communication Technologies* (Vol. 3). Bern, Switzerland: Peter Lang.

Visweswaran, K. (1994) *Fictions of Feminist Ethnography*. Minneapolis, MN.: University of Minnesota Press.

Wajcman, J., Brown, J. and Bittman, M. (2008) 'Intimate connections: The impact of the mobile phone on work life boundaries', in G. Goggin and L. Hjorth (eds),

Mobile Technologies: From Telecommunications to Media. London and New York: Routledge, pp. 9–22.

Wallis, C. (2013) *Technomobility in China: Young Migrant Women and Mobile Phones*. New York: New York University Press.

Warde, A. (2005) 'Consumption and the theory of practice', *Journal of Consumer Culture*, 5 (2): 131–54.

Warde, A. (2011) 'Cultural hostility re-considered', *Cultural Sociology*, 5 (3): 341–66.

Warde, A. (2014) 'After taste: Culture, consumption and theories of practice', *Journal of Consumer Culture*, 14 (3) 279–303.

Waterman, C.A. (1990) *Juju: A Social History and Ethnography of an African Popular Music*. Chicago. The University of Chicago Press.

Wellman, B. et al. (2003) 'The social affordances of the Internet for networked individualism', *Journal of Computer-Mediated Communication*, 8 (3), available at: http://jcmc.indiana.edu/vol8/issue3/wellman.html (accessed 15 October 2014).

Wellman, B. and Leighton, B. (1979) 'Networks, neighborhoods and communities' *Urban Affairs Quarterly*, 14: 363–90.

Wenger, E. (1998) *Communities of Practice: Learning, Meaning and Identity*. Cambridge: Cambridge University Press.

Whitehead, N. L., and Wesch, M. (2012) *Human no more: Digital Subjectivities Unhuman Subjects, and the end of Anthropology*, Boulder, CO: University Press of Colorado.

Whyte, W.F. (1943) *Street Corner Society: The Social Structure of an Italian Slum*. Chicago, IL: University of Chicago Press.

Wilding, R. (2006) '"Virtual" intimacies? Families communicating across transnational contexts', *Global Networks: A Journal of Transnational Affairs*, 6 (2): 125–42.

Wilk, R. (2009) 'The edge of agency: Routines, habits and volition', in E. Shove, F. Trentmann and R.R. Wilk (eds), *Time, Consumption and Everyday Life: Practice, Materiality and Culture*. Oxford and New York: Berg, pp. 143–56.

Williams, R. (1974) *Television: Technology and Cultural Form*. London: Collins.

Williams, R. (1977) *Marxism and Literature*. Oxford: Oxford University Press.

Willis, P. (1977) *Learning to Labour: How Working Class Kids Get Working Class Jobs*. New York: Columbia University Press.

Witkowski, E. (2012) 'On the Digital Playing Field How We "Do Sport" With Networked Computer Games', *Games and Culture*, 7 (5): 349–74.

Wittel, A. (2000) 'Ethnography on the move: From field to Net to Internet', *Forum: Qualitative Social Research*, 1(1), available at: www.qualitative-research.net/index.php/fqs/article/view/1131/2517 (accessed 17 November 2014).

Wittel, A. (2001) 'Toward a network sociality', *Theory, Culture & Society*, 18 (6): 51–76.

Wulff, H. (2007) *The Emotions: A Cultural Reader*. Oxford and New York: Berg.

Young, M. and Wilmott, P. (1957) *Family and Kinship in East London*. London: Routledge.

Index

Figures are indicated by page numbers in bold print.